PHILOTHEA *or*
An INTRODUCTION
to the DEVOUT LIFE

Nihil Obstat:
Joseph A. M. Quigley
Censor Librorum
Philadelphia
November 5, 1942

Imprimatur:
✠D. Cardinal Dougherty
Archbishop of Philadelphia
Philadelphia
November 7, 1942

PHILOTHEA *or*
An INTRODUCTION
to the DEVOUT LIFE

SAINT FRANCIS DE SALES
Bishop, Confessor and Doctor of the Church

With an Introduction by
Father John C. Reville, S.J., Ph.D.

*"The parting words of St. Louis, when on his
deathbed, to his son, were: 'Make frequent confession, and choose thee a good confessor, who shall
faithfully teach thee in the way of salvation.'"*
—St. Francis de Sales (p. 11)

TAN·CLASSICS

TAN Books is an imprint of Saint Benedict Press, Charlotte, North Carolina.

An Introduction to the Devout Life was published in this edition by Joseph F. Wagner, Inc., New York, New York, in 1923, and again by The Peter Reilly Company, Philadelphia, Pennsylvania, in 1942. Retypeset and published by Saint Benedict Press, TAN Books, in 2010.

Published with the assistance of The Livingstone Corporation. Cover and interior design by Mark Wainright, The Livingstone Corporation. Typeset by Saint Benedict Press, TAN Books.

Cover Image: *The Angelus*, 1857–59 (oil on canvas), Millet, Jean-Francois (1814–75). Musee d'Orsay, Paris, France. Giraudon, The Bridgeman Art Library International.

Library of Congress Catalog Card No.: 94-60603

ISBN: 978-0-89555-228-0

Printed and bound in United States of America.

12 11 10 9 8 7 6 5 4 3

www.tanbooks.com
www.saintbenedictpress.com

TAN·CLASSICS

*"But even as Josue and Caleb declared that
the Land of Promise was good and fair,
and that the possession of it would be easy and pleasant;
so the Holy Spirit, speaking by all the Saints,
and our blessed Lord Himself assure us that
a devout life is a lovely, a pleasant, and a happy life."*
—St. Francis de Sales

CONTENTS

INTRODUCTION   xvii

PART FIRST
*Counsels and Exercises for the Guidance of the
Soul from Its First Desire after a Devout Life
unto a Full Resolution of Pursuing the Same*

CHAPTER ONE   3
True Devotion Described

CHAPTER TWO   6
Fitness and Excellence of Devotion

CHAPTER THREE   9
Devotion Suitable to All Kinds of Vocations and Professions

CHAPTER FOUR   11
Necessity of a Spiritual Guide for Progress in the Devout Life

CHAPTER FIVE   14
The First Step—Purifying the Soul

CHAPTER SIX   16
First Purification—That of Mortal Sin

CHAPTER SEVEN   18
Purification—From the Affection to Sin

CHAPTER EIGHT   20
How to Effect this Second Purification

CHAPTER NINE   22
Meditation One: Creation

CHAPTER TEN   25
Meditation Two: The End for which We Are Created

CHAPTER ELEVEN   27
Meditation Three: The Mercies of God

CHAPTER TWELVE   30
Meditation Four: Sin

CHAPTER THIRTEEN   32
Meditation Five: Death

CHAPTER FOURTEEN   35
Meditation Six: Judgment

CHAPTER FIFTEEN   38
Meditation Seven: Hell

CHAPTER SIXTEEN   40
Meditation Eight: Paradise

CHAPTER SEVENTEEN   42
Meditation Nine: The Choice of Paradise

CHAPTER EIGHTEEN   44
Meditation Ten: The Soul's Choice of a Devout Life

CHAPTER NINETEEN   47
General Confession

CHAPTER TWENTY   49
A Protest for the Purpose of Fixing in the Mind a Resolution
to Serve God, and to Conclude Your Penitential Acts

CHAPTER TWENTY-ONE   51
Conclusion of the First Purification

CHAPTER TWENTY-TWO   53
We Must Also Lay Aside Our Disposition towards Venial Sins

CHAPTER TWENTY-THREE   55
We Must Purify Ourselves from the Taste for Useless and
Dangerous Things

CHAPTER TWENTY-FOUR   57
Purifying Ourselves from Evil Inclinations

PART SECOND
*Counsels Concerning the Soul's Approach
to God in Prayer and the Sacraments*

CHAPTER ONE   61
The Necessity of Prayer

CHAPTER TWO   64
A Short Plan for Meditation. Concerning the Presence of God:
The First Point of Preparation

CHAPTER THREE   67
Of Invocation: The Second Part of Preparation

CHAPTER FOUR   68
Setting Forth the Mystery: The Third Point of Preparation

CHAPTER FIVE   70
Second Part of Meditation—Reflections

CHAPTER SIX   71
Third Part of Meditation—Affections and Resolutions

CHAPTER SEVEN   73
   The Conclusion

CHAPTER EIGHT   75
   Further Rules for Meditation

CHAPTER NINE   78
   The Dryness which May Trouble Meditation

CHAPTER TEN   80
   A Morning Exercise

CHAPTER ELEVEN   82
   The Evening Exercise, and Examination of Conscience

CHAPTER TWELVE   84
   Spiritual Retreat

CHAPTER THIRTEEN   87
   Aspirations, Ejaculatory Prayers, and Holy Thoughts

CHAPTER FOURTEEN   92
   Holy Mass, and How to Hear It

CHAPTER FIFTEEN   95
   Other Public Services

CHAPTER SIXTEEN   97
   The Invocation of Saints

CHAPTER SEVENTEEN   99
   How to Hear and Read the Word of God

CHAPTER EIGHTEEN   101
   How to Receive Inspirations

CHAPTER NINETEEN   104
   Holy Confession

CHAPTER TWENTY   107
   Frequent Communion

CHAPTER TWENTY-ONE   111
How to Communicate

PART THIRD
Rules for the Practice of Virtue

CHAPTER ONE   117
The Selection of Virtues to Be Practiced

CHAPTER TWO   121
Choice of Virtues (Continued)

CHAPTER THREE   124
Patience

CHAPTER FOUR   128
External Humility

CHAPTER FIVE   131
Inward Humility

CHAPTER SIX   136
Humility Makes Us Love Our Own Abasement

CHAPTER SEVEN   140
How to Preserve a Good Reputation Together with the Practice
of Humility

CHAPTER EIGHT   144
Meekness and the Remedies for Anger

CHAPTER NINE   148
Gentleness towards Ourselves

CHAPTER TEN   151
We Must Be Careful in Our Business Without Over-Eagerness
or Solicitude

CHAPTER ELEVEN   154
Obedience

CHAPTER TWELVE   157
The Necessity of Chastity

CHAPTER THIRTEEN   161
Rules for the Preservation of Chastity

CHAPTER FOURTEEN   163
Poverty of Spirit in the Midst of Wealth

CHAPTER FIFTEEN   166
How to Practice Real Poverty, While Being Actually Rich

CHAPTER SIXTEEN   170
The Practice of Spiritual Riches amidst Real Poverty

CHAPTER SEVENTEEN   172
Friendship—First, of Bad and Frivolous Friendships

CHAPTER EIGHTEEN   174
Flirtations

CHAPTER NINETEEN   177
True Friendship

CHAPTER TWENTY   180
The Difference between True and False Friendships

CHAPTER TWENTY-ONE   183
Counsels and Remedies against Evil Friendships

CHAPTER TWENTY-TWO   186
Further Counsels Concerning Friendship

CHAPTER TWENTY-THREE   189
The Practice of External Mortification

CHAPTER TWENTY-FOUR   194
Society and Solitude

CHAPTER TWENTY-FIVE   197
Propriety in Dress

CHAPTER TWENTY-SIX   199
Conversations: and First, of Conversation Concerning God

CHAPTER TWENTY-SEVEN   201
Modesty in Conversation, and Becoming Reverence

CHAPTER TWENTY-EIGHT   203
Rash Judgment

CHAPTER TWENTY-NINE   208
Detraction

CHAPTER THIRTY   212
Further Counsels Concerning Conversation

CHAPTER THIRTY-ONE   214
Amusements: First, of Those Which Are Lawful

CHAPTER THIRTY-TWO   216
Forbidden Games

CHAPTER THIRTY-THREE   218
Balls and Recreations Which Are Lawful but Dangerous

CHAPTER THIRTY-FOUR   220
When We May Play or Dance

CHAPTER THIRTY-FIVE   222
We Must Be Faithful in Things Great and Small

CHAPTER THIRTY-SIX   225
The Necessity of a Just and Reasonable Mind

CHAPTER THIRTY-SEVEN   228
Desires

CHAPTER THIRTY-EIGHT   231
Advice to Married Persons

CHAPTER THIRTY-NINE   237
Further Instructions to the Same

CHAPTER FORTY   240
The Widowed

CHAPTER FORTY-ONE   245
A Word to the Unmarried

PART FOURTH
Some Needful Remedies against Ordinary Temptations

CHAPTER ONE   249
We Must Not Give Heed to "What Will the World Say?"

CHAPTER TWO   252
We Must Be of Good Courage

CHAPTER THREE   254
The Nature of Temptation, and the Difference between
Feeling It and Yielding to It

CHAPTER FOUR   257
Illustration of This Principle

CHAPTER FIVE   259
Encouragement for the Tempted Soul

CHAPTER SIX   261
How Temptations and Attraction May Become Sinful

CHAPTER SEVEN   263
Remedies for Great Temptations

CHAPTER EIGHT   265
The Importance of Resisting Small Temptations

CHAPTER NINE   267
How to Remedy Such Temptations

CHAPTER TEN   269
How to Arm the Heart against Temptation

CHAPTER ELEVEN   271
Anxiety

CHAPTER TWELVE   274
Sadness

CHAPTER THIRTEEN   277
Actual and Spiritual Consolations, and How to Receive Them

CHAPTER FOURTEEN   284
Dryness and Spiritual Barrenness

CHAPTER FIFTEEN   289
An Example and Illustration

PART FIFTH

*Counsels and Exercises for the Renewing of the Soul,
and Her Confirmation in Devotion*

CHAPTER ONE   295
How We Should Each Year Renew Our Good Intentions
by Means of the Following Exercises

CHAPTER TWO   297
The Mercy of God in Calling Us to His Service, and Our
Consequent Pledge

CHAPTER THREE   300
Examination of Our Soul, as to Its Progress in the Devout Life

CHAPTER FOUR   302
Examination of the State of Our Soul towards God

CHAPTER FIVE   305
Examination of Your Condition with Regard to Yourself

CHAPTER SIX   307
Examination of the Soul as Regards Our Neighbor

CHAPTER SEVEN   308
Examination of the Soul's Affections

CHAPTER EIGHT   310
Affections after the Examination

CHAPTER NINE   311
Reflections Suitable to the Renewal of Our Good Resolutions

CHAPTER TEN   312
First Reflection: The Excellence of the Soul

CHAPTER ELEVEN   314
Second Reflection: The Excellence of Virtue

CHAPTER TWELVE   315
Third Reflection: The Example of the Saints

CHAPTER THIRTEEN   317
Fourth Reflection: The Love That Jesus Christ Bears Us

CHAPTER FOURTEEN   319
Fifth Reflection: God's Eternal Love for Us

CHAPTER FIFTEEN   320
General Affections Following These Reflections, and
Conclusion of the Exercise

CHAPTER SIXTEEN   322
The Feelings to Be Retained after This Exercise

CHAPTER SEVENTEEN   323
Answer to Two Objections Which May Be Made against
This Introduction

CHAPTER EIGHTEEN   325
Three Final and Chief Rules

INTRODUCTION

THE "Introduction à la Vie Dévote," is here offered plus the title of *Philothea*, the name under which the original French of the work was published, by its author, St. Francis de Sales, in 1608. It first saw the light, just about the time Shakespeare was giving to the world "Antony and Cleopatra," Captain John Smith his "True Relation," Middleton "A Mad World." In the year of its publication John Milton was born and Quebec founded. It is not likely that at any time during his life the saintly Bishop of Geneva ever heard of the plays of the greatest of English poets, nor can we imagine, that, man of taste and lover of letters though he was, he would have much relished the tempest and turbulence of passion as painted by the Elizabethan dramatist. Yet, like Shakespeare, the writer of the *Philothea* was an admirable psychologist and could read and analyze character with unerring instinct. But Shakespeare did not move on the same plane of thought and vision. Francis lived in a world of supernatural ideas, and there is much, we imagine, in the world of the creator of Falstaff and the Merry Wives of Windsor, in the philosophy even of "Hamlet" and the crudities of "Timon of Athens," that would have shocked him. But long before Shakespeare's name had met with anything like general recognition, either from his own countrymen, or, more especially from circles abroad, before any foreign translations of his plays existed, "L'Introduction à la Vie Dévote" had been done into almost every language of cultured Europe, and the Saint's name and work were better known among Frenchmen and foreigners than those of the Englishman, in Cumberland or Lincolnshire.

The *Philothea* wears well, like all great classics. It is now more than three hundred years old, and though everything has changed around us, the very language in which it was written, the styles, fashions and manners, the politics, the social fabrics of the times, it has still the freshness and vigor of its first youth. For the Saints, who seem to be so cloistered from the world and to look out upon it, as might some holy nun through the iron grille of a Carmelite chapel, with ethereal gaze and as in a waking trance, really understand the world better than the worldling. They unerringly chart its course and accurately take the soundings of its treacherous waters, they plummet its depths far better than those whose bark is tossing on their restlessness. Their vision is clearer, their compass is more accurately set. Hence it is that any really great spiritual book has, of its nature, one of the first qualities required for a world-classic. It deals in truth and power with the vital questions that affect the lives of men, it enters into the sanctuary of the heart, it brings light, the sometimes blinding light of God's truth into the neglected shrine of inner consciousness and sends the echoes of forgotten principles ringing through the awakened soul.

Hence the immortality of such a book as the *Confessions of St. Augustine*. Its author had sounded all the depths and shoals of human pleasure and triumph. The African rhetorician knew the world, he had tasted its emptiness. An honored, petted and rose-garlanded guest, he had sat at its banquet table, amidst wine and song. But, with what Libyan, almost uncontrolled and fiercely burning passion, he bewails his follies and sins, his pride, the world's evil fascination! What lyric raptures over the goodness of a merciful God who saved him from its snares! The author of the *Imitation of Christ*, the Flemish recluse of the fifteenth century, is the very antithesis of St. Augustine. In him, the style, the thought do not pour forth like molten lava from the panting heart. He is uniformly serene, calm, self-poised and he writes like a hermit venturing abroad into the haunts of men, with hands thrust into the long sleeves of his habit, his head covered with enfolding cowl, with apparently unseeing eyes, with slow and rhythmic step, a hieratic figure of meditation and solitude. But how he too knows the world! How well he reads the heart! What a diagnostician of the maladies of the soul! How gently, yet how ruthlessly he places his finger on the wound, hidden perhaps to ourselves, and with infinite tenderness and the sternness and unflinching sincerity of true love tells us, almost with a smile, as if we were told something we already but too well suspected: "Here, brother, thou ailest. Friend, here thou art dangerously ill. Here—be brave my son—thou shalt have to apply the knife, to cut and to burn, for thy very life is at stake." Wisest of monitors and kindliest of friends! What treasures of heavenly lore, yea even of true worldly wisdom hast thou stored in the pages of thy little book.

To the *Imitation* we must add another little volume dear to St. Francis de Sales, and which he is said even to have preferred to it, *The Spiritual Combat* of the Theatine, Lorenzo Scupoli. Nor must we forget *The Sinner's Guide* by the Venerable Louis de Granada, the *Names of Christ* of the Venerable Louis de Leon, nor the drill-book of the soldier of Christ, *The Spiritual Exercises* of Saint Ignatius, that made as many Saints, as Francis de Sales used to say, as it contained letters, nor the *Christian Perfection* of Alphonso Rodriguez, the manual on whose solid precepts so many seculars and religious have been trained.

At no time in the history of the Church have masters of the ascetic life failed to point out its principles, its end and the practical methods by which it must be attained. In the very age which saw the germs of wide-spread spiritual decay, in the lives of Catholics, while Voltaire was undermining so many things sacred by his sarcasms and sneer, St. Alphonsus de Liguori was writing those masterpieces of asceticism which still guide thousands in the pursuit of holiness.

The spiritual book, the *Philothea*, now given to our readers is from the pen of one of the greatest men of the seventeenth century in France, and one of the noblest and most lovable Saints in the Church of God. Francis de Sales was born at Thorens in Savoie, August 21, 1567, of a noble family, illustrious in the annals of his native province. His father and mother brought him up in the strictest principles of the Catholic Faith, the more so, as nearby Geneva, where the family counted many friends, was the central stronghold of Calvinism. The boy had for daily spectacle, and almost for playfellows, the snow-clad Alps, theme of Guiraud's, Byron's and Coleridge's song, ever sublime, ever fascinating, whether the bridal veil of the mists garlands their brows, or their bastions bear the burden of everlasting snows.

The young nobleman's education was that of the youths of his class in the last years of the sixteenth century. His mother taught him his prayers and catechism. He made his first studies near his native place at the college of Annecy in Savoie; later, under the Jesuits in Paris. To the study of rhetoric and philosophy, he added that of theology, Scripture and Hebrew. At the age of twenty, the young man, handsome, cultured, and courtly, the perfect type of the gentleman of his time, went to Italy and heard the lectures of the famous Pancirola, in the law school of the University of Padua. The world smiled before him, pleasure beckoned him on, the highest honors of the State were dangled before his eyes. He made hosts of friends by his refined manners, his kindly humor, his eloquence, his wit, his unfailing kindness and his all-winning gentleness and sweetness. He made enemies, alas, by his uncompromising fidelity to the principles of his faith, his scorn of all that was base, his loyalty to the standards of honor and purity he had learnt in the ancestral home. His enemies, thinking no doubt they might terrify him from the paths of virtue from which they could not wheedle him, set upon him to cow him into submission. But the gentle Francis de Sales was not to be cowed by threat or blow, and when attacked by a band of assailants he whipped out his rapier and drove his enemies in headlong flight through the tortuous streets of old Padua. Gentle Francis de Sales! Yes, in truth. But he won the right to be so called because he had disciplined a naturally fiery temperament with the curb and bit of Christian self-control.

The degree of Doctor *utriusque juris*, of civil and canon law, crowned the career of Francis in dreamy Padua. Yielding for the moment to his father's wish, he accepted office before the local Senate of his native province at Chambéry. Twice he refused the senatorial dignity. In 1593 he was named, while still a layman, Provost of the Episcopal Chapter of Geneva, and the same year was ordained priest. His heart was now satisfied.

If ever there was a priestly soul, it was that of Francis de Sales. His life was stainless. His character was balanced. His intellectual gifts were of a high order, his mental vision clear, his fancy playful, his imagination creative, his learning extensive. His love of God burned like a poetic flame; it was tender and childlike; it was the very breath of his apostolate. With an almost feminine tenderness, he loved all men and because he loved them he wished all to know and to love God. But he was strong. In his strength, he was tolerant of men's weaknesses, of their peculiarities, their narrow views, their whims, their oddities, their ill-founded judgments, their inconsistencies and their faults, provided only, these did not essentially interfere with their solemn obligations towards God. He taught that a courtier might be a faithful attendant on his prince and yet serve God; that a woman might keep her social rank and defer to its reasonable demands and conventions, and at the same time preserve the grace of God in her heart.

When he first preached to the mountain villages of the Chablais, his simple popular eloquence, full of parables, homely allusions and illustrations, won all hearts. He spoke to the people and for their needs. They listened to him with rapt attention and heard the "Provost's" sermons with something like amazement. Never had the mountain folk of the Chablais ever suspected even that they could be spoken to in such homely yet truly priestly and dignified phrase. Conversions from Calvinism became numerous and the name of the young apostle was soon known throughout the length and breadth of France.

Francis, although disliking controversy, held several conferences with the Calvinist Théodore de Bèze, but as they seemed to lead nowhere, they were soon abandoned. In 1602 he was appointed Bishop of Geneva. But the Calvinist capital offered but a cold welcome and limited opportunities for the evangelization of his immediate Catholic flock, and he transferred the main theater of his labors to Annecy, where he lived like any poor priest and where he has left up to this day a lasting and fragrant memory.

His work as Bishop, as founder with St. Jane Frances de Chantal of the Order of the Visitation, his labors as reformer of ecclesiastical discipline in Savoie and in France, his influence at court with Henry IV and his son Louis XIII, his unbounded charity, his zeal for souls, his gentleness and at the same time the heroism which he displayed in the most trying tasks, his unswerving fidelity to the Chair of Peter, his contempt for the honors of the world, his constant refusal to accept from Henry IV and Louis XIII of France far greater honors than the Dukes of Savoie could offer him—all this belongs to the history of the Church in the seventeenth century. They need not be recounted here. But they soon wore out the brave champion of Christ who scaled the snow-clad Alps to seek out his erring sheep. Obedient to the orders of his sovereign, the Duke of Savoie, who had sent him on a confidential mission to Avignon, he stopped on his return at Lyons. There he saw Madame de Chantal, whom he had long directed in the secrets of the spiritual life and led to the heights of sanctity. Worn out by his labors and suffering intense pains, which he bore without a murmur, he here passed away, December 28, 1622. The body of the Saint rests in his beloved Convent of the Visitation at Annecy. The Lyonnese kept his heart in their city for over a century and a half, but at the time of the French Revolution it was carried to Venice, where it is venerated today. Francis was beatified in 1661 and canonized by Pope Alexander VII in 1665. In 1877 he was proclaimed by Pius IX, Doctor of the Universal Church.

Among the Saint's principal works are the *Controversies*, first printed as hand-bills and leaflets and scattered among the inhabitants of the Chablais mountains who either could not or would not come to hear him preach. The Saint was one of the first in modern times to use this peculiarly twentieth-century publicity device for mission purposes. The *Controversies* form a popular treatise on the fundamental articles of the Catholic Faith. The authority of the Church and the Primacy of Peter are particularly insisted on. "The Defense of the Standard of the Cross" exposes the reasons for the devotion to the Cross and the meaning of the Sign of the Cross; it is a simple exposition of one of the most popular of Catholic practices. *The Treatise on the Love of God* is with the "Philothea" the one masterpiece which fully reflects the mind and heart of the Bishop of Geneva as those of a great genius and a great Saint. The first four of its twelve books explain the theory of Divine Love, its birth, growth, perfection in the soul, and how it may be lost there; the fifth defines what is meant by the love of complacency and the love of benevolence; the sixth and seventh treat of *affective* love; the eighth and ninth of *effective* love, which is naught else but submission and conformity in practice to the will of God. The last three books resume this teaching and suggest practical methods for its application to daily life. If, in the first part of the work, there is a little dryness when the Saint enters into the explanation of the faculties of the soul, as the work proceeds, it rises into the realms of true mystic poetry, and its pages are clothed in language of the purest lyricism, which caused it to be compared by Sainte-Beuve to the finest passages of Lamartine. The *Philothea* (1608) may not in vastness of conception be the equal of the *Treatise on the Love of God*, but it is perhaps better suited to the average reader, and as a spiritual book stands in the very first rank of great religious treatises.

In order that the memory and example of the saintly Bishop of Geneva might be still more honored than in the past, Pope Pius XI, on the occasion of the tercentenary of the Saint's death, issued a special Encyclical Letter, dated January 26, 1923. In that Encyclical *Rerum Omnium*, he solemnly designated St. Francis de Sales, heavenly patron of Catholic writers and journalists. In the course of his Letter the Holy Father refers to the book now edited, the *Philothea* or *Introduction to the Devout Life*, and counsels the men and women of our day to read its simple, homely, but ennobling lessons. He singles it out with special and whole-hearted approbation, so that we may well call it the chosen "Spiritual Guide of the Holy Father." He is fully aware, no doubt, that it has a special mission in our own times, just as it had in the seventeenth century, and that it can bring, both the priest at the altar and the nun in her cell, the statesman in office, the highborn lady of the world and the humblest handmaid at her work, rich and poor alike to the highest sanctity, provided they follow its golden lessons. "Philothea," as its Greek etymology implies, is the "God-loving" soul, any soul that sincerely wishes to serve its Creator and Lord, in no matter what rank of society, under any circumstances of fortune, in any walk or state of life. The original "Philothea" seems to have been a lady of high rank, Madame de Charmoisy, equally distinguished by birth, fortune and piety, whom the pious Bishop of Geneva had met on one of his visits to Paris and in whom he found an apt pupil in the ways of perfection.

The *Philothea* or *Introduction to the Devout Life* is meant for all Christians. St. Francis himself tells us that too many spiritual authors addressed themselves in their writings to priests only, to religious men and women living under a special rule that obliged them to aim at a higher perfection. These authors did not address the vast majority of their brethren who had no other guide but the Gospel. They had cloistered the principles of sanctity and made asceticism a closed book to them. Yet Our Lord had preached that perfection was meant for all men. He had called all to perfection, that perfection at least which they might attain in their various states of life. "Be ye perfect as your Heavenly Father is perfect." It is the special merit of the Bishop of Geneva to have opened the too rigidly barred gates of asceticism; to have given asceticism, devotion an open entrance into the court, the camp, the farmhouse, the fashionable salon or parlor, the workshop of the laborer; to have taught with unsurpassed authority, sweetness and charm, that the very height of sanctity and perfection might be attained by any man or woman who, in the fear of God and His Love, fulfills all the duties of the state of life in which his lot has been cast. In the *Philothea* then, Francis intends to lead the soul living in the world, on the paths of devotion, to true and solid piety. It is an error, a heresy even, says the Saint, to hold, that piety is incompatible with any state of life. In the first part of the book, the Saint helps the soul to divest itself from all affection to sin. In the second, he teaches it how to be united to God by prayer and the use of the Sacraments; in the third he drills it in the practice of virtue. He then strengthens it against temptation, and finally teaches it how to form its resolutions and to persevere. The "Introduction" is a masterpiece of psychology, of practical morality, built upon the solid foundation of the Gospel and the teaching of the Fathers and great ascetical writers.

Philothea is addressed, as we have said, to every rank and class of society, to the religious, the priest, the nun, the artisan; to the widow, the mother, the bride. It is written with the directness, the plainness of phrase and allusion, characteristic of the Saints, and which at times might shock an over-fastidious ear. But the holy Bishop looks at life steadily and sees it with the purified vision of a stainless soul. Simple and solid, it is also clothed with that "incommunicable charm" of the great writer, as Newman says, who has something close to his heart and must carry it in its entirety to his readers. It is no wonder that Pius XI singled it out as peculiarly appropriate to the needs of our present society. Few other books teach the lessons of the Gospel with the same authority and charm, and are so eminently practical.

St. Francis is not only a master of the spiritual life, he is a great writer and one of the fountainheads undefiled of the noble French literature of the seventeenth century. He is by his quaintness, simplicity, richness of imagination and originality of thought, by his sprightliness and picturesqueness of phrase, the connecting link between Montaigne and Amyot on the one hand and Fénelon and La Fontaine on the other. There is a winged grace in his words, a twinkle, a joyance, subdued and tender in his eyes, that immediately disarm the most critical reader. His French, like that of La Fontaine, loses its delicate aroma, even in the best translation. His "Letters" remind us of those of St. Teresa. The curling iron has not given them that too artificial, if graceful Marcel wave sometimes seen in those of Madame de Sévigné; but they are as French in their freedom, simplicity and grace as those of Voltaire, Joseph de Maistre or Louis Veuillot.

"Les grandes pensées viennent du coeur," wrote the Marquis de Vauvenargues. The heart of the Bishop of Geneva was filled with the love of the beautiful and the true. God for him was Beauty, Truth and Love. The noblest thoughts sprang from the rich soil of his generous nature. He expressed them with the spontaneity of a child. Like a child he loves to talk of marvels and strange beasts, and relying too much on Pliny and old "Bestiaries" he draws many of his illustrations from the "Natural Philosophy" of the Roman writer, and charming though the illustrations be, modern science must reject the foundation on which they rest. He loves to speak of doves and bees, lions, partridges. "Phoenixes, unicorns and salamanders," says Gamaliel Bradford in his appreciative essay "Portrait of a Saint," included in his volume, "A Naturalist of Souls," play a large part in his menagerie, and his botany is too often in a class with Falstaff's camomile: "Honors, rank, dignities, are like the saffron plant, which the more it is trodden on, the faster it grows." Yet we read it all with never-failing delight.

Mr. Bradford's essay reminds us of Leigh Hunt's delightful essay on the Bishop of Geneva, "The Gentleman Saint." The title, however, is an unhappy one, for no Saint, whether Simon Stylites or Benedict Joseph Labre, can really deserve the name that does not also possess the essential characteristics of the gentleman even though he might not know all the complexities of modern etiquette. St. Francis de Sales has found no enemies. A Protestant sovereign, James I of England, one of the scholars of his age, said that he wrote more like an angel than a man. Great French critics and littérateurs, from Sainte-Beuve to Strowski, Henri Bordeaux and Amédée de Margerie, Lanson, Brunetière and Faguet, linger with delight over the polished yet homely and simple ease of his phrase. Like Samuel Johnson, Francis had his faithful, but fortunately not too prolix Boswell, and in "L'Esprit de Saint François de Sales," his friend Camus, Bishop of Belley, painted an intimate portrait of a great servant of God, whose winning smile, tender words, humility, sweetness and charity won countless souls to a newer and fuller understanding of the service of God. Through the *Philothea* St. Francis speaks to the men and women of our own times. Those who will read the book will heartily reëcho the wish of the Holy Father: "Would that this book, the most perfect of its kind in the judgment of his contemporaries, as it was at one time in the hands of all, were now read by all, so that true piety might everywhere flourish again, and the Church of God might rejoice in seeing sanctity common among her sons."

JOHN C. REVILLE, S.J.

PART FIRST

———•———

Counsels and Exercises for the
Guidance of the Soul from Its First Desire
after a Devout Life unto a
Full Resolution of Pursuing the Same

CHAPTER ONE

True Devotion Described

———————— • ————————

YOU aim at true devotion, my dear Philothea, because, as a Christian, you know how acceptable it is to the Divine Majesty. But inasmuch as trifling errors at the outset of any undertaking are wont to increase rapidly as we advance, frequently becoming almost irreparable, it is needful that, first of all, you should ascertain wherein lies the virtue of devotion; for there are many counterfeits, but only one true devotion; and, therefore, if you do not find that which is real, you will but deceive yourself, and vainly pursue an idle, superstitious form.

Aurelius gave to all his works of art the countenance of the women he loved; and so every one colors his devotion according to his tastes and inclinations. One is given to fasting, and whilst he fasts he holds himself to be devout, although his heart is full of bitterness; and whilst he will not touch his lips with wine, nor even with water for abstinence' sake, he scruples not to sully them with his neighbor's blood in slander and calumny. Another would fain be devout because he daily repeats many prayers, although, at the same time, he gives way to angry, proud, and injurious language amongst his servants or associates. Another willingly opens his purse to give alms to the poor, but he cannot open his heart to forgive his enemies. Another forgives his enemies, but only force obliges him to do justice to his creditors. Such men may pass for devout, but they are not really so.

When the messengers of Saul sought David, they found only an image in his bed, which, being dressed by Michol in David's garments, deceived them so that they imagined it to be David himself. Thus many persons clothe themselves with a garb of external devotion, and the world believes them to be really devout and spiritual, whilst in truth they are mere statues or phantasms of devotion.

True, living devotion, my Philothea, implies the love of God. Indeed it is itself a true love of Him in the highest form, for whereas divine love enlightening our soul is called Grace, and makes us pleasing in His sight; so giving us power to do good, it is called Charity; and when it reaches that point of perfection wherein it not only causes us to do good, but to do it earnestly, frequently, and readily, then it is called Devotion. The ostrich never flies, the common fowl flies but seldom, and then heavily and near the ground; but the swallow, the dove, and the eagle are ever on the wing, they fly far and easily. Even so sinners rise not to God, but always grovel on the earth in pursuing earthly things; well-meaning people who are as yet not truly devout, mount up to God in good works, but rarely, slowly, and heavily; whilst the devout fly to Him perpetually, soaring lightly. In short, devotion is spiritual agility and vivacity, by means of which charity works in us, or we in her, with love and readiness; and as charity leads us to obey and fulfill all God's commandments, so devotion leads us to obey them with promptitude and diligence. Therefore no one who fails to observe all these commandments can be truly virtuous or devout, since to that end he must have charity, and further, thorough readiness and eagerness to fulfill the laws of charity.

And as devotion consists in perfect charity, so it not only makes us active, ready, and diligent in keeping God's commandments, but furthermore it stimulates us to the eager and loving performance of all the good works we can attain unto, even such as are not enjoined us, but only suggested or counseled. Even as a man just recovered from an illness walks on his journey only as far as is absolutely necessary, with pain and difficulty, so the repentant sinner treads in God's ways heavily and slowly until, having attained the grace of devotion, he resembles the healthy and light-hearted traveler, who not only proceeds on his way, but runs, and leaps with joy in the way of God's commandments, hastening into the paths of His heavenly counsels and inspirations. In truth, charity and devotion differ no further than flame and fire, for charity is a spiritual fire which when it flames brightly, becomes devotion; and devotion adds to the fire of charity a flame which renders it ready, active, and diligent, not only in keeping His commandments, but in carrying out His heavenly inspirations and counsels of perfection.

CHAPTER TWO

Fitness and Excellence of Devotion

———————————•———————————

THOSE who would have hindered the Israelites from journeying into the Land of Promise, described it as a "land that devoureth the inhabitants thereof," that is of so noxious an air that the life of men therein was short, and that its inhabitants were giants, in whose sight the children of Israel were but as grasshoppers. (*Num.* 13). Even so, Philothea, does the world calumniate holy devotion, representing devout persons with a gloomy, sad, and irritable countenance, and pretending that religion creates melancholy and unsocial men. But even as Josue and Caleb declared that the Land of Promise was good and fair, and that the possession of it would be easy and pleasant; so the Holy Spirit, speaking by all the Saints, and our blessed Lord Himself assure us that a devout life is a lovely, a pleasant, and a happy life.

The world sees only how the devout fast, pray, and bear reproach; how they nurse the sick, give alms to the poor, restrain their temper, repress and extinguish their passions, refrain from sensual delights, and perform similar actions which in themselves, and taken alone, are hard and painful. But the world does not see the internal, hearty devotion which renders all such actions easy, pleasant, and grateful. Watch the bees, how they suck from thyme a bitter juice, but as they suck it is converted into honey, for such is their property. Tell the worldly man, in truth the devout find many hardships in their works of mortification, but in the performance they become easy and welcome; even as the stake, the fire, the sword, and the wheel, were as perfumed flowers to the martyrs of old, because they were devout, and if devotion can soften torture and death itself, can it not lighten the daily path of duty?

Sugar sweetens unripe fruits, and neutralizes the acidity of those which are already ripe—so true devotion is a spiritual sugar which takes away the bitterness of mortification, and the danger of gratification; it counteracts the poor man's discontent, and the rich man's self-satisfaction; the loneliness of him that is oppressed, and the vainglory of the successful; the sadness of him that is alone, and the dissipation of him that is in society; it is as fire in winter, and dew in summer; it knows how to abound, and how to suffer need; it draws some good alike from honor and contempt, it accepts both joy and suffering with an even spirit, and fills us with a marvelous sweetness. Consider Jacob's ladder (which is a faithful representation of the devout life): the two sides between which we ascend, and which support the steps, are prayer, which brings the love of God, and the Sacraments which confer it; the steps are but the various degrees of charity by which we advance from virtue to virtue, either descending in action to the aid of our neighbor, or ascending in contemplation to a loving union with God. Observe, further, those who tread this ladder: they are men with angels' hearts, or angels with human forms. They are not young, yet they seem youthful, being full of vigor and spiritual activity. They have wings whereon to mount up to God in prayer, but they have also feet whereon to tread the path of men in all holy and loving converse; their countenances are open and mild, for they meet all things with gentleness and meekness; their heads and limbs are uncovered, inasmuch as their thoughts, their affections, and deeds have no aim or motive but to please God; their bodies are covered with light shining garments, for they of a truth use this world and its good things, but after a pure and holy fashion, and no more than is requisite. Such are the truly devout. Believe me, dear Philothea, devotion is the crown of sweetness, the queen of virtues, the perfection of charity. If charity is milk, devotion is the cream; if charity is a plant, devotion is the flower; if charity is a precious stone, its brilliancy is devotion; if charity is a costly balsam, devotion is its fragrance, an odor of sweetness, which consoles men and makes the angels to rejoice.

CHAPTER THREE

Devotion Suitable to All Kinds of Vocations and Professions

———————— • ————————

IN THE creation God commanded the plants of the earth to bring forth fruit, each after its kind; and in a similar way He commands Christians, who are the living plants of His Church, to bring forth the fruits of devotion, each according to his calling and vocation. There is a different practice of devotion for the gentleman and the mechanic; for the prince and the servant; for the wife, the maiden, and the widow; and still further, the practice of devotion must be adapted to the capabilities, the engagements, and the duties of each individual. It would not do were the Bishop to adopt a Carthusian solitude, or if the father of a family refused like the Capuchins to save money; if the artisan spent his whole time in church like the professed religious; or the latter were to expose himself to all manner of society in his neighbor's behalf as the Bishop must do. Such devotion would be inconsistent and ridiculous. Yet this kind of mistake is not unfrequently made, and the world being either not able, or not willing, to distinguish between true devotion and the indiscretion of false devotees, condemns that devotion which nevertheless has no share in these inconsistencies.

No, my Philothea, true devotion hinders no one, but rather it perfects everything, and whenever it is out of keeping with any person's legitimate vocation, it must be spurious. Aristotle says that the bee extracts honey from the flowers without injuring them, leaving them as fresh and whole as she finds them; but true devotion does still better, for it not only hinders no duty or vocation, but on the contrary it adorns and purifies them. Throw precious stones into honey, and the natural color of each will wax more brilliant; and so every individual adorns his vocation by following it with devotion; domestic peace is assured, conjugal love strengthened, fidelity to our sovereign more closely treasured, and all occupations rendered more acceptable and agreeable.

It is not merely an error but a heresy to suppose that a devout life is necessarily banished from the soldier's camp, the merchant's shop, the prince's court, or the domestic hearth. Doubtless that form of devotion which is purely contemplative, monastic and religious, will not accord with their vocations, but there are other forms of devotion suitable to perfect a secular life. This we may learn from the example of Abraham, Isaac, and Jacob, David, Job, Tobias, Sarah, Rebecca, and Judith in the Old Dispensation and in the New from St. Joseph, Lydia and St. Crispin in their trades; from St. Anne, St. Martha, St. Monica, Aquila and Priscilla in their households; Cornelius, St. Sebastian and St. Maurice in their military charges; and from Constantine, St. Helena, St. Louis, and St. Edward, on their thrones. Some even have prospered better amidst the multitude which seems so ill-suited for holiness, than in solitude which appears its most likely soil. Thus St. Gregory remarks that Lot remained chaste whilst in Sodom, and fell into sin after he had forsaken it. Wheresoever we may be, we may and should aim at a life of perfect devotion.

CHAPTER FOUR

Necessity of a Spiritual Guide for Progress in the Devout Life

───────●───────

THE young Tobias being commanded to go to Rages, replied, "I know not the way," and his father answered, "Seek thee a man who may go with thee." And so I say to you, Philothea, if you desire heartily to follow a devout life, seek a holy guide and conductor. Seek where you will (so spoke the devout Avila), and you will never so safely find the will of God as in the path of humble obedience, so well trodden by all the Saints of old. When St. Teresa saw what great penances were practiced by Catherine of Cordova, she longed to imitate her, and was tempted to disobey her confessor in so doing, but God said to her, "Daughter, thou art in a safe and good path, I prize thy obedience higher than her penance," and so great was her love of obedience that, beyond what she owed to her ordinary superiors, she took a vow of special obedience to a holy man, obliging herself to follow his guidance, which was an infinite blessing to her; and many other pious souls, both before and after her, to subject themselves more perfectly to God, have submitted their will to that of His servants, which is highly commended by St. Catherine of Siena. The pious princess St. Elizabeth of Hungary submitted with entire obedience to Conrad; and the parting words of St. Louis, when on his deathbed, to his son, were: "Make frequent confession, and choose thee a good confessor, who shall faithfully teach thee in the way of salvation."

Holy Writ says that, "a faithful friend is as a strong defense, and that he that hath found him hath found a treasure. A faithful friend is the medicine of life and immortality, and they that fear the Lord shall find him." (*Ecclus.* 6:14-16).

These words (as you may see by the context) regard chiefly our eternal interests, in which above all we require this faithful friend, who will guide our actions by his warnings and counsels, and thereby protect us from the snares and delusions of the Evil one; in all our sorrows, our sadness, our falls, he will be as a treasure of wisdom to us; he will be as a physician to give ease to our hearts, and help in our spiritual diseases; he will preserve us from evil, and forward us in what is good, and when we are conquered by some infirmity, he will save us from being overwhelmed, and will raise us from our prostrate condition.

But who can find such a friend? The wise man answers, "They that fear the Lord," that is to say, those who are lowly in heart and earnestly desire their spiritual advancement. And be sure, my daughter, that since it is so all-important for you to begin this holy course of devotion led by a safe guide, if you heartily pray that God would give you such, He will supply your need in His own way; doubt not that He who sent an angel to guide the young Tobias, will provide you with a good and faithful guide.

And when found, he should be to you as an angel; do not regard him as an ordinary man, nor trust in him as such, nor in his human knowledge, but in God, who will Himself guide you through His appointed channel, prompting him to do and say that which you most require; therefore count him as an angel come from Heaven that he may conduct you thither. Have towards him an open heart in all faithfulness and sincerity, laying bare to him alike your evil and your good without pretense or dissimulation. By this means what is good in you will be examined and established; what is evil remedied and corrected. You will be relieved and comforted in your sorrows; moderated and restrained in your prosperity. Place entire confidence in him, mingled with sacred reverence, so that neither reverence should hinder your confidence, nor confidence lessen your reverence. Trust in him with the love of a daughter for a father, esteem him with the confidence of a son towards his mother; in short, let this friendship be at once loving and firm, wholly sacred, divine, spiritual, holy.

And for such you must choose amongst thousands, for there are but few suited to such an office. He must be filled with charity, knowledge, and discretion; where any of them are lacking, there is danger. But ask such of God, and when you have found what you need, thank His Divine Majesty, and be content; seek no more, but go on simply, humbly, and trustingly, and your journey will be safe and blessed.

CHAPTER FIVE

The First Step—Purifying the Soul

———————— • ————————

"THE flowers have appeared in our land," says the Divine Spouse (*Cant.* 2:12), and the time for pruning is come. What, my daughter, are the flowers of our heart, but good desires? Therefore so soon as they appear we need the sickle which shall prune away from our conscience all dead works and superfluities. Before the captive maiden might be espoused to the Israelite, she was obliged to shave her head, and pare her nails, and put the raiment of her captivity from off her (*Deut.* 21:12), and so the soul which aspires to be the bride of Christ must put off the old man, and forsaking sin be clothed with the new man; paring and shaving away all hindrances which come between it and the love of God; such a purging of our corruption is the foundation of future health. St. Paul was purged with a perfect purification in a moment, as were St. Mary Magdalen, St. Catherine of Genoa, St. Pelagia, and some others, but such purifications are miracles of grace, even as the resurrection of the dead was a miracle in nature, and we dare not aspire to such. Ordinary purification and healing, whether of body or soul, are accomplished by little and little, progressing slowly and often hardly at all.

The angels who ascended and descended on Jacob's ladder had wings, yet they flew not, but trod the successive steps of the ladder. We may compare a soul rising from sin to holiness to the dawn which, as it rises, does not at once dispel darkness, but advances gradually. It is an old saying, that a slow cure is a certain cure. Spiritual diseases like those of the body come mounted and at full speed, they return on foot and creeping. We must be patient and courageous. It is sad to see those who, finding their attempts after the devout life hindered by various infirmities, begin to grow uneasy, to fret and be disheartened, almost ready to yield to the temptation of forsaking their aim and falling back; but on the other hand their danger is great, who at the very outset persuade themselves that their imperfections are purified, at once esteem themselves perfected, and seek to fly without wings. Truly, my daughter, having too soon cast aside the physician's care they are in great danger of a relapse. Arise not until the light cometh, saith the Prophet, rise not till ye have rested: and he himself practices this lesson, and having been already washed and cleansed, prays that he may be washed more thoroughly.

The discipline of purification can and must cease only with our life, therefore be not discouraged by infirmities; our perfection consists in struggling against them, which we cannot do unless we perceive them, neither can we conquer unless we come into collision with them. Victory does not lie in ignoring our infirmities, but in resisting them.

Therefore being grieved by them is not consenting to them—our humility is at times tested by the wounds which we receive in this spiritual combat, but we are never conquered unless we lose our courage or our life. And our spiritual life can be extinguished only by mortal sins—not by imperfections and venial sins—therefore we have the more need to watch that these do not destroy our courage. "Deliver me, O Lord," said David, "from cowardice and faint-heartedness." It is a favorable feature of this war, that so long as we will fight, we must be victorious.

CHAPTER SIX

First Purification—That of Mortal Sin

———•———

T HE first purification to be made is that of sin, and the means—the holy Sacrament of Penance. Seek the best confessor that you can, take some one of the books prepared for the aid of conscience, read it carefully, and observe minutely wherein you have sinned from the earliest period up to the present time, and if you distrust your memory, write down what you discover. Having thus examined and collected the sinful wounds of your conscience, detest them, and with your whole heart reject and abhor them by contrition; remembering these four things, *viz.*, that by sin you have lost God's grace, forfeited Heaven, merited Hell, and renounced the eternal love of God. You see, Philothea, that I am now speaking of a General Confession of the whole past life, which although not always absolutely necessary, I still hold to be a most profitable beginning, and recommend it strongly. The ordinary Confessions of those who live a commonplace material life are full of faults. Frequently they make little or no preparation, and come without the requisite contrition; and therefore confess with a tacit intention of repeating their sins, since they will neither avoid the occasions of falling, nor take the needful steps for amending their lives; to all such a General Confession is requisite to assure the soul. Furthermore, it increases our self-knowledge, incites a healthy sorrow for our past sins, fills us with admiration of the patience and mercy of God, calms our heart, relieves our mind, excites in us good resolutions, enables our spiritual Father to guide us with more certainty, and opens our heart to speak fully and with confidence in our future Confessions. Therefore, in preparing for an entire renewal of the heart, and dedication of our soul to God, in commencing a devout life, I do not hesitate to recommend as a first step this General Confession.

CHAPTER SEVEN

Purification—From the Affection to Sin

———— • ————

ALL the children of Israel actually departed from Egypt, but
they did not all depart heartily, wherefore in the desert some
of them regretted the flesh, the melons, the leeks, and onions of Egypt.
(*Num.* 11). And so some penitents, though they forsake sin outwardly, do
not forsake the love of sin; that is to say, they resolve to sin no more,
but it is with reluctance that they abstain from the fatal delights of sin,
their hearts renounce it, and seek to depart, but they frequently look
longingly behind them, as did Lot's wife. They abstain from sin as a
sick man abstains from dainties, which the physicians tell him will be
fatal to him if he eats thereof, he abstains but most unwillingly, he
talks about them, and measures how far he may transgress, at least he
would fain behold what he desires, and envies those who can indulge in
what is forbidden to him. Thus these weak cowardly penitents for a while
refrain from sin, but reluctantly—they would fain be able to sin and
yet escape condemnation—they have still all the taste for forbidden
gratification, and count those happy who enjoy it.

Thus a man who is bent on revenge will change his mind whilst
he is in Confession, but directly after he will find a satisfaction in dis-
cussing the subject of his dispute amongst his friends, saying, that
but for the fear of God he would do so and so—that it is hard to

forgive—would he might lawfully seek revenge, and so forth. Is not this man still hindered with the inclinations of sin, and although he has come out from Egypt, are not his tastes and affections lingering there with its leeks and garlic? So, also, with the woman who having abandoned her unlawful attachments still delights in admiration. Alas, such persons are in great danger!

But you, my daughter, since you desire to commence the devout life, must not only forsake sin, but wholly cleanse your heart of all attachments to sin; for besides the danger of relapse, these wretched affections enfeeble the spirit, and weigh it down so that you cannot be ready, constant, and diligent in performing good works, in which lies the very essence of devotion. A soul which having forsaken actual sin is yet always encumbered with this languishing inclination, reminds me of a person who is not ill, and yet is pale, ailing in all his functions—eating without appetite, sleeping without rest, laughing without gladness, and who instead of walking briskly, drags himself wearily along. Such a soul performs good actions, but with such spiritual languor as to deprive them of all grace, and to make them scanty and ineffective.

CHAPTER EIGHT

How to Effect This Second Purification

———•———

T HE first impulse to this second purification is a clear and hearty consciousness of the exceeding evil of sin, by which means we attain deep and earnest contrition. For as a feeble contrition (if it is true), and especially if united to the holy Sacraments, serves to purify us from actual sin, so deep and hearty contrition purifies us from all the affections of sin. A feeble dislike or antipathy makes us feel repugnant to its object, and glad to shun it; but a strong mortal hatred causes us not only to abhor and fly from its object, but fills us with disgust for it, so that we cannot endure to approach any person or thing in the remotest degree connected with, or reminding us of it. So when the penitent hates his sin with but a feeble (although it may be a sincere) contrition, he resolves to sin no more, but when he hates it with a hearty, vigorous contrition, he detests not only the sin itself, but every affection, circumstance, and inducement which tends towards it. Therefore, my daughter, we should seek to enlarge our contrition and repentance till they extend to everything appertaining to sin. Thus when Magdalen was converted she so lost all delight in her former sins and their pleasures, that she never again thought of them; and David declared not only that he hated sin, but that he utterly abhorred all false and evil ways (*Ps.* 118:104), and in this lies that spiritual renewal of which the same prophet speaks, saying, "thy youth shall be renewed like the eagle's." (*Ps.* 102:5).

In order to obtain this sensitiveness and contrition, exercise yourself carefully in the following meditations which, if well practiced, will, by the grace of God, uproot from your heart both sin and the affections of sin. I have prepared them to that end; and would have you take them in order, one daily, and as early in the morning as possible, for that is the fittest time for such exercises, then ponder and ruminate over it during the rest of the day. Further on, you will find due instructions if you are not already in the habit of making meditation.

CHAPTER NINE

Meditation One—Creation

———•———

Preparation

1. Place yourself in the presence of God.
2. Entreat Him to inspire you.

Reflections

1. Reflect for how many years you were not in the world, and you had no being. Where wert thou, O my soul, at that time? The world had existed so long, but thou wert unheard of.

2. God brought you out of nothing, and made you what you are out of His sole goodness, without requiring any assistance on your part.

3. Consider the being which God has given you, for it is the principal being of this visible world, capable of eternal life, and of perfect union with His Divine Majesty.

Affections and Resolutions

1. Humble yourself profoundly before God, saying from your heart with the Psalmist, "My substance is as nothing before Thee" (*Ps.* 38:6), "and how hast Thou been mindful of me to create me?" Alas, my soul, thou wert once a thing of naught, and even such wouldst thou be still,

unless God had called thee into being. What then would thus have become of thee?

2. Render thanks to God. O great and good Creator, how much do I owe to Thee, since out of my nothingness Thou hast made me what I am? How can I ever worthily bless Thy holy name, and thank Thine infinite goodness?

3. Humble yourself. But alas, O my Creator, instead of uniting myself to Thee by my love and service, my ill-regulated affections have made me rebel against Thee, separating and estranging me from Thee, leading me into sin, and causing me to forget Thy goodness and that Thou art my Creator.

4. Prostrate thyself before God. O my soul, know that the Lord He is Thy God, it is He that hath made thee, and not thou thyself. O God, I am the work of Thy hands. Therefore I would no more rest in myself, who am naught. Wherein shouldst thou glory, O dust and ashes? Wherefore exalt thyself, O thing of naught? In humiliation I will do such and such things, endure such and such contempt, I will live a new life following from henceforth in God's holy ways, and glorifying in the existence He has given me, I will employ it wholly in obeying His Will as I shall learn it, and as my spiritual father shall enjoin.

Conclusion

1. Thank God. Bless God, O my soul, and let all that is in me praise His holy Name, for His goodness has raised me out of nothing, and His loving kindness has created me.

2. Make an offering. O my God, I offer Thee with my whole heart that being which Thou hast given me: to Thee I dedicate and consecrate it.

3. Pray. O God, strengthen me in these affections and resolutions. Holy Virgin, commend them together with all for whom I ought to pray to the mercy of thy Blessed Son. *Our Father. Hail Mary.*

When your prayer is ended gather together the essence of your devout meditations, as it were in a little nosegay, and keep it before you throughout the day.

CHAPTER TEN

Meditation Two—The End for which We Are Created

———————•———————

Preparation

1. Place yourself in the presence of God.
2. Entreat Him to inspire you.

Reflections

1. God did not create you because He had any need of you, for you are wholly useless to Him, but only that He might exercise towards you His goodness, bestowing on you His grace and glory. To accomplish this, He has given you an understanding to know Him, a memory to remember Him, a will to love Him, an imagination to recall His mercies, eyes to see the wonders of His works, a tongue to praise Him, and so with all your other faculties.

2. Therefore being created and placed in the world for this purpose, you should avoid and reject all actions which are contrary to it; and despise as idle and superfluous all which do not promote it.

3. Consider the wretchedness of the world which forgets this, and goes on as though the end of creation were to plant and to build, to amass wealth, and live in frivolity.

Affections and Resolutions

1. Humble yourself, reproaching your soul with her past neglect in reflecting so little on this. Alas! O my God, where were my thoughts when I forgot Thee? What did I love when I loved not Thee? When I should have been nourished and fed with truth, I filled myself with vanity, and served that world which is made to be my servant.

2. Abhor your past life. I renounce you, O vain thoughts and idle meditations! I abjure you, O evil and detestable remembrances! I renounce you, false and treacherous friendships, lost labors, empty pleasures, miserable, deluding satisfactions.

3. Turn to God. And Thou, my God, my Saviour, henceforth, Thou alone shalt fill my thoughts; no more will I wander amidst reflections which displease Thee. My memory shall daily recall the greatness of Thy loving-kindness, so graciously displayed towards me. Thou shalt be the delight of my heart, and the sweetness of my affections.

Henceforth I will detest the frivolities and amusements, the empty pursuits which occupied my time; such and such affections which absorbed my heart I will renounce—to which end I will seek such and such remedies.

Conclusion

1. Thank God who has made you for so good an end. Thou hast made me, O Lord, for Thyself, and that I may forever share the immensity of Thy glory! When shall I be worthy of Thy goodness, and thank Thee worthily?

2. Offering. I offer to Thee, O my Creator, all my affections and resolutions, with all my heart and all my soul.

3. Pray. I beseech Thee, O Lord, accept these my desires and vows, and give Thy blessing to my soul, so that I may have strength to accomplish them through the merit of the blood of Thy Son shed upon the Cross for me.

Weave a little nosegay of devotion.

CHAPTER ELEVEN

Meditation Three—The Mercies of God

———•———

Preparation

1. Place yourself in the presence of God.
2. Entreat Him to inspire you.

Reflections

1. Consider the personal gifts which God has given you: your body, the means of preserving it, health and enjoyments, friends, helpers. Then compare yourself with many who deserve more than you, and yet are deprived of these mercies; some imperfect in health, or in their bodily frame and members, others suffering under contempt, dishonor, and injustice; others struggling with poverty. From all this God has preserved you.

2. Consider your mental gifts: how many there are in the world who are idiots, fools, or madmen. Why are you not amongst them? God has been very gracious to you, for whilst many are brought up in negligence and utter ignorance, His Providence has given you a good and valuable education.

3. Consider your spiritual gifts. You are a child of the Church, and have been trained in its doctrines from childhood. How often has God

granted you to partake of His Sacraments? What inspirations, inward enlightening, correction, has He given for your amendment? How often has He forgiven your sins? How often has He delivered you from the dangers into which your willfulness led you? And all your past life, has it not been a means of advancing the welfare of your soul? Count and see how gracious the Lord has been to you.

Affections and Resolutions

1. Admire the goodness of God. Oh, how good is my God to me! How rich in mercy, how abounding in loving-kindness is His heart! O my soul, never be thou weary of recounting His mercies!

2. Consider your own ingratitude. But what am I, O Lord, that Thou rememberest me? How great is my unworthiness! Alas! I have trodden Thy mercies underfoot, I have abused Thy goodness, and despised Thy sovereign grace, I have opposed the depth of my ingratitude to the depth of Thy favor and grace.

3. Excite thy gratitude. Arise then, O my soul! Be no more faithless, ungrateful, and disloyal to thy mighty Benefactor. What! Shall not my soul henceforth be subject to God who has worked such marvels of grace in me and for me?

4. Then, my daughter, leave off these thy besetting sins; subject thy whole body to the service of God, who has done such great things for it. Apply thy soul to know and approach Him, through the appointed channels. Avail thyself carefully of the means provided by the Church for thy advancement towards salvation and the love of God; be frequent in prayer and in receiving the Sacraments, in hearing God's Word, in heeding all inspirations and counsels.

Conclusion

1. Thank God for the knowledge which He has given thee of thy duty, and for all His past benefits.

2. Offer to Him thy heart together with all thy resolutions.

3. Pray that He will give thee strength to pursue them faithfully,

through the merits of the death of His Son, and ask the intercession of the Blessed Virgin and the Saints.

Our Father. Hail Mary.

Form a spiritual nosegay.

CHAPTER TWELVE

Meditation Four—Sin

———•———

Preparation

1. Place yourself in the presence of God.
2. Entreat Him to inspire you.

Reflections

1. Recollect how long you have sinned, and take note how long the sins of your heart have multiplied; how they have daily accumulated in thought, word, deed, and imagination against God, yourself, and your neighbor.

2. Think over your corrupt inclinations, and how you have yielded to them. And these two reflections will prove that your faults are more in number than the hairs of your head, or the sands of the sea.

3. Consider separately the sin of ingratitude towards God, which is a sin that finds its way through all the others, and aggravates them infinitely. Recount all the mercies He has bestowed upon you, and how you have in return abused them; above all how many inspirations you have despised, how many good impulses you have neglected. How many Sacraments have you received, and where are their fruits? Where are those precious jewels with which your Heavenly Spouse adorned

you? With what preparation have you received them? Think over all this ingratitude, and how God has ceaselessly sought you to save you, whilst you have always fled from Him that you might lose yourself.

Affections and Resolutions

1. Abhor yourself in your wretchedness. O my God, how dare I come before Thine eyes? Alas! I am but a mass of impurity, a very sink of ingratitude and iniquity. Is it possible that I have been so utterly faithless that there is no one of my senses or intellectual powers that I have not sullied and defiled? That no day of my life has passed in which I have not so grievously offended? Was this a meet return for the mercies of my Creator, and the blood of my Redeemer?

2. Ask pardon. Throw yourself at our Saviour's feet, like the Prodigal Son, like Mary Magdalen, like the woman taken in adultery. O Lord, have mercy upon me, a sinner! O living Fountain of Compassion, look upon Thine unworthy child in pity!

3. Purpose amendment. By the help of Thy grace never more will I yield to my sin, O Lord. Alas, I have loved it too well, now I abhor it and cleave to Thee. O Merciful Father, I will live and die in Thee.

4. In order to do away with my former sins I will boldly accuse myself, and suffer none to rankle within my breast.

5. I will do my utmost to uproot them wholly from my heart, especially such a one and such a one, which have chiefly hindered me.

6. And for this end I will faithfully obey the counsels I receive, acknowledging that I can never sufficiently repair my many faults.

Conclusion

1. Thank God for having brought you to this hour, and for giving you these good desires.

2. Offer Him your heart that they may be fulfilled.

3. Pray to Him to strengthen you, etc.

CHAPTER THIRTEEN

Meditation Five—Death

———————●———————

Preparation

1. Place yourself in the presence of God.

2. Entreat His grace.

3. Imagine yourself to lie in extremity on your deathbed, without hope of recovery.

Reflections

1. Consider the uncertainty of your dying day. O my soul, some day must thou quit this body. When will it be, summer or winter? In town or in the country? By day or by night? Will it be suddenly or after due warning? Will it be in sickness or by an accident? Wilt thou have time to confess thy sins or not? Will thy spiritual father be present to assist thee? Alas! Of all this we know nothing; this only is certain, that die we must, and that for the most part sooner than we expect.

2. Consider that then the world is at an end, so far as regards you; there is none any more for you. Everything will then be reversed, all pleasures, vanities, worldly joys, and vain attachments will then appear as mere phantoms and vapors. Woe is me, for what delusive trifles have I offended my God! Then will you discover that you have forsaken God

for nothing! On the other hand, how beautiful and desirable will good works and devotion then appear; why have you not followed on that holy and blessed road? Truly at that hour sins which before seemed as trifles will wax great as the mountains, and how faint, how weak, will your devotion then appear!

3. Consider the painful and final farewell which your soul must take of this lower world. It must take leave of wealth, of vanities and vain society, of pleasure, of amusements, of friends and neighbors, of parents and children, of husband and wife, in short of everything earthly. Last of all it must take leave of the body, which it will leave pale and sunken, forsaken, hideous, and vile.

4. Consider the haste with which that body will be hidden beneath the ground, and when that is done the world will scarcely bestow another thought upon you. You will in your turn be forgotten, as you have forgotten others. God rest his soul, will be said, and no more. O death, how unsparing, how pitiless thou art!

5. Consider that when the soul quits the body, it must go either to the left hand or the right. Whither will yours go? Which will be its path? Even such as it has chosen whilst on earth.

Affections and Resolutions

1. Pray to God, and cast yourself upon Him. Lord, in that dreadful day receive me into Thy care! Turn that hour into blessedness to me, and then let all the previous hours of my life be bitter and sad.

2. Despise the world. Since I know not, O world, at what hour I must quit thee, I will not attach myself to thee. O dear friends, treasured hopes, grant me only to love you with a holy friendship which may endure throughout eternity. Why should I be bound to you with ties that must be severed here?

I will prepare for this hour, and make fitting preparation to accomplish the journey well; I will diligently strive to make my conscience clear, and to set in order its deficiencies.

Conclusion

Thank God for enabling you so to resolve, offer your resolutions to His Majesty, and repeatedly implore Him to grant you a happy death, through the merits of His Son. Implore the help of Our Lady and the Saints. *Pater. Ave.*

Weave a nosegay of myrrh.

CHAPTER FOURTEEN

Meditation Six—Judgment

— • —

Preparation

1. Place yourself in the presence of God.
2. Entreat Him to inspire you.

Reflections

1. At the end of the time appointed by God for the world to last, and after many signs and terrible wonders which shall fill all men with fear and terror, a deluge of fire will come and consume the whole earth, sparing nothing of all that we behold.

2. After this fiery deluge and scorching heat, all men, except those already risen, shall rise up from their graves, and at the Archangel's summons appear in the valley of Josaphat. But there will be a great difference amongst them, for the bodies of some will be glorious and shining, those of others horrible and vile.

3. Consider the majesty in which the Sovereign Judge will appear surrounded by all the Saints and Angels, and with His Cross shining brighter than the sun, symbol of grace to the good and of condemnation to the wicked.

4. This Sovereign Judge by His omnipotent decree will in an instant

separate the good from the bad—placing the former on His right hand, the latter on His left—an eternal separation, after which the two companies will never meet again.

5. After this separation, all consciences shall be laid bare, and the wickedness of the bad will be clearly seen, and how they have despised God; as will the penitence of the good, and the results of God's grace working in them; for then nothing shall be hid. O my God, how great will be the confusion of the one, and the bliss of the others!

6. Consider the final sentence of the bad, "Depart from Me, ye cursed, into everlasting fire, prepared for the devil and his angels." Weigh well these most weighty words. "Depart," it is a sentence of final abandonment which God speaks—banishing them forever from His presence. He calls them "cursed." O my soul, what a malediction! A malediction comprising all woes! Irrevocable! For all time and eternity—and "into everlasting fire." Contemplate, my soul, this eternity. O eternal eternity of woe, how fearful art thou!

7. Consider the opposite sentence of the good, "Come," saith the Judge (O blessed word of salvation! By which God draws us to Himself and receives us within the circle of His grace), "Come, ye blessed of My Father" (O benediction above all benedictions!), "possess you the kingdom prepared for you from the foundation of the world." My God, what a favor, for that kingdom has no end!

Affections and Resolutions

1. Tremble, O my soul, at this thought. My God, who shall support me in that day when the very heavens shall pass away?

2. Abhor your sins which alone can destroy you at that fearful day. Let me judge myself now, that I be not judged then; let me examine my conscience, and condemn myself; let me accuse and correct myself, that the Judge may not condemn me in that dreadful day—let me then hasten to Confession, and adopt the needful remedies.

Conclusion

1. Thank God, who has given you the means of being secure on that day, and who has granted you time for repentance.

2. Offer Him your heart in penitence, and beseech Him to give you grace to repent worthily. *Pater. Ave.*

3. Make your nosegay.

CHAPTER FIFTEEN

Meditation Seven—Hell

———— • ————

Preparation

1. Place yourself in the Divine Presence.

2. Humble yourself, and implore His assistance

3. Imagine yourself in a dark city, burning with brimstone and sulphur, and filled with citizens who cannot escape.

Reflections

1. The damned are in the infernal abyss as in this miserable city, where they endure unutterable torments in every sense and in every member; because, as every sense and member has participated in their sin, so must they participate in its punishment. The eyes, as the reward of their false and evil gazing, will endure the horrible sight of devils and of Hell; the ears, which delighted in unholy conversation, will never hear aught save weeping, lamentations, and despair, and so with the other senses.

2. Besides all these torments there is one yet greater, namely, that they are forever deprived of God and of His glory. If Absalom sorrowed more over the absence of his father David than over his exile (*2 Kings* 14:32), what shall be the regret of those who are forever deprived of the

sight of Thy sweet and gracious countenance, O Lord?

3. Consider, above all, the eternity of suffering which alone would make Hell insupportable. How a trifling annoyance, a slight fever, makes a short night appear long and grievous to us here! What, then, will be the night of eternity with its torments? That eternity whence arise eternal despair, blasphemy, and rage.

Affections and Resolutions

"Which of you can dwell with devouring fire? Which of you shall dwell with everlasting burnings?" (*Is.* 33:14). Take warning from these words. O my soul, couldst thou live forever amidst these torments? Wilt thou indeed forsake thy God forever? Confess that you have repeatedly deserved so to lose Him. Henceforth I will follow the other path, why should I go down into Hell? I will therefore make such and such efforts to avoid the sins which will bring me to eternal death.

Thank God. Make an offering of thyself. Pray.

CHAPTER SIXTEEN

Meditation Eight—Paradise

——— • ———

Preparation

1. Place yourself in the presence of God.
2. Invoke Him.

Reflections

1. Represent to yourself a beautiful serene night, and consider how pleasant it is to behold the sky with all that multitude and variety of stars; then add to that beauty the glory of a bright day, yet so that the brilliancy of the sun should not overpower the brightness either of the moon or the stars; and then remember that assuredly all this collected beauty falls immeasurably short of Paradise. Oh, what a blessed and desired home it is! How precious a city!

2. Consider the grandeur, the beauty, and the multitude of the citizens and inhabitants of that happy land, the millions and millions of angels, Cherubim and Seraphim, the glorious company of Apostles, martyrs, confessors, virgins, and matrons: the multitude is innumerable. Oh, what a blessed company, of whom the least is greater than the whole world! What will it be to behold them all? O my God, how blessed are they, forever singing the glad song of eternal love, forever

enjoying perpetual gladness, mutually rejoicing in each other, and sharing the delights of a friendship which can never know any interruption.

3. Consider further how they forever rejoice in God, beholding His gracious countenance, which sheds into their hearts a never-ceasing depth of sweetness. What a thing it is never to be separated from their King! They are like happy birds, hovering and singing *forever* in the atmosphere of Divinity, which surrounds them with unspeakable delights. There with envy they rival one another in singing the praises of their Creator! Blessed be Thou forever, O loving and sovereign Creator and Saviour, who art so merciful towards us and givest us so abundantly of Thy glory. And in His turn God bestows a perpetual benediction on all His Saints: Blessed be ye forever, O my children, who have served Me, and now praise Me eternally with unutterable love and joy.

Affections and Resolutions

1. Admire and praise this heavenly country. Blessed art thou, O Jerusalem, and blessed are thine inhabitants within thee.

2. Reproach your own heart with its want of resolution in steadily following the road which leads to this blessed land. Why have I so neglected my supreme bliss? Woe is me, for trivial unsatisfying pleasures I have a thousand times forsaken these eternal and infinite delights. How could I despise so great good, and prize such vain and contemptible things?

3. Earnestly aspire after this blessed Home. O my good and gracious Lord, since it hath pleased Thee to lead me back into Thy paths, never more will I depart from them. Forward then, O my soul! Let us hasten onwards to this everlasting rest, let us press forward to this blessed Land of Promise. Why do we linger here in Egypt? Henceforth I will forsake all things that can hinder me, or cause me to lose my way, and will do only such things as shall forward me on this road.

Give thanks. Offer thyself. Pray.

CHAPTER SEVENTEEN

Meditation Nine—The Choice of Paradise

———————————●———————————

Preparation

1. Place yourself in the presence of God.
2. Humble yourself before Him, and ask His inspiration.

Reflections

Imagine yourself in a wide plain alone with your Guardian Angel (as was young Tobias on his way to Rages), and that he displays to you Paradise above, and all its delights on which you have been meditating—beneath you Hell and all its torments: having realized this, kneel down before your Guardian Angel and consider—

1. That you are truly placed between Heaven and Hell, and that both are waiting for you to choose whither you will go.

2. Consider that the choice you make of either in this life will last forever in the next.

3. Consider further, that although the choice depends upon yourself, yet God, who is ready to give the one through His justice, the other through His mercy, desires above all that you choose Heaven, and your good Angel urges you to that choice with all his might, offering to your aid a thousand graces from God, a thousand means of help.

4. Jesus Christ looks down from Heaven in love upon you, and calls you tenderly. Come, O my beloved, come to eternal rest within My loving arms, which are waiting for thee with immortal pleasures and unfailing love. Behold with thy spiritual sight the Blessed Virgin watching thee with a mother's love. Be brave, my daughter, despise not the longings of my Son, nor the sighs which I pour out for thee, desiring thine eternal salvation. Behold the Saints warning thee, and millions of holy spirits watching thee, desiring ardently that thou mayst join them in praising God forever, and pleading with thee that the heavenward path is not so difficult as the world would fain make thee believe. Be of good courage, they repeat: whoever will consider the pathway of devotion, by which we have arrived here, will see that we attained this happiness through a sweetness far greater than any the world can give.

Choice

1. Hell, I detest thee now and forever. I abhor thy torments and thy pains; thy terrible and wretched eternity, and above all the eternal maledictions and blasphemies which thou pourest forth against my God. And gazing upon thee, O lovely Paradise, eternal glory, everlasting gladness, I choose my home forever amidst thy blessed and glorious mansions, within thy holy and precious tabernacles. O my God, I bless Thy mercy, and accept the choice it has pleased Thee to offer me. O Jesus, my Saviour, I accept Thine everlasting love, and thank Thee that Thou hast obtained for me a place within the heavenly Jerusalem, where above all other delights I shall love and bless Thee forever.

2. Accept the aid of the Blessed Virgin and the Saints, promise to follow in their steps; and give up yourself to your good angel, that he may lead you onwards in the way you have chosen.

CHAPTER EIGHTEEN

Meditation Ten—The Soul's Choice of a Devout Life

———— • ————

Preparation

1. Place thyself in the presence of God.
2. Prostrate thyself before Him, and seek His aid.

Reflections

1. Once more imagine yourself in a wide plain alone with your good angel; and on the left hand behold the devil sitting on a high and lofty throne, surrounded by infernal spirits, and by a troop of worldly men who with uncovered heads acknowledge him and do homage to him, some by one sin, some by another. Examine the countenances of these unfortunate courtiers of an abominable king: some raging with hatred, passion, and envy; some murdering their neighbors; some pale, thoughtful, and absorbed in the accumulation of wealth; others engrossed in vanity and empty, useless pleasures; others corrupt and lost in their vile passions; see how all live alike without rest, without order, without grace. See how they despise one another, and how their friendship is but counterfeit. In short you see a miserable gathering, tyrannized over by an accursed king, a sight meet to move your pity.

2. On the right hand behold the crucified Saviour, who with fervent

love prays for these wretches, that they may escape from their tyrant, and come to Him. Behold how He is surrounded by holy men and women and their good angels. Contemplate the beauty of the kingdom of holiness. How lovely this band of virgins, both men and women, purer than the lily; this company of widows full of holy mortification and humility; this body of husbands and wives who live in such harmony and mutual love, the fruit of charity. Consider how they unite the care of their external duties with that of their hearts, conjugal love with love of the Heavenly Spouse. Look all round; everywhere you will behold a gentle, holy, loving aspect, whilst they hearken to their Lord, and seek to retain Him within their very inmost hearts. They rejoice, but with a holy, charitable, well-regulated joy; they love one another, but with a holy, pure love. Some amongst them have sorrows, but they do not fret under them and are not discouraged, for they seek their consolation from their Saviour, and forever look up to Him.

3. You have already forsaken Satan and his pitiable company by the good desires which God has given you; nevertheless, you have not as yet attained to Jesus our King, or joined His blessed and happy company of holy men; therefore, you are still standing between the two.

4. The Blessed Virgin with St. Joseph, St. Louis, St. Monica, and thousands of those who once were living in the world, invite and encourage you.

5. The crucified King calls you by name: Come, O my beloved, come that I may crown thee.

Choice

1. O world, sad company, never will I join thy standard. I have forever forsaken thy treacheries and vanities! Proud king, infernal spirit, I renounce thee with all thy pomps, I abhor thee with all thy works.

2. And turning to Thee, O Blessed Jesus, King of eternal glory and happiness, I embrace Thee with my whole soul, I adore Thee with my whole heart. I adopt Thee as my King now and forever, and by my

inviolable fidelity, I give myself up to Thee forever, I submit forever to Thy holy laws and precepts.

3. O holy Virgin, dearest Lady, thou shalt be my guide and teacher; I offer to thee my special reverence and love.

O Guardian Angel, conduct me to this blessed assembly; leave me not until I attain to that happy company with whom I would say now and ever in confirmation of my choice: Jesus, be Thou my Lord forever!

CHAPTER NINETEEN

General Confession

———•———

HAVING then gone through this course of meditation, approach your General Confession with humility, yet confidently; but do not allow yourself to be perplexed with fears. The scorpion's bite is venomous, but from its substance is extracted a remedy which heals that very bite: so our sins are shameful when we commit them, but when they are turned to confession and penitence they are a source of spiritual benefit and welfare. Contrition and confession are so lovely and acceptable, that they efface the stain and disperse the stench of sin.

Simon the leper called Magdalen a sinner, but our Saviour spoke not of her sins, but only of the precious ointment which she poured out, and of the fullness of her love. If we are truly humble, Philothea, we shall grieve bitterly over our sin because it offends God, but we shall find sweetness in accusing ourselves, because in so doing we honor Him; and we shall find relief in fully revealing our complaints to our physician. When you are before your spiritual father, suppose yourself to be on Mount Calvary, at the feet of the Crucified Jesus, whose Precious Blood drops upon you to purify your iniquities. For although it is no longer His very blood, nevertheless, it is the virtue of His blood-shedding, which so plentifully descends upon the penitent in the confessional. Hesitate not then to open your heart fully in Confession, for in proportion as your sins go forth, the precious merits of Christ's Passion will come in and fill you with all blessings.

Speak simply and ingenuously, and thoroughly lighten your conscience. After this give heed to the warnings and the directions of God's minister, and say in your heart: Speak, Lord, for Thy servant heareth. It is God Himself who speaks to you, my daughter, inasmuch as He has said, "He that heareth you heareth Me." (*Luke* 10:16). Then take the following protestation as a conclusion of your contrition, and having previously studied it carefully, read it with attention and as much feeling as you can.

CHAPTER TWENTY

A Protest for the Purpose of Fixing In the Mind a Resolution to Serve God, And to Conclude Your Penitential Acts

———————— • ————————

I, the undersigned, standing before the presence of the Eternal God and His heavenly host, having reflected upon the boundless mercy of His divine goodness towards me, His weak unworthy creature, whom He has created out of nothing, preserved, sustained, delivered from so many dangers, and loaded with so many gifts: but, above all, having considered the incomprehensible mercy and compassion with which this good God has endured my iniquities, inspiring me with good desires, winning me on to amendment, and waiting so patiently until this period for my repentance in spite of all my ingratitude, disloyalty, and faithlessness, through which by delaying my conversion and despising His grace, I have so deeply offended Him, having further considered that in my Baptism I was happily and solemnly dedicated to God as His child, and that in spite of the profession then made in my name, I have so often wickedly profaned and sullied my soul, going contrary to His divine will, now at last coming to myself, prostrate in heart and soul before the throne of His justice, I own, acknowledge, and confess that I am thoroughly convicted of treason against God, and am guilty of the death and Passion of Jesus Christ, through the sins which I have committed and for which He died, enduring the Cross—therefore I own myself worthy of death and damnation.

But I look towards the throne of infinite mercy of this same Eternal God, and detesting the sins of my past life with all my heart and all my strength, I humbly beseech pardon and mercy and entire absolution of my sins, through the merits of the death and Passion of this same Lord and Redeemer of my soul. Resting on Him as the sole foundation of all my hopes I hereby repeat and renew the solemn profession made by me to God in my Baptism, renouncing the world, the flesh, and the devil, abhorring their hateful vanities, lusts, and passions, henceforth and forever. And turning to my compassionate and merciful God, I desire, purpose, resolve, and deliberately dedicate myself to serve and love Him now and for all eternity; seeking His pleasure, devoting and consecrating my mind with all its faculties, my soul with all its powers, my heart with all its affections, and my body with all its senses, to His service. And I resolve never again to pervert any part of my being to disobey His Will and Sovereign Majesty to which I spiritually immolate and sacrifice myself, purposing ever to be His faithful and obedient child, without hesitation or change! But if, alas, through human infirmity or the power of the enemy, I should in any way infringe this my steadfast resolution, I now protest that through the grace of the Holy Spirit I will return the moment I perceive my error, once more offering myself to the divine mercy without limitation or delay. This is my will, my intention, my inviolable and irrevocable resolution, which I profess and confirm without exception or reserve in the sacred presence of God, before the Church Triumphant, and my Mother the Church Militant, who receives this declaration in the person of her appointed minister now present. Be pleased, O Eternal God, Omnipotent and Merciful Father, Son, and Holy Ghost, to confirm my resolutions, and accept favorably this my heart's offering. And as it has pleased Thee to give me the desire and will to serve Thee, give me likewise grace and strength to do so. O God, Thou art the God of my heart, of my soul, and of my spirit: I will acknowledge and adore Thee, now, and for all eternity. Amen.

CHAPTER TWENTY-ONE

Conclusion of the First Purification

———————————•———————————

HAVING made this declaration, open the ears of your heart and listen attentively, that your soul may hear the absolution which the Saviour on the throne of His mercy will pronounce before all the Saints and angels, when in His Name the priest absolves you here on earth. All that blessed company will rejoice with you, will sing their heavenly song with unutterable gladness, and in spirit will embrace you, restored to grace and renewed holiness.

My daughter, what a treaty is this, whereby you enter into covenant with God, giving yourself to Him, and gaining both Himself and yourself for life everlasting! It only remains now in all sincerity to take the pen in your hand and sign your protestation, and then to approach the holy altar, where God will on His part sign and seal your absolution and the promise of Paradise, placing His Sacrament as a sacred seal upon your renewed heart. Thus, daughter, your soul will be cleansed from sin and the desires of sin. But forasmuch as these desires are easily reawakened in the heart, owing to our infirmity and proneness to evil, which may be repressed but never extinguished whilst we are on earth, I will give you certain rules, by the observance of which you may henceforth be preserved from mortal sin and its affections, so that they may never find entrance into your heart. In order that these rules may serve as a still further purification, I will first speak concerning the state of absolute purity, to which I would lead you.

CHAPTER TWENTY-TWO

We Must Also Lay Aside Our Disposition towards Venial Sins

———————•———————

A S THE light waxes fuller we see the more plainly in our mirror the stains and specks upon our face. Even so as the Holy Spirit enlightens our conscience we perceive more clearly and distinctly the sins, inclinations, and imperfections which hinder us in attaining to true devotion. The same light which discovers to us these tares and weeds, also kindles us with the desire to cleanse and purify our hearts from them.

You will discover then, my daughter, that besides mortal sins and their affections from which you are now purified, there yet linger in your heart various inclinations and dispositions to venial sin. I do not say that you will discover venial sins, but you will find a disposition and inclination to them, which is a very different thing, for we can never be wholly free from venial sins, at least not for any length of time, but we can be without affection for them. There is a wide difference between a chance falsehood concerning some trivial matter, which is the result of carelessness, and taking pleasure in falsehood or deliberately telling lies.

Therefore I say we must purify the soul from all inclination to venial sins, that is to say, we must never willingly admit or continue in any kind of venial sin whatever. It would indeed be a fearful thing wittingly to burden our conscience with anything so offensive to God as a will to displease Him. And venial sin, however slight, does displease Him, although not so grievously as to make Him condemn and destroy us for it. If therefore venial sin so displeases God, all consent and affection on our part to it is nothing less than a willingness to displease His Divine Majesty. Can any pious soul not only offend God, but take pleasure in so doing?

All such inclinations, my daughter, are directly opposed to devotion, as inclinations to mortal sin are opposed to charity: they enfeeble the spirit, hinder divine consolations, and open the door to temptation; so that, though they do not slay the soul, they wound it grievously. "Dying flies" (says the wise man) "spoil the sweetness of the ointment" (*Eccles.* 10:1); by which he means that when the flies only pass over the surface of the ointment and eat as they go, what remains is uninjured, but if they remain in it, they putrefy and spoil it all. So the venial sins of a devout soul which find no resting-place, do no great injury, but if they are harbored and delighted in, they destroy the sweetness of the ointment, that is, of pure devotion.

Spiders do not kill bees, but they spoil and corrupt their honey, covering the combs with their webs, by which if they remain the bees are hindered in their work. So venial sins do not destroy the soul, but they hinder devotion, and so clog the powers of the soul with bad habits and inclinations that it loses that active charity which is the lifespring of devotion—always supposing that we willingly harbor venial sin in our conscience. Some slight falsehood, some lack of self-control in word or action, in dress, in occupation, in amusement—these will leave no lasting evil if, like spider's webs, they are banished from our conscience as soon as perceived, just as the bees drive out the intruding spider. But if we permit them to remain, still more if we take any pleasure in them and suffer them to multiply, soon our honey will be lost, and the hive of our conscience will be soiled and damaged. But I ask again, what sincere soul could ever take delight in offending God, rejoice in displeasing Him, and persist in willing that which He forbids?

CHAPTER TWENTY-THREE

We Must Purify Ourselves from the Taste for Useless and Dangerous Things

———————•———————

SPORTS, balls, festivities, display, the drama, in themselves are not necessarily evil things, but rather indifferent, and capable of being used or abused. Nevertheless, there is always danger in these things, and to care for them is much more dangerous. Therefore I should say that although it is lawful to amuse yourself, to dance, dress, hear good plays, and join in society, yet to be attached to such things, is contrary to devotion and extremely hurtful and dangerous. The evil lies not in *doing* the thing, but in *caring* for it. It is a pity to sow in our heart such vain and idle inclinations which occupy the place of better things, and hinder our soul from devoting all its energies to higher pursuits.

Thus of old the Nazarenes abstained not only from everything which could intoxicate, but also from grapes and from vinegar of wine (*Num.* 6:3), not that these could produce intoxication, but because the taste of the one might excite a desire for the taste of the other. I do not say that we must not use these dangerous things, but I do say that we can never take delight in them without periling our devotion. When the stag has grown too fat, he hides himself in the thickets, knowing that he is not able to fly with sufficient speed from the hunter: so the heart of man, if it is encumbered with these useless attachments which are both superfluous and dangerous, cannot readily, easily, and gladly rise up to God—in which readiness true devotion consists. Children run eagerly after butterflies, and no one blames them, because they are but children; but is it not a ridiculous and a melancholy sight to see men eager and earnest in pursuit of such unworthy trifles as those of which I speak, which besides their own insignificance run the risk of discomposing and injuring us whilst we follow after them? Therefore, my daughter, shake off all such attachments, and be assured that if the actions themselves are not contrary to devotion, to take delight in them is most hurtful to it.

CHAPTER TWENTY-FOUR

Purifying Ourselves from Evil Inclinations

———————•———————

FURTHERMORE, we have certain inclinations which, as they do not arise from our individual sins, are not precisely either mortal or venial sins, but rather imperfections, and their results are faults and deficiencies. For instance, St. Jerome relates that St. Paula was naturally so disposed to sadness and melancholy, that when she lost her husband and children she nearly died of grief. This was an imperfection, not a sin, as it was against her desire and will. Some are naturally light of purpose, some disputatious; others are disposed to impatience, to anger, or to softness—indeed there are few in whom we do not perceive some such imperfections. But although they are natural infirmities, still by care and watchfulness they may be restrained and corrected, and at last overcome and cured. And this, my daughter, you must do. We have discovered that by cutting the foot of the tree and letting the sap escape, we can change the bitter almond tree into that which bears pleasant fruit: shall we not also be able to get rid of our perverse inclinations and acquire better? There is no disposition so good by nature that it cannot acquire bad habits, neither is there any disposition naturally so perverse that by the grace of God, united to diligence and industry, it may not be conquered and subdued. To this end I shall counsel you, and furnish you with exercises whereby to purify the soul of dangerous inclinations, imperfections, and tendencies to venial sins, and to be more and more strengthened against mortal sins. May God give you grace to use them profitably!

PART SECOND

———•———

*Counsels Concerning the Soul's
Approach to God
in Prayer and the Sacraments*

CHAPTER ONE

The Necessity of Prayer

PRAYER brings our mind into the brightness of divine light, and exposes our will to the warmth of divine love. Nothing else can so purge our mind from its ignorance, and our will from its depraved affections. It is a blessed fountain which, as it flows, revives our good desires and causes them to bring forth fruit, washes away the stains of infirmity from our soul, and calms the passions of our hearts.

Above all, I would recommend mental prayer, the prayer of the heart; and that drawn from the contemplation of our Saviour's life and Passion. If you habitually meditate upon Him, your whole soul will be filled with Him, you will learn His expression, and learn to frame your actions after His example. He is the Light of the world, it is therefore in Him, by Him, and for Him, that we must be enlightened and illuminated: such meditation is the Desired Tree, under the shadow of which we must repose: it is Jacob's well wherein we may wash away all our stains. Do not children as they hearken to their mother, and, lisping, imitate her, gradually learn to speak her language? And so if we remain close to the Saviour, meditating upon Him, and giving heed to His words, His actions, and His affections, we shall gradually, by the help of His grace, learn to speak, to act and will like Him. There we must stop, for, believe me, Philothea, we can approach God the Father by no other door: just as we could see no reflection in a mirror were it not covered at the back with lead or tin, so should we be unable in this world to contemplate the Divinity were it not united to our Blessed Lord's Sacred Humanity, His life and death being the most suitable, sweet, blessed, and profitable subject which we can choose for our constant meditation. He did not call Himself "the Bread which cometh down from heaven," without a meaning: just as men eat bread, with whatever other meat they may have, so in all our prayers and actions we should seek, dwell upon, and meditate on our Saviour. His life and death have been divided and arranged for meditation by several authors: those whom I recommend to you are St. Bonaventure, Bellintani, Bruno, Capilla, Grenada, and Da Ponte.

Devote one hour daily to mental prayer—if you can, let it be early in the morning, because then your mind is less cumbered and more vigorous after the night's rest. Do not spend longer than an hour in this exercise unless expressly desired to do so by your spiritual father.

If you can perform it in church, so much the better, and surely no one, father or mother, husband or wife, or any one else, can object to your spending an hour in church, and perhaps you could not easily insure an uninterrupted hour at home.

Begin all prayer, whether mental or vocal, by placing yourself in the presence of God. Adhere strictly to this rule, the value of which you will soon realize.

I recommend you to say the Lord's Prayer, Hail Mary, and Creed in Latin. But you must at the same time thoroughly understand the words in your own language: so that whilst you join in the universal language of the Church, you may appreciate the blessed meaning of those holy prayers, which you must say, fixing your thoughts steadily, and arousing your affections, not hurrying in order to say many prayers, but endeavoring that what you say may come from your heart. For one Lord's Prayer said with devotion is worth more than many recited hastily.

The Rosary is a most useful kind of prayer, if you know how to say it rightly; to which end use one of the little books which explain it. The

Litanies of Our Lord, of the Blessed Virgin, and of the Saints, and all the other prayers which you find in the authorized manuals and primers are useful. But if you have the gift of mental prayer, mind and make that the chief thing, so that if from press of business or other causes you are hindered from vocal prayer, you will not be distressed, but will rest satisfied with saying, before or after your meditation, the Lord's Prayer, the Angelic Salutation, and the Apostles' Creed.

If during vocal prayer your heart is drawn to mental prayer, do not restrain it, but let your devotion take that channel, omitting the vocal prayers which you intended to say: that which takes their place is more acceptable to God, and more useful to your own soul. Of course this does not include the Church's Office if you are bound to recite it.

If your morning passes away without this holy exercise of mental prayer, from either excessive occupation or any other cause (though such interruptions should be avoided as far as possible), try to repair the omission later in the day—but not directly after a meal, as then you might make it heavily and sleepily, and might even injure your health. If through the whole day you cannot perform it, you must try to make amends by multiplying ejaculatory prayer, and by reading some devotional book, or by some penitential acts in order to avert the consequences of your omission; to which add a firm resolution to do better the next day.

CHAPTER TWO

A Short Plan for Meditation.
Concerning the Presence of God:
The First Point of Preparation

———————— • ————————

YOU may perhaps not understand how to practice mental prayer, for unfortunately at the present time it is too much neglected. I will therefore give you some short and simple instructions concerning it. First, I would notice the preparation, which may be divided into two parts—placing yourself in the presence of God, and invoking His help. To the first end, placing yourself in the presence of God, I will give you four chief means, whereby to begin.

The first consists in a keen and attentive realizing of God's omnipresence; that He is in all and everywhere: that there is no place nor thing in the world where He is not; so that, as the birds, let them fly where they will, always meet the air, so we, let us go where we will, be where we will, shall always be where God is. We all know this as an intellectual truth, but we do not always receive and act upon it. A blind man does not see his sovereign, but if he is informed of his presence he maintains an attitude of reverence: yet not seeing the object of respect he easily forgets that it is present, and so forgetting soon loses his reverence. So with us, we do not see God, and although faith warns us that He is present, yet not seeing Him with our own eyes we soon forget it, and act as though He were afar off. For though as a mere matter of reasoning we know that He is everywhere, if we do not think about it, the result is the same as if we did not know it. For this reason we should always, before we pray, excite our souls to an attentive recollection of the presence of God. Thus, David says, "If I ascend into heaven, Thou art there: if I descend into hell, Thou art present." (*Ps.* 138:8). And so may we use the words of Jacob, who when he had beheld the holy ladder of angels, exclaimed, "How terrible is this place! Indeed the Lord is in this place, and I knew it not!" (*Gen.* 28:16, 17). That is, he had not thought about it, for surely he knew that God was everywhere. When, therefore, you would pray, say to your heart, and with your whole heart, "Surely God is in this place."

The second means by which you may realize this Sacred presence, is to remember that not only is God in the *place* where you are, but that He is also specially within your heart and spirit, which He animates and quickens with His divine presence; the Heart of your heart, the Spirit of your spirit; for just as the soul animates the whole body, yet above all inhabits the heart, so God being present everywhere is yet specially present with our spirit. Therefore David calls God the "God of his heart" (*Ps.* 72:26), and St. Paul says, that "in Him we live, and move, and are." (*Acts* 17:28). This reflection will excite deep reverence within your heart for that God who is ever so close to you.

The third means is to reflect upon our Saviour, who in His Humanity looks down from Heaven upon all men, but chiefly on Christians, who are His children: and still more especially on those who pray, to whose thoughts and actions He gives careful heed. Nor is this a mere supposition, but an assured truth: for although we see Him not, He is ever looking down upon us. The martyr St. Stephen beheld Him thus; and we may say with the Bride, "Behold He standeth behind our wall, looking through the windows, looking through the lattices." (*Cant.* 2:9).

The fourth means is in imagination to behold the Saviour in His Sacred Humanity as actually present with us; just as we do with the friends we love, saying, "I can see him doing or saying such and such things." But if the Blessed Sacrament be present, this Presence becomes no longer imaginary, but actual; for hidden under the veil of bread and wine the Saviour is really present, beholding and watching us, although we cannot see His bodily Presence. Before you pray, then, make use of some of these methods whereby to place your soul in the presence of God, and do not attempt to use them all at once, but one at a time, and let what you do be short and simple.

CHAPTER THREE

Of Invocation:
The Second Part of Preparation

———————•———————

INVOCATION is as follows: having placed your soul in the presence of God, you must humble it with deep reverence, acknowledging yourself unworthy to approach His Sovereign Majesty, yet knowing that His goodness would have you draw near, and therefore asking of Him grace to serve and worship Him in your meditation. To this end you can use some such brief and earnest petitions as those of David, when he said, "Cast me not away from thy face: and take not thy holy spirit from me." (*Ps.* 50). "Make thy face to shine upon thy servant: and teach me thine ordinances." (*Ps.* 118:135). "Give me understanding, and I will search Thy law: and I will keep it with my whole heart." (*ibid.* 34). "I am thy servant, O give me understanding" (*ibid.* 125), and many other such. Furthermore, it will help you to invoke your Guardian Angel, and those saints most especially connected with the subject of your meditation; thus in meditating on the death of Our Lord, you might invoke Our Lady, St. John, St. Mary Magdalen, the Penitent Thief, so that the holy inspirations which prompted them may be communicated to you; and in meditating on your own death, you would invoke your Guardian Angel, who will then be present, so that he may help you to reflect suitably, and so on with other mysteries.

CHAPTER FOUR

Setting Forth the Mystery:
The Third Point of Preparation

---•---

AFTER these two ordinary points in meditation, comes a third, which is not common to all meditation, and which is by some called the *Compositio loci,* or composition of place, and by others the inward lesson.

This is simply representing to ourselves by the aid of the imagination the mystery on which we would meditate, as though it were actually going on before our eyes. For instance, if the subject of your meditation is the crucified Saviour, imagine yourself on Mount Calvary, beholding and hearing all the events of His Passion; and represent to yourself all that the Evangelists describe. So, when you meditate on death, or on Hell and similar mysteries which concern visible things of sense; for when we come to the mysteries of God's greatness, the excellence of goodness, the end of our creation, and such invisible things, we cannot employ this active imagination. We can certainly use similitudes and comparisons to assist our reflections; but there is some effort in this, and I would have you act with great simplicity, and not fatigue your mind with labored thoughts.

By the help of this vivid imagination we can the better fix our mind upon the proposed subject of meditation, and refrain from wandering thoughts; just as a bird is confined in a cage, or a hawk by its jesses, so that it may not quit the wrist. There are some who will tell you that it is better to use the pure thoughts of faith, and a simple apprehension altogether mental and spiritual in the representation of these mysteries, but I consider that too hard and subtle a process at first, and until it pleases God to lead you higher, I counsel you, Philothea, to rest satisfied with the humble means which I have indicated.

CHAPTER FIVE

Second Part of Meditation—Reflections

———————•———————

AFTER this act of imagination, there follows an act of the understanding, which we call meditation. It consists of one or more reflections made with the view of exciting our affections towards God and the things of Heaven. And the difference between meditation and study or any other processes of thought, is that the latter have not virtue and the love of God for their end, for their object is temporal, such as the acquisition of knowledge, for purposes of discussion, composition, etc., etc. Having then confined your mind to the appointed subject (by imagination, if the subject be corporeal, or by simple thought if it is purely spiritual), begin to make reflections upon it in the way that I have already shown you in the preceding meditations. If your mind finds sufficient food and light in one reflection, then dwell upon that only, imitating the bee, which does not leave a flower until it has sucked thence all the honey. But if you do not find sufficient matter for reflection in the first topic, proceed after some efforts to another, but let all be done quietly and without haste.

CHAPTER SIX

Third Part of Meditation—Affections and Resolutions

———————•———————

MEDITATION fills our will, the affective part of the soul, with good impulses, such as the love of God and of our neighbor, the desire of Heaven and its glories, zeal for the salvation of souls, imitation of the life of our Saviour, compassion, veneration, holy joy, fear of God's displeasure, of judgment and Hell, hatred of sin, confidence in the mercy and goodness of God, repentance for our past sins. And we should seek to enlarge and confirm our souls as much as possible in these affections. To that end take the first volume of the *Meditations* of Don Andrew Capilla, and study his preface, in which he shows how to expand the affections, as Father Arias does at greater length in his *Treatise on Prayer*.

Nevertheless, Philothea, you must not rest satisfied with general desires and aspirations, but rather turn them into special resolutions for your individual correction and amendment. For instance, when you meditate upon the first of our Saviour's words from the Cross, you will assuredly feel a desire to imitate Him, to forgive and love your enemies. But that desire is worth little unless you proceed to some practical resolution, such as "I will no longer be angry at the irritating words which such a one says to me or of me; nor at the annoyance caused me by another; on the contrary, I will do and say all I can to soothe and win them"—and so forth. In this way you will soon correct your faults, whereas mere desires will have but few and tardy results.

CHAPTER SEVEN

The Conclusion

———————•———————

FINALLY, you must conclude your meditation with three acts, which should be made with the utmost humility.

First, an act of thanksgiving, thanking God for giving us good desires and resolutions, and for His mercy and goodness which have been made known to us in meditation.

Secondly, an act of oblation, in which we offer to God His own mercy and goodness, the death, the blood, and merits of His Son, and in union with these our own affections and resolutions.

Thirdly, an act of intercession, by which we entreat God to impart to us the graces and virtues of His Son, and to bless our desires and resolutions, so that we may faithfully fulfill them: and further, we must pray for the Church, for our pastors, relations, friends, and all others, making use of the intercession of Our Blessed Lady, the Saints and angels—concluding with the *Our Father* and *Hail Mary*, the universal and never-failing petition of the faithful. To this I would add that we should gather a little nosegay of devotion. When we walk in a beautiful garden we usually gather some few choice flowers, inhale their fragrance, and carry them away with us, retaining and enjoying them through the day. So when our mind has fed upon some mystery by meditation, we should select some few points which especially strike us, and are most calculated to benefit us, and dwell upon them, inhaling their spiritual fragrance. And this we should strive to do in the place in which we have been engaged in meditation, or in solitude afterwards.

CHAPTER EIGHT

Further Rules for Meditation

———————— ● ————————

ABOVE all, Philothea, you must be careful to retain the resolutions to which you have come through meditation, on your return to active duties. Without this chief fruit of meditation it becomes not only useless but positively hurtful, for our mind is apt to rest satisfied with the consideration instead of the practice of virtues, till we persuade ourselves that we *are* what we have *resolved to be*—this is all very well if our resolutions are active and solid, but if not, it is a vain and dangerous error—therefore we should always endeavor to put them in practice, and seek every occasion for so doing. For instance, if I have resolved to win those who annoy me by my gentleness, I will seek the opportunity of addressing them kindly, but if the occasion does not present itself, I will speak well of them, and pray for them.

On leaving this fervent prayer, you must beware of giving your heart any sudden jar, which might spill the precious balm with which devotion has filled it. I mean that if possible you should remain some brief season in quietness, and gradually pass from prayer to your needful occupations, seeking to retain as long as possible the holy thoughts and inclinations you have been exercising. A man who has received a costly vessel full of some precious cordial would carry it most carefully. He would walk slowly, and not look idly about him, but keep his eyes now on the road before him for fear some stone or false step should endanger him, now at his vase for fear he should spill its contents. Do the like when you cease your meditation; do not at once plunge into distractions, but merely look straight before you; if you must of necessity enter into worldly conversation, you cannot help yourself, but you can be on the watch, and mount guard over your heart, so that you may lose as little as possible of the precious cordial you have obtained in prayer.

You must accustom yourself to go from prayer to whatever occupations may be involved by your station or profession, even though they may seem far distant from the feelings excited in you by that prayer. Thus the lawyer must go from prayer to his pleadings, the merchant to his trade, the wife to her conjugal and household duties, with perfect calm and tranquillity; for since these duties as well as that of prayer are imposed on us by God, we must pass from one to the other in a devout and humble spirit.

Perhaps sometimes directly after your preparation you may find your affections greatly kindled towards God, and then I would have you yield to them without heeding any formal method, for the object of that is to excite the affections, and if the Holy Spirit gives you that warmth of affection and resolution without studied reflection, you have no need of it. In short, whenever pious affections are stirred up in you, receive and welcome them, whether before or after reflection. I have only classed the affections after reflection, in order the better to divide the several parts of prayer, for it is an established rule never to restrain the affections, but always to yield to them when they are kindled. And this equally applies to the acts of thanksgiving, of oblation, and intercession, which must not be withheld at any time, although they should always be repeated at the conclusion of your meditation. But you should always make your resolutions after such affections, and last of all before concluding your meditation, because as they relate to common, every-day matters, they would be very likely to distract and disturb you earlier.

Amongst our affections and resolutions it is well to speak colloquially to our Saviour, the angels, the persons connected with the mysteries, the Saints, ourselves, our hearts, sinners, and even inanimate creatures, after the example of David in the Psalms, and other saints in their meditations and prayers.

CHAPTER NINE

The Dryness Which May Trouble Meditation

S HOULD you find neither delight nor consolation in meditation, do not be disheartened, but have recourse occasionally to vocal prayer, tell your trouble to the Lord, confess your unworthiness, and say with Jacob, "I will not let thee go except thou bless me"; or with the Canaanitish woman, "Yea, Lord, yet the dogs eat of the crumbs which fall from their master's table." Else take a book, and read attentively until your mind is quickened and reassured; or stir up your heart by the help of some outward action or gesture—prostrating yourself, crossing your hands upon your breast, embracing the crucifix (taking it for granted that you are alone).

But if these things avail you nothing, do not be disheartened, however great your dryness, only continue to present yourself devoutly before God. How many courtiers daily appear before their sovereign without a hope of speaking with him, content to be seen by him, and offer their homage? So, Philothea, we must pray purely and simply in order to do homage to God, and show our faithfulness. If it pleases His Divine Majesty to speak with us, to hold converse with us by His holy inspirations and inward consolations, it is doubtless a great honor and unspeakable delight; but if He vouchsafes not so to favor us, neither speaking, nor even appearing to perceive us, as though we were not in

His Presence; yet we must not therefore leave it: on the contrary, we must remain devoutly and meekly before His sovereign goodness, and then He will assuredly accept our patience, and observe our assiduity and perseverance, so that when we again come before Him, He will look favorably on us, and reward us with His consolations, bidding us taste the sweetness of devout prayer. But if not, let us rest contented, remembering that we are unworthy even of the honor of standing before Him and in His sight.

CHAPTER TEN

A Morning Exercise

———— • ————

IN ADDITION to the complete mental prayer of which I have spoken, and the other vocal prayers which you should say once in the day, there are five shorter sorts of prayer, which are as it were the forerunners and servants of the principal devotion. The first of these is the morning prayer, which is a general preparation for all the duties of the day. You should perform it as follows:

Thank and adore God for His mercy in preserving you through the past night, and if, during it, you have anyways offended Him, ask forgiveness.

Consider that the present time is given you that you may win that which is to come: make therefore a firm resolution to employ the day now beginning, to that end.

Foresee in what business, what intercourse, and what occasions you may be able this day to serve God, and by what temptations you may be in danger of offending Him, whether through anger, vanity, or any other fault. Then make a pious resolution to embrace all means whereby you may serve God, and promote your own devotion, and on the other hand prepare to shun, resist, and overcome all that may hinder your salvation and the glory of God. Do not rest satisfied with making the resolution, consider beforehand how you will execute it.

For instance, if I know that I shall be obliged to come into contact with some hasty, passionate person, I will not only resolve not to be irritated, but I will prepare to meet him with gentle, soothing words, or provide the intervention of someone else who can control him. If I am likely to visit some sick person, I will arrange my hour, and prepare the assistance or the help I shall convey to him, and so on with other things.

After this, humble yourself before God, acknowledging that of yourself you can perform nothing which you propose, either in doing what is good or avoiding what is bad. And taking, as it were, your heart in your hands, offer it and all its desires to His Divine Majesty, entreating that He will take it under His protection, and strengthen it for His service, saying some such words as these, "O Lord, behold this poor weak heart, which through Thy grace has conceived some good desires, but, alas, is too wretched and feeble to carry them into effect unless Thou givest it Thy blessing, which I therefore ask, O loving Father, through the merits of Thy Son's most precious death, to whose honor I would dedicate this day, and all the rest of my life." Then call on the Blessed Virgin, your Guardian Angel, and the Saints to help you.

These spiritual actions should be briefly and heartily performed before you leave your room, so that by this means all you do throughout the day may be refreshed by the blessing of God. Therefore, I beseech you, Philothea, never to omit this practice.

CHAPTER ELEVEN

*The Evening Exercise, and
Examination of Conscience*

———————— • ————————

A S BEFORE your morning meal you made a spiritual meditation suitable to the beginning of the day, so now before your evening meal you must make a little devout and spiritual meal corresponding. To this end arrange a season of leisure before bedtime, and, prostrating yourself before God, collect your mind before Jesus Christ crucified (whom you will inwardly place before you), kindle anew the flame of your morning's meditation by the help of some hearty aspirations, acts of humility and love towards your Saviour, either repeating chosen points of your previous meditation, or stirring yourself afresh with some other subject, according as you find best.

The examination which you should make of your conscience before going to rest is very simple.

Thank God for preserving you through the day.

Examine how you have conducted yourself through the hours that are past, and for that purpose remember where you have been, with whom, and how occupied.

If you have done anything that is good, thank God for it; if you have sinned in thought, word, or deed, ask His forgiveness, resolving to make confession of the same at the first opportunity, and diligently to amend.

Afterwards commend to the divine protection your soul and body, the Church, your relations and friends: ask the Blessed Virgin, your Guardian Angel, and the Saints, to watch over you and for you, and with God's blessing seek that rest which He has ordained for you.

Never omit this exercise any more than that of the morning, for as by the latter you open the windows of your soul to the sun of righteousness, so by these evening devotions you close them against the darkness of Hell.

CHAPTER TWELVE

Spiritual Retreat

———————— • ————————

O N THIS subject, Philothea, I would require your most earnest attention to my counsels, for it involves one of the most important means towards your spiritual advancement.

As often as you can through the day, recall your mind to the presence of God by some one of the four methods I have mentioned. Consider what He is doing, and what you are doing. You will always find His eyes fixed upon you with unchangeable love. Then say, O my God, why cannot I be ever looking up to Thee, even as Thou art ever looking down upon me? Why dost Thou ever remember me, whilst I, alas, so often forget Thee? O my soul, thy true rest is in God, art thou seeking it there only?

Just as the birds have their nests to which they can retreat, and the stag shelters himself in the thick forest, seeking shade and refreshment when the summer is hot, even so, Philothea, should our hearts daily seek a resting-place on Mount Calvary or in the wounds of our Blessed Lord, or in some other spot close to Him, whither to retire on all occasions, there to rest from their worldly cares, and to find protection and strength against temptation. Happy the soul which can sincerely say to the Lord, "Thou art my House of defense, my strong Tower, my Shelter against the storm, and my Refuge against the heat."

Remember then frequently to retire into the solitude of your heart, even whilst you are externally occupied in business or society. This mental solitude need not be hindered though many persons are around you, for they do but surround your body, not your heart, which should remain alone in the presence of God. This was what King David did throughout his numberless cares, and we find him in the Psalms perpetually exclaiming, "My God, Thou art ever before me! The Lord is ever on my right hand! To Thee, O Lord, have I lifted up mine eyes! O Thou that dwellest in the heavens! Mine eyes are ever looking to the Lord."

We are rarely so engaged in intercourse with others as to be unable from time to time to recall our hearts into this blessed solitude. When St. Catherine of Siena was deprived by her parents of all suitable time and place wherein to pray and meditate, Our Lord inspired her with the thought of making an oratory in her heart whither she could retire mentally, and amidst external distractions enjoy internal solitude. And later, when the world troubled her, she was noways discomposed, saying that she could always retire into the closet of her heart, and seek consolation with her Heavenly Spouse, and she afterwards recommended her spiritual children to do the same.

From time to time then, gather your spirit into the solitude of your heart, where, separate from all men, you can lay open your soul and speak face to face with God, and say with David, "I am become like a pelican of the wilderness: I am like a night-raven in the house. I have watched, and am become as a sparrow all alone on the housetop." (*Ps.* 101:7, 8). In these words, we find (beyond their literal meaning, whence we gather that the pious King devoted a part of his time to solitude and spiritual contemplation) the description of three excellent kinds of retreat, as it were, three hermitages, where in our solitude we can imitate our Saviour who, on Mount Calvary, resembled the pelican of the wilderness, which revives its dying young ones with its own blood. By His birth, in a desolate stable, He was like the lonely owl, bemoaning our sins; and in His Ascension He resembled the sparrow flying up to heaven, which may be called the roof of the earth. Amidst the worry and vexations of the world, then, we may seek a retreat in any of these resting-places. When the Blessed Elzear, Count of Arian in Provence, had been long absent from his pious and chaste Delphine, she sent a messenger to bring her news concerning his health, by whom he replied—"I am well, dear wife, and if you would see me, seek for me in the wounded side of our sweet Jesus, for there I dwell, and there will you find me: in vain do you seek elsewhere"—truly he was a Christian knight!

CHAPTER THIRTEEN

Aspirations, Ejaculatory Prayers, and Holy Thoughts

———————•———————

WE MAKE our retreat in God, because we aspire after Him, and we long for Him in order that we may so retire. Therefore a longing after God and spiritual retreat mutually advance one another, and both arise from holy thoughts: do not fail therefore to long frequently for God by short but ardent efforts of your heart. Admire His beauty, invoke His aid, cast yourself in spirit at the foot of His Cross, adore His goodness, often inquire of Him concerning your salvation; a thousand times in the day offer your soul to Him; fix your inward eyes upon His sweetness; hold out your hand to Him as a child to his father, that He may guide you; lay Him on your breast as a fragrant bundle of myrrh. (*Cant.* 1:13). Establish Him as the standard of your soul, and in every way excite your heart to the love of God and to a tender, ardent love for your Heavenly Spouse. It is thus that St. Augustine recommended ejaculatory prayer to the pious matron Proba. The spirit thus dwelling on the grandeur of God, and sharing an intimate communion with Him, will be perfumed with His perfections. Neither is it a difficult practice: such prayer may be interwoven with all our business and occupations without hindering them in the slightest degree. Indeed, our external pursuits are rather helped than hindered by spiritual retreat and short devotions of the soul. When the traveler pauses to taste a drop of wine which will refresh and reinvigorate him, such a slight delay does not hinder his journey, but rather gives him new strength whereby to expedite and lighten it—he stops only that he may go forward the better.

There are many useful collections of vocal aspirations, but I would advise you not to confine yourself to any formal words; rather use those which are prompted by the feelings of your heart, as you need them: they will never fail you. Undoubtedly, there are some sentences which surpass all others and satisfy the heart, such as the ejaculations found throughout the Psalms of David, the various invocations of the Name of Jesus, and the ardent expressions of love in the Canticle of Canticles: sacred hymns have a similar effect if they are devoutly used.

Those who are filled with an earthly love are ever thinking of the object of their attachment, their heart brims with affection for it, their mouth is full of its praises; when absent they constantly speak of their love in letters, and engrave the treasured name on every tree: just so those who love God are never weary of thinking upon Him, living for Him, yearning for Him, and talking of Him, and they would fain grave the holy and blessed Name of Jesus upon the hearts of every human being throughout the world.

To such as these everything speaks of Him, and His whole creation joins them in lauding their Beloved. The whole world (says St. Augustine, following St. Anthony) speaks to them in a silent but intelligible language of their love, everything excites them to holy thoughts, whence arise countless and elevating aspirations after God. Thus St. Gregory Nazianzen relates to his flock, how, as he walked by the seaside, he watched the waves as they deposited on the beach all manner of shells, seaweeds, mussels, and various other products of the sea, which the sea discharged as it were from its bosom; then other waves flowing over the same beach swallowed up and again carried away this light deposit, whilst the surrounding rocks stood firm and unshaken, although the waves dashed rudely against them. Thence he drew this beautiful reflection, that the faithless, like these shells and weeds, are carried hither and thither in grief or joy by the waters and waves of fortune; but the faithful remain firm and unshaken through the severest storms; whence he turns to the cry of David, "Save me, O God: for the waters are come in even unto my soul. I stick fast in the deep mire, and there is no sure standing; I am come into the depth of the sea, and the tempest hath overwhelmed me." St. Gregory was at that time under suffering himself, Maximus having sought to usurp his bishopric.

When St. Fulgentius, Bishop of Ruspa, found himself in the midst of a general assembly of the Roman patricians who were paying court to Theodoric, King of the Goths, beholding the splendor of the nobles who were stationed according to their rank, he exclaimed, "O my God! If earthly Rome is so magnificent, what must the heavenly Jerusalem be? And if in this world such splendor is granted to those who follow after vanity, what glory must be in store for those who behold the Truth?"

It is told of St. Anselm, Archbishop of Canterbury, whose birthplace we esteem an honor to our mountains, that he was much given to such holy thoughts. One day as he was traveling, a hare, being closely run by the hounds which pursued it, took refuge between his horse's feet, and the dogs remained yelping around unable to molest their prey in this its strange sanctuary. His followers were highly entertained at so novel a spectacle, but St. Anselm groaned and wept. "You may laugh," he said, "but the poor hare does not laugh: and even thus do the enemies of the soul pursue it and drive it into all manner of sins, until at the last they can kill and devour it; and whilst the terrified soul seeks for some refuge and help, its enemies mock and laugh if it finds none!" and then sighing, he went on his way.

Constantine the Great wrote with deference to St. Anthony, at which his monks expressed surprise. "Do you marvel that a king should write to a subject?" he asked of them, "marvel rather at the goodness of God who hath written His law for man, and has spoken face to face with them in the person of His Son."

St. Francis, seeing a sheep alone amongst a herd of goats, said to his companion, "Look at that poor sheep, how gentle it is amongst the goats—even so our Blessed Lord was gentle and lowly amidst the Pharisees." And another time seeing a tender lamb devoured by a boar, "Ah, little lamb!" he exclaimed with tears, "thou settest forth to me the death of my Saviour." So a pious man of our own age, Francis Borgia, then Duke of Gandia, delighted to indulge in holy thoughts whilst out hunting. "I was reflecting," he said on his return from hawking, "how obediently our hawks return to the wrist and submit to be tied and hooded, whilst men are so rebellious to the Voice of God."

The great St. Basil says that the rose amidst the thorns remonstrates thus with men: "All that is sweetest in this world, oh, mortals, is tinged with bitterness; no bliss is pure, sadness ever mingles with joy, widowhood follows marriage, care burdens abundance, ignominy glory, trouble honor, disgust pleasure, sickness health. It is a lovely flower this same rose," he continues, "but it fills my heart with sadness—recalling my sin for which the earth is doomed to bring forth thorns."

A holy man contemplating a river on a calm night, and beholding how the sky and its many stars were mirrored therein, exclaimed, "O my God, when Thou takest me to Thy blessed mansions, these stars will be beneath my feet! Surely as the stars of heaven are reflected here on earth, so we men are reflected in Heaven in the Living Fountain of divine charity." So, another, as he watched a rolling river, cried out, "My soul shall never rest until it is lost in the ocean of Divinity whence it came forth."

St. Frances, as she knelt beside a pleasant brook, being greatly enchanted, repeated often, "Even so sweetly and pleasantly flows the grace of my God!" Another, as he gazed on some flowering trees, said with a sigh, "Why do I alone bear no flowers in the garden of the Church? Another beholding a hen brooding over her young ones prayed thus, "O Lord, keep us ever under the shadow of Thy wings," and noticing a sunflower, "When, O my God," he cried, "will my soul even thus follow the drawings of Thy grace?" Remarking the garden heart's-ease, which is very beautiful but scentless, "Alas," he said, "even so are the thoughts of my heart, fair to outward show, but without use or fragrance!"

Thus, Philothea, may we extract holy thoughts and pious aspirations from all the varying circumstances of our mortal life. Woe be to those who convert the works of the Creator into sin: thrice happy they who turn all things to His glory, and use their very weakness to promote His honor. "I am always wont to turn all things to my spiritual welfare," says St. Gregory Nazianzen. Read the pious epitaph which St. Jerome framed for St. Paula—it is striking from the abundance of holy thoughts and aspirations with which she ever abounded. This habit of spiritual retirement and ejaculatory prayer is the keystone of devotion, and can supply the defects of all your other prayers; but nothing else can supply its place. Without it you cannot follow the contemplative life well, nor the active life without danger. Without it repose is but idleness, labor but trouble: therefore, I beseech you, cleave steadily to it, and never forsake it.

CHAPTER FOURTEEN

Holy Mass, and How to Hear It

———————●———————

I HAVE as yet said nothing concerning the Sun of all spiritual exercises, which is the most holy, sacred and royal sacrifice and Sacrament of the Eucharist, the center of the Christian religion, the heart of devotion, the soul of piety; an ineffable mystery which embraces the untold depths of divine charity, and in which God, giving Himself to us, bestows upon us freely all His favors and graces.

Prayer, united to this Divine Sacrifice, has unutterable power, so that in it the soul overflows with celestial grace, as leaning upon her Beloved, He fills her with fragrance and spiritual sweetness, until, in the words of Solomon, she is "like a pillar of smoke of aromatical spices, of myrrh and frankincense, and of all powders of the perfumer." (*Cant.* 3:6). Endeavor, if possible, to be present daily at the Holy Mass, that, together with the priest, you may offer the Sacrifice of your Redeemer to God His Father in your own behalf and that of the whole Church. The holy angels are always present in great numbers to honor this holy mystery, St. Chrysostom says; and we may hope to be made partakers of their holiness, when we are gathered together with them to the same intent: and the choirs of the Church Triumphant as well as the Church Militant join themselves to Our Lord in this divine action, that with Him, in Him, and by Him, we may as it were take God by storm, and obtain His mercy and love. What a privilege to be united in so blessed and mighty an action!

If you are unavoidably prevented from being present at the celebration of this great Sacrifice by a real and bodily presence, do not fail to join in it by a spiritual communion. So that if you cannot go to church and join actually, at least go thither in the spirit, unite your intention to all your brethren, and offer the same spiritual service that you would offer were you able to be present actually before the Altar. In order to join profitably, whether actually or spiritually, adopt the following rules:

1. Begin with due preparation, whilst the priest is at the foot of the altar, placing yourself in the presence of God, acknowledging your unworthiness, and asking pardon for your faults.

2. When he goes up the steps, and to the Gospel, meditate generally on the birth and life of our Saviour.

3. From the Gospel until after the Creed, reflect upon His teaching, and renew your resolution to live and die in the obedience and faith of the Holy Catholic Church.

4. From the Creed to the Lord's Prayer, apply your mind to the words of Christ, in union with the death and Passion of the Redeemer, which are essentially and actually set forth in this holy Sacrifice, which, together with the priest and all present, you offer to God the Father for His glory and your salvation.

5. From the *Pater Noster* to the Communion, offer earnestly the prayers of your heart, ardently desiring to be forever joined and united to our Saviour by an eternal love.

Then to the conclusion, thank Him for His Incarnation, His life, His death, His Passion, and the love He shows to us in this blessed Sacrifice; beseeching Him through it to look graciously upon you, your relations, friends, and the whole Church; and then meekly and humbly receive the divine blessing which our Saviour gives you through His priest.

If you wish to make your daily meditation at this time, then do so instead of these several acts; only turn your mind to offering this adorable Sacrifice through your prayer and meditation—for all the acts I have suggested are actually or tacitly implied in devout meditation.

CHAPTER FIFTEEN

Other Public Services

———————•———————

O N SUNDAYS and festivals especially you should assist at the
Divine Office as much as you are able, for these days above all
are dedicated to God, and on them it is well to offer Him a more abundant service than on other days. Thus you will experience the blessings
of public worship like St. Augustine, who records in his *Confessions*
that when in the beginning of his conversion he heard the psalmody of
the Church, his heart melted within him, and his eyes streamed with
holy tears. Moreover, there is always greater benefit and comfort to be
derived from the public service of the Church than from private devotion, God having promised a special blessing to this union of hearts
and souls.

Take advantage of the societies (or confraternities) which exist where
you are, especially those whose rules abound most in good works and
edification; this obedience is pleasing to God, for though the Church
does not enjoin such ties, she highly recommends them, in witness
of which she grants indulgences and other privileges to confraternities; and it is always profitable to be joined to others and cooperate in
good works. And although you might perform equally pious exercises
by yourself, and perhaps with more self-gratification, yet God is more
glorified by our being united to our friends and neighbors.

I say the same of all public prayers and good works, in all of which we ought, as far as may be, to consider the benefit to our neighbors of a good example and our own zeal for the glory of God and the common welfare.

CHAPTER SIXTEEN

The Invocation of Saints

———•———

SINCE God often sends us His inspirations by means of His angels, we ought frequently to offer Him our aspirations through the same channel. The souls of the holy dead who are in Paradise with the angels, and of whom our Saviour has taught us that they are like to and equal with them, also assist us by their holy prayers.

Let us then unite our hearts to these celestial spirits and blessed souls, so that as the young nightingale learns to sing from the older ones, surely by the sacred communion which we have with the Saints we may the better pray and praise our God. "I will sing praise unto Thee," said David, "in the sight of the angels." (*Ps.* 137:1). Honor, reverence, and love the holy and glorious Virgin Mary, for she is the Mother of Our Lord, and therefore our Mother also. Fly to her as her child, and cast yourself at her knees with a perfect confidence at all times, and on all occasions. Call on this dear Mother, appeal to her maternal love, and strive to imitate her virtues. Familiarize yourself with the thought of the holy angels, and honor especially the angel guardian of the diocese in which you live, and those of your neighbors, and above all your own. Call on them and honor them frequently, and ask their help in all your affairs, temporal as well as spiritual.

The holy Peter Lefèvre, first priest, preacher, and lector in theology, of the Society of Jesus, and earliest companion of St. Ignatius its founder, on returning one day from Germany where he had done great things for the glory of Our Lord, happened to pass his birthplace which was in this diocese. He related that in journeying through districts infected by heresy he had received many consolations through a practice he had adopted of saluting the Guardian Angel of each parish on his entering it; and he said that he sensibly experienced their help both in guarding him from the ambushes of the heretics, and also in rendering several souls mild and docile to receive the doctrines of salvation. And this he related with so much earnestness that a gentlewoman, who, when very young, had heard it from his own mouth, repeated it only four years ago with extraordinary feeling, although it was 60 years since she heard him tell it. I had the consolation last year to consecrate an altar on the spot where it had pleased God that this holy man should be born, in the little village of Villaret, amidst some of our most rugged mountains.

Choose as your patrons some saints in particular, to whose life and imitation you feel most drawn, and in whose intercession you feel an especial confidence. The Saint whose name you bear is already assigned you from your Baptism.

CHAPTER SEVENTEEN

How to Hear and Read the Word of God

———●———

ALWAYS give good heed to the Word of God, whether you hear or read it in private, or hearken to it when publicly preached: listen with attention and reverence; seek to profit by it, and do not let the precious words fall unheeded; receive them into your heart as a costly balsam; imitate the Blessed Virgin who "kept all the sayings" concerning her Son "in her heart." And remember that according as we hearken to and receive God's words, so will He hearken and receive our supplications.

It is well always to have at hand some good devotional works, such as those of St. Bonaventure, Gerson, Denis the Carthusian, Blosius, Grenada, Stella, Arias, Pinelli, Da Ponte, Avila, the *Spiritual Combat*, the *Confessions of St. Augustine*, the *Epistles of St. Jerome*, and other such, and to read some portion daily, counting them as letters from the Saints in Heaven intended to show you the road thither and give you courage to follow it. Also study the lives of the Saints, in which you will behold a portrait of the true Christian's life as in a mirror, and you can adapt their examples to your own life. For although those who live in the world cannot in all things imitate the Saints, yet all may in some measure follow in their blessed steps: as, for instance, in your spiritual retirement you can imitate St. Paul, the first hermit; in self-imposed poverty, the poverty of St. Francis, and so on with others. Some are more suited than others to guide our life, such as the life of the holy St. Teresa, those of the first Jesuits, of St. Charles Borromeo, Archbishop of Milan, St. Louis, St. Bernard, the Chronicles of St. Francis, and such like. Others are rather calculated to attract our wonder than our imitation, such as St. Mary of Egypt, St. Simon Stylites, and the two Saints Catherine, of Siena and of Genoa. These, nevertheless, may serve to excite us to a warmer desire after the holy love of God.

CHAPTER EIGHTEEN

How to Receive Inspirations

———————•———————

BY INSPIRATIONS I mean all the affections, attractions, inward reproaches and regrets, perceptions and illuminations with which God moves us, working in our hearts through His Fatherly love and care in order to awaken, to kindle, lead and draw us to heavenly love and holy desires; in short, all that forwards our eternal welfare. These are the voice of the Beloved knocking at the door, speaking to the heart of His bride, wakening her when she sleeps, calling to her when she is absent, offering her the honey, the milk, and the fruits of His garden, filling her ears with the sound of His most sweet and lovely voice. (*Cant.*).

To draw a comparison from our common life. Before a marriage is arranged, first the marriage proposal must be made to the bride; secondly, she hearkens to the proposition; and thirdly, she gives her consent. So when God would work in us, by us, and with us, some good work, He begins by suggesting it by His inspiration. Next we receive the suggestion, and lastly we consent to it.

There are three steps downwards towards sin—temptation, delight, and consent; and in the same way three steps upwards towards virtue—inspiration as opposed to temptation, pleasure in the inspiration as opposed to delight in temptation, and consent to inspiration as opposed to consent to temptation.

Though the inspiration should continue during our whole life, it is of no avail unless we take delight in it, but rather we the more offend God, as did the Israelites with whom He strove for 40 years, seeking to convert them, whilst they hardened their hearts and would not hear; so that He swore in His wrath that they should not enter into His rest; just as one who had long loved a woman would feel injured if, after all, she were to set aside his attachment.

It is a great step towards glorifying God when we delight in His inspirations, and in so doing we begin to please Him; for although such delight falls short of entire consent, yet it shows an inclination to it; and just as it is a good sign when we take pleasure in hearing God's Word, which may be called an outward inspiration, so is our delight in His inward inspirations a pleasing and acceptable thing in His sight. Of this kind of pleasure the spouse in the Canticle said, "My soul melted when he (my Beloved) spoke." (*Cant.* 5:6). And so an earthly lover is content when he sees that his love is esteemed and prized.

But the perfection lies in consent, for if after receiving inspiration, and that gladly, we still refuse to consent to it, we greatly offend God, and despise His goodness. So it was with the bride, for although the voice of her Beloved had reached her heart, yet she delayed to open the door to Him, offering an idle excuse, and so He withdrew Himself and departed (*Cant.* 5); and so an earthly lover who had been received and encouraged would feel more aggrieved if afterwards he was rejected than if he had never been encouraged at all. Resolve then gratefully to receive all God's inspirations, and make haste to receive them with reverence as the ambassadors of the Heavenly King, who would espouse you to Himself. Hearken meekly to their words, cultivate the love you feel, and cherish the holy inspiration.

Consent to it fully, lovingly, and ceaselessly, for then God, Whom we cannot place under an obligation, will yet hold Himself greatly obliged to your love. But before you act upon these inspirations in any important or unusual matters, take counsel of your spiritual guide, that he may judge whether your inspiration is true or false; for when the enemy sees a soul ready to consent to inspirations, he often seeks to deceive it, an evil which will never happen so long as you are obedient to your director in all humility.

Having consented, be diligent to procure the fruits in good works, which are the crowning point of virtue; for consent in the heart producing no outward results is like a vine that bears no fruit. Your morning exercise well performed will greatly promote this, inasmuch as it leads you not only to general, but to specific, good actions.

CHAPTER NINETEEN

Holy Confession

———————•———————

OUR Saviour has left in His Church the Sacrament of Penance and Confession, in order that as often as our souls are stained with sin we may cleanse and purify them. Since then you have so sure and simple a remedy at hand, never permit your heart to remain long sullied by sin. If by chance the lioness' path is crossed by a leopard, she hastens to free herself from the offensive odor he imparts, lest it should irritate the lion. So the soul which has consented to sin should abhor itself, and hasten to be cleansed, remembering that the Everlasting Eyes are upon it; and why should we die a spiritual death, since we have so sovereign a remedy at hand?

You should make your Confession humbly and devoutly once a week, always if possible before receiving Holy Communion, even although your conscience be not burdened with any mortal sin; for by Confession you not only receive absolution for the venial sins which you confess, but also great assistance in henceforward avoiding them, new light to perceive them, and abundant grace to win back the ground you have lost owing to them. Further, you practice the virtues of humility, obedience, simplicity, and love, so that by the act of confession you exercise more virtues than by any other means.

Always entertain a sincere hatred of the sins you confess, even though they be trifling, and a heartfelt resolution to amend. Some mechanically and from mere habit confess their venial sins, without thinking of correcting them, and continuing in them, lose much spiritual good. If, therefore, you make confession of untruthfulness through want of thought, of hasty words, or self-indulgence, repent heartily, and firmly resolve to amend, for it is an abuse of the confessional to confess any sins, either mortal or venial, without purposing to get rid of them.

Do not rest satisfied with general vague Confessions. "I have not loved God as much as I ought—I have not prayed with sufficient earnestness, I have not shown due charity towards my neighbor—I have not received the Sacraments with the reverence that I ought," and so forth: for by such Confessions you in no degree enlighten your confessor as to the true state of your conscience, since all the Saints now in Paradise, and every living being might confess the same. Examine for what particular reason you have to accuse yourself of these faults, and having ascertained it, accuse yourself honestly and simply of the special omission or commission. For instance, you say you have not treated your neighbor with due charity, perhaps, because having seen a poor man in great need whom you might easily have succored, you neglected to do so. Well, then, specify your neglect—say, "I saw a needy brother, and either through negligence or indifference, or hardness of heart" (as the case may be) "I forbore to relieve him." Again, do not accuse yourself in general of being cold in your devotions; but if you have voluntarily yielded to distractions, or neglected to seek the fitting time, place, or circumstances, for thoughtful prayer, say so at once according to the facts, without keeping to those useless, lukewarm generalities.

Again, do not content yourself with confessing the fact of venial sins, but mention likewise the motive which induced the sin. Thus, instead of simply confessing that you have told a falsehood which did not injure your neighbor, say whether it was from vanity, in order to screen yourself from blame or win praise, or whether it was from thoughtlessness or perversity. If you have exceeded in amusements, explain whether it was from being engrossed by society, or vanity, and so on. Say whether you persisted long in your fault, for duration aggravates sin, and there is a wide difference between the passing vanity which surprised us for a quarter of an hour, and that which has engrossed our heart for a day or more; therefore be particular in confessing the fact, the cause, and the duration of your faults. For although we are not bound to so strict a confession of venial sins, yet those who are really anxious to cleanse their souls and attain to pure devotion should carefully disclose every slight symptom to their spiritual physician, that he may heal them.

Be careful also to mention those details which explain the nature of your fault, such as the cause which excited your anger, or led you to encourage what was wrong. Thus someone whom I dislike has said some trifles in jest, which I took amiss and was angry with him. But if a person I liked had said something more offensive, I should not have taken it amiss. Therefore I will not spare myself, but own that I gave way to anger, not on account of what was said, but because I disliked the speaker; and if it is necessary in order to explain that you repeat the very words, I would have you do so, for by thus honestly confessing all, you not only disclose your actual faults, but also the bad inclinations and habits, and similar roots of sin which lurk within you. By this means your spiritual father obtains a more perfect knowledge of the heart he has to deal with, and of the treatment to be adopted. But as far as possible avoid naming any third person in your Confessions.

Watch over the many faults which often exist and hold sway insensibly in your conscience, in order that you may confess them and conquer them: and to this end study the 6th, 27th, 28th, 29th, 35th, and 36th chapters of the Third Part, and the 7th chapter of the Fourth Part. Do not lightly change your confessor; but having once selected one be punctual in opening your conscience to him at the appointed times, telling him simply and honestly all your faults. And from time to time—say every one or two months—manifest the state of your inclinations although you may not have sinned by them; such as that you are assailed by sadness or gloom, Or that you are tempted by excitement to greed, or any similar dispositions.

CHAPTER TWENTY

Frequent Communion

————— • —————

I T IS said that Mithridates, king of Pontus, having invented the mithridate, was so strengthened by means of it, that when at a later period he tried to poison himself in order to escape the Roman yoke, he found it impossible. Our Blessed Lord has instituted the most holy Sacrament of the Eucharist, wherein is His Flesh and His Blood, that whosoever eats thereof may have eternal life. Therefore he who frequently and devoutly feeds thereon, so strengthens the life and health of his soul that it can scarcely be poisoned by any evil passions. No one can be fed with the Bread of Life, and yet live upon dead affections, and as in Eden there was no death for the body owing to the living fruits which God had placed there, so those who eat of this Sacrament of Life shall find no death for their souls.

If the most delicate and perishable fruits, such as strawberries, cherries, and apricots, can easily be preserved the whole year by means of sugar or honey, surely it is no great marvel that our hearts, albeit frail and weak, should be preserved from the corruption of sin when they are immersed in the sweetness of the incorruptible Body and Blood of the Son of God. O Philothea, surely those Christians who are condemned at the Last Day will be able to make no reply when the Judge reproaches them with their spiritual death, since they might so easily have preserved both life and health by feeding upon His Body given to them for that intent. Unhappy men, He will say, why would ye die, when the fruit of life lay within your grasp?

I neither exhort you to receive the Blessed Sacrament daily, nor do I forbid it. But I do exhort every one to communicate at least every Sunday, if his heart be pure from affection to sin. In this I follow St. Augustine, who neither enjoined nor blamed the practice of daily Communion, leaving that to the judgment of each person's spiritual guide, for on so nice and important a point it is scarcely possible to give any general rule. Inasmuch as the requisite dispositions for so great a privilege may often be found in some pious and devout persons, it is best neither to counsel it generally, nor dissuade, but leave it to be decided according to the individual needs of each. For whilst it would be unwise indiscriminately to recommend daily Communion, it would be equally unwise to blame any one for it, especially when under the guidance of a prudent director.

When fault was found with St. Catherine of Siena on account of her frequent Communion, and St. Augustine brought forward as an authority who neither enjoined nor condemned it as a daily practice— "Well, then," she replied, "if St. Augustine did not condemn it, I entreat you not to condemn it either, and I shall be content."

But St. Augustine strongly recommends and exhorts us to communicate every Sunday, therefore adhere to that rule. If, as I doubt not, you have no sort of affection to mortal sin, and no consent to venial sin, you are in that frame of mind which St. Augustine requires; and even more, if you not only give no consent to sin, but have no attachment to any kind of sin, you may communicate as much oftener as your spiritual father permits. Nevertheless, there are certain lawful impediments which may arise without any fault of yours, but through those with whom you live, which may induce a wise director to hinder you from such frequent Communion. For instance, if you are in a dependent position, and those to whom you owe obedience and reverence are so ignorant or so unaccommodating as to be dissatisfied at your frequent

Communions, it may, under peculiar circumstances, be well for you to condescend to their weakness, and not communicate oftener than once a fortnight, but only in case you can by no other means overcome the difficulty. But this is another point concerning which I can give no general rule, but must leave such to the direction of their own spiritual father; only, I should say that no one who really desires to seek God in the devout life can communicate less than once a month at the very least.

If you give good heed, neither father nor mother, husband nor wife will really oppose your frequent Communions, for you will be careful that they do not interfere with the duties of your station. You will be still kinder and more gentle in your demeanor towards your neighbors, and not refuse them any service or assistance, so that they can hardly seek to interfere with what causes them no inconvenience; unless they are extremely fanciful and unreasonable, in which case your director may advise that you should yield to them.

I must say here a word to the married. In the Old Law God disapproved that creditors should exact their debts upon festival days, but He never disapproved of debtors paying that which was owing if demanded on these days. This rule should be the guide of the married in regard to their mutual obligation. It is unbecoming to ask on the day of Communion that which however it would be meritorious to pay if demanded. No one, therefore, should be debarred from Holy Communion by compliance in this matter, if their devotion causes them to desire it. In the primitive Church Christians communicated every day although they were married and blessed with children. Whence I infer that frequent Communion is by no means inconsistent with the state of a parent, husband or wife, provided that the person who communicates be discreet and prudent. As to bodily maladies there are none which lawfully impede Communion, save such as cause frequent vomiting.

Those who would communicate weekly must be free from all mortal sin, and all affection to venial sin, desiring earnestly to communicate, but those who would daily approach the holy altar must still further have overcome in great part their evil inclinations—nor should any come without the advice of their spiritual guide.

CHAPTER TWENTY-ONE

How to Communicate

———————•———————

B EGIN your preparation for Holy Communion on the preceding evening with aspirations and ejaculations of love, retiring earlier than usual to your room in order to rise earlier the next morning. And if you wake in the night, let your heart and mouth break forth in holy words, wherewith your soul may be perfumed and ready to receive the Bridegroom, who watches whilst you sleep, and makes ready countless graces and favors for you, if you do but dispose yourself to receive them. Rise joyfully in the morning, thinking of the great happiness which awaits you, and after Confession go with full confidence and deep humility to receive that Heavenly Food which will nourish you unto life everlasting. And when you have said, Lord, I am not worthy that Thou shouldst come unto me, do not again move either your head or your lips, either in prayer or sighs, but raising your head so as to enable the priest to see what he does, open your mouth gently and moderately, and then resigning yourself wholly to the reception of that great blessing, wait for the ministering priest to give It to you, and in faith, hope, and charity, receive Him in Whom, by Whom and for Whom you believe, hope, and love. Believe that as the bee having gathered the dew of heaven and the sweets of earth from the flowers, and converted them into honey carries it safely to its hive, so the priests having taken from the altar His Body, the Son of God, the Saviour of the world, Virgin born, coming forth as a flower from the soil of humanity, feeds your body and soul with this Bread of sweetness. Having received It, offer your devout homage to the King of our salvation, lay bare to Him all your inmost heart and its concerns, and cherish His presence within you for your exceeding benefit. In short, give Him the best welcome that you can, and let it be seen by the holiness of all your actions that God is with you. When you are unable actually to receive Him in the Holy Eucharist, then unite yourself by the earnestness of your desires to this life-giving flesh of the Saviour, and communicate spiritually in your heart.

Your chief aim in Holy Communion should be to advance, strengthen, and comfort yourself in the love of God; receiving for love's sake, what love alone can give. There is nothing in which the love of Christ is set forth more tenderly or more touchingly than in this Sacrament, by which He, so to say, annihilates Himself for us, and takes upon Him the form of bread, in order to feed us, and unite Himself closely to the bodies and souls of the faithful.

If men of the world ask why you communicate so often, tell them that it is in order that you may learn to love God, that you may be purified from your imperfections, delivered from your perplexities, comforted in your sorrows, strengthened in your weakness. Tell them that there are two classes of men who need frequent Communion—those who are perfect, since surely they above all men should draw near to the Source and Fountain of all perfection, and the imperfect, in order that they may learn to be perfect; the strong that they may not lose strength, the weak that they may become strong; the sick in order to be healed, the healthy that they may not be sick; and that you who are imperfect, weak, and diseased need constant intercourse with your Perfection, your Strength, and your Physician. Tell them that those who are not encumbered with worldly business should take advantage of their leisure, and communicate frequently; and those who, on the contrary, are pressed and harassed require it the more, for he who labors long and hard needs solid and abundant food. Tell them that you receive the Blessed Sacrament that you may learn to receive it rightly, for what we do but seldom we do ill. Therefore communicate as often as you have permission, and remember that as the hares amidst our snowy mountains grow white from living in the snow, so by perpetually worshiping and adoring beauty, goodness, and purity in this Divine Sacrament, you too will become beautiful, good, and pure.

PART THIRD

———————•———————

Rules for the Practice of Virtue

CHAPTER ONE

The Selection of Virtues to Be Practiced

———————•———————

THE queen bee never settles in a hive without being surrounded by her swarm, and charity never takes possession of a heart without bringing in her train all other virtues, exercising and bringing them into play as a general his troops. But she does not call them forth suddenly, all at once, nor in all times and places. The good man is like a tree planted by the water-side that will bring forth its fruit in due season, because when a soul is watered by charity, it brings forth good works seasonably and with discretion. That music which in gladness rejoices our hearts, is an intrusion in the time of heaviness. There are some who make a great mistake in striving after some special virtue, by acting upon it at unsuitable times. They are like those philosophers of old who insisted on always laughing or always crying; and, what is worse, such persons find fault with those who differ from them. The Apostle bids us weep with them that weep and rejoice with them that rejoice, and charity is patient, benevolent, liberal, prudent, and kind.

But there are some virtues of universal application, and which should infuse their own spirit into everything. We have but rarely opportunities for the practice of courage, magnanimity, and great sacrifices. But every action of our daily life should be influenced by gentleness, temperance, humility, and purity. Some qualities may be more

117

eminent, but these are the most needful. Sugar is more agreeable than salt, but salt is in much more universal requisition. Therefore we should be rich in these everyday virtues, of which we stand in such perpetual need.

We ought always to give the preference to those virtues which are most incumbent on us, and not to those which are most agreeable to our inclinations. St. Paula took delight in the practice of bodily mortification, thereby enhancing her spiritual consolations; but obedience to her superior was a higher duty, and therefore St. Jerome allows that she was wrong in fasting immoderately contrary to the direction of her bishop. So the Apostles, who were commissioned to preach the Gospel and feed the souls of men with the Bread of Life, rightly judged that they must not forsake this duty in order to minister to the bodily needs of the poor, although in itself that was so sacred a duty. (*Acts* 6). Every station in life imposes some peculiar obligation; different virtues are incumbent upon a bishop, a prince, or a soldier—the wife has her duties and the widow hers, and although all should practice every virtue, still each should seek chiefly to advance in those peculiarly required by the state of life to which God has called him.

Amongst those virtues not especially involved by our position, we should cultivate the most excellent rather than the most showy. Comets ordinarily appear larger than the stars, and attract our eyes more, but they are not really to be compared to the stars either in grandeur or quality, and only appear larger to us because they are so much nearer the earth, and their substance is less pure than that of the stars. In the same way there are some virtues which approach our senses, and are, so to say, material, and are, therefore, highly esteemed and preferred by ordinary men, who thus will exalt temporal almsgiving above spiritual, or fasting, discipline and bodily mortifications above gentleness, cheerfulness, modesty, and other acts of discipline of the heart, which are in truth greatly preferable. Do you, Philothea, seek the highest virtues, not those most lauded; the best, not the most obvious; the truest, and not the most showy.

It is a good practice to select some particular virtue at which to aim—not neglecting the others, but in order to give regularity and method to the mind. There appeared once to St. John, Bishop of Alexandria, a beautiful virgin, arrayed in royal robes, shining brighter than the sun, and crowned with an olive wreath. She spoke to him, saying, "I am the King's eldest daughter, and if thou wilt make me thy friend I will lead thee into His presence." Then he knew that this was God Himself teaching him to have mercy upon Christ's poor, and from that time he devoted himself to the practice of that virtue, so that he has been always known as St. John the Almoner. Eulogius the Alexandrian, seeking specially to dedicate himself to God, and not having resolution either to embrace the solitary life or perpetual obedience, brought a wretched, diseased man into his house, as an occasion for practicing charity and mortification, vowing to serve and honor him as a servant his Lord. After a while both parties being disposed to separate, they referred their case to St. Anthony the Great, who replied, "Beware, my sons, that you part not, having so nearly approached the end of your journey, for if the Angel of Death does not find you together, both are in danger of losing their crowns."

The king St. Louis regularly visited his hospitals, and ministered with his own hands to the sick. St. Francis loved poverty above all things, calling her his bride. St. Dominic specially devoted himself to preaching, and hence the name of the Order of Preachers. St. Gregory the Great took great delight in welcoming pilgrims, therein imitating the Patriarch Abraham, and like him receiving the King of Glory under a pilgrim's form. Tobias adopted the charitable habit of burying the dead. St. Elizabeth loved to set aside her royal independence by the entire subjection of herself and her whole will. When St. Catherine of Genoa became a widow she devoted herself to serving in the hospital. Cassian relates how a certain devout woman, desiring to practice the virtue of patience, had recourse to St. Athanasius, who assigned to her as a companion a poor widow of a fretful, irritable, passionate temper, who, rendering herself almost insupportable to the pious maiden, afforded her ample scope for the practice of forbearance and gentleness. So amongst the servants of God, some have devoted themselves to tending the sick, some to visiting the poor, others to the advancement of Christ's religion amongst little children, others to the restoration of lost and wandering souls—some to the especial care of the church and altars, others to the promotion of peace and concord amongst men; thus resembling embroiderers who work their gold, silver, and silk on to various materials, thereby producing all manner of beautiful flowers. For these pious souls who adopt some especial practice of devotion use it as the groundwork whereon they embroider countless other virtues, thus regulating and giving method to all their good works and affections by means of this their chief object, and arraying their soul "in a vesture of gold, wrought about with divers colors."

If we are hindered by some particular vice, we should as far as possible strive to cultivate the opposite virtue, making all things tend to it; for by this means we shall subdue the enemy, and not cease to advance in all virtue. If I am specially tempted with pride or anger, I must, above all things, seek to practice humility and gentleness, and call in all my other devout acts of prayer, the Sacraments, prudence, perseverance, and temperance to my aid! For even as the wild boar whets his tusks by the help of his other teeth, thereby sharpening them also, so the good man who seeks to perfect himself in that virtue of which he stands most in need, should whet and sharpen it by the practice of other virtues, which will thus themselves become stronger and brighter. So it was with Job, who, whilst specially seeking to learn patience under temptation, became very holy and grounded in all other goodness. And St. Gregory Nazianzen says that by the help of one virtue heartily practiced men may attain to all holiness; instancing Rahab, who having practiced the duty of hospitality received such glory of God. But for this we require great devotion and exceeding fervor and charity.

CHAPTER TWO

Choice of Virtues (Continued)

———— • ————

S T. AUGUSTINE says well, that when men are beginning to lead a
devout life they commit errors which are, strictly speaking, against
the laws of perfection, but which, nevertheless, are valuable as indica-
tions of future piety, to which they often conduce not a little. The low,
groveling fear whence arises over-scrupulousness in the minds of those
who are but just forsaking sin, is a quality not to be despised, inasmuch
as it is the forerunner of future purity of conscience, but the same feeling would be blameable in those further advanced in holiness, whose
hearts should be filled with love which will gradually banish such ser-
vile fear.

Originally St. Bernard was exceedingly severe and rigorous towards
those whom he directed, telling them when they came to him to leave
their bodies, and come with the spirit only. Hearing their Confession,
he treated all, even the least fault, with such severity, and so pressed
his poor novices in perfection, that instead of urging them forward
he kept them back; for they were dismayed and discouraged at being
thus rudely driven up so steep and rugged a path. This was the result
of the Saint's own ardent zeal and great purity, and zeal is assuredly a
virtue, yet in this case it became an evil. But God vouchsafed to correct
it, filling St. Bernard's heart with gentleness, tenderness, and mildness,

so that changing his whole system he reproached himself bitterly with his former exacting severity, and became so tender and forbearing that he was like St. Paul, all things to all men, that he might gain them all. St. Jerome records of his beloved daughter in the Faith, St. Paula, that she not only was extravagant in her bodily mortifications, but also self-willed in persisting in them contrary to the advice of St. Epiphanius, her bishop; and further, that at the death of those she loved, she indulged in such excessive grief, as to endanger her own life. "It will be said," he continues, "that instead of praising this holy woman, I am condemning her, but I call Jesus, her master and mine, to witness that I speak the whole truth both good and bad, representing her as she really was, according as one Christian should write of another, that is to say, I write her memoir, not her panegyric; and truly her faults would be another's virtues." That is to say, that St. Paula's faults and imperfections would have counted as virtues in one less holy, and, indeed, there are many actions which we hold as imperfections in the perfect, which, in the imperfect, would pass for great virtues. It is a good sign when the legs of one recovering from sickness begin to swell, as denoting that reviving nature is throwing out what is corrupt in the system, but in a healthy man it would be a bad sign, indicating that nature had not strength to absorb her own superfluities.

Philothea, we must esteem highly those who abound in virtues, even though mingled with imperfections, remembering that so it has been with saints; but for ourselves we must practice all virtues faithfully and watchfully, and give good heed to the Wise Man's counsel, and not rely on our own wisdom, but on that of the guides God has given us.

There are some things which pass current as virtues, but are really quite otherwise, such as ecstasies, raptures, insensibilities, impassibilities, deific unions, elevations, transformations, and similar perfections, which are the subject of certain books. These promise to exalt the soul to a purely intellectual contemplation, to an essential application of the spirit, and a super-eminent life. But these are not virtues; they are rather the reward of those virtues, or foretastes of the bliss of a future existence, which are sometimes granted to men in order to kindle their longings for the perfect blessedness of Paradise. But it is safer not to seek such favors, which are no ways necessary in order to serve and love God truly, which should be our only aim. Neither, indeed, can they be obtained by a labored search, since they are rather emotions than actions, which we can receive, but not originate. Our aim is to become good, devout, pious men and women, and to that end we must labor; then if it should please God to give us angelic perfections, we should, doubtless, be good angels, but, meanwhile, let us simply, humbly, and devoutly practice those lowly virtues, the acquisition of which has been appointed by our Saviour as our daily task, such as patience, cheerfulness, a mortified heart, humility, obedience, poverty, chastity, kindness towards our neighbor, forbearance towards his faults, diligence, and holy fervor. Let us cheerfully leave preeminent graces to preeminent souls; we do not deserve so high a post in God's service, too happy if we can obtain the humblest office in His household, whence He in His own good time, if He sees fit, will bid us, come up higher.

Yes, Philothea, this glorious King does not reward His servants according to the dignity of their office, but according to the humility and love with which they fulfill that appointed them. Whilst Saul sought his father's asses, he found the kingdom of Israel; Rebecca, whilst watering Abraham's camels, became his son's bride; Ruth gleaning after the reapers, and lying at Booz's feet, was raised up to be his wife. Undoubtedly, high pretensions are very liable to illusions, deceits, and errors, so that sometimes those who would fain be angels are not really even good men, and there is more of elevation and holiness in their words and expressions than in their heart and deeds. Nevertheless, we should never be hasty with our contempt or censure; but whilst we thank God for the exalted favors He bestows on others, remain humbly in our own lower sphere—lower, indeed, but safer and better, more suited to our weakness and insufficiency, certain that if we walk therein, humbly and faithfully, God will exalt us to real greatness.

CHAPTER THREE

Patience

———•———

"PATIENCE is necessary for you, that, doing the will of God, you may receive the promise" (*Heb.* 10:36), says the Apostle; and Our Lord Himself declared (*Luke* 21:19), "In your patience you shall possess your souls." The great happiness of man, Philothea, is thus to possess his soul; and the more perfect our patience, the more perfectly do we possess our souls. Call to mind frequently that it was by suffering and endurance that Our Lord saved us, and that it is meet that we too on our part must work out our salvation by sufferings and afflictions, bearing injuries, contradictions, and annoyances with the greatest calm and gentleness.

Do not limit your patience to this or that kind of injury or trouble, but let it embrace every sort of trial that God sends or permits to come upon you.

There are some persons who are willing to suffer, provided the sufferings are of a kind that bring honor with them, as, for example, to be wounded or taken prisoner in war, to be ill-treated on account of their religion, to bear the losses entailed by a legal decision given in their favor. But such persons are lovers, not of the trials, but of the honor that accompanies them. The truly patient servant of God bears the troubles that bring contempt no less willingly than those that are esteemed honorable. To be despised, reproached, and accused by the wicked is no great trial to a man of good heart; but to be condemned, despised, and ill-treated by the good, by friends, or by relations, is a real test of progress. I think much more of the meekness with which the great St. Charles Borromeo for a long time bore the public attacks made upon him from the pulpit by an eminent preacher of a certain religious Order, more than his patience under all other injuries. For just as the sting of a bee is more painful than that of a fly, so the contradiction and opposition of good men is far harder to bear than that of the ungodly; and yet it often happens that two men, each meaning well in their opposing opinions, are very bitter in contradicting and persecuting one another.

Be patient, not only under the great and heavy trials which come upon you, but also under the minor troubles and accidents of life. "I am quite content to become poor," one man says, "if only it did not hinder me from educating my children and assisting my friends and living respectably." And another, "I should not mind it, but that the world will lay the blame on me." Another would willingly be calumniated, and would bear calumny with patience, on condition that no one believes the calumny. Others again are willing to endure some troubles, but not all—they are content to be sick, they say, but are dissatisfied because they have not wherewithal to procure advice, or because those around them are disconcerted by their illness. But to such I would say, "We must be patient not only under sickness, but further, we must bear the particular complaint which God sends us; take the place where He wills us to be amongst those with whom He surrounds us, and under the privations He appoints for us, and so on with all other trials." When you are overtaken by some misfortune, seek the remedies which God affords you, for not to do so would be tempting His Divine Providence, but having done so, await the result He may appoint with perfect resignation. If He sees fit to permit the remedies to overcome the evil, thank Him humbly; but if, on the other hand, He permits the evil to overcome the remedies, patiently bless His holy Name and submit.

I say with St. Gregory, if you are justly accused of some fault which you have committed, humble yourself, and acknowledge that you deserve the accusation; if you are falsely accused, excuse yourself meekly, denying your guilt, for so much you owe to truth, and the edification of your neighbor. But if after your true and honest excuse your accusers persist, give yourself no further trouble, and do not persevere in your defense, for having paid tribute to truth, now pay tribute to humility. By this means you will alike do justice to the claim which your reputation has upon you, and to that quietness, humility, and lowliness of heart which are so important.

Do not complain of the injuries done to you more than you can help, for undoubtedly, as a general thing he who complains, errs; inasmuch as our self-love always magnifies our injuries; but above all, do not make your complaints to those who are easily excited to anger and ready to think ill of others. If it is necessary to complain at all, either for redress, or in order to relieve your own mind, let it be to some one of a peaceable disposition who truly loves God; for others, instead of soothing you, will only excite you still more: instead of extracting the thorn from your foot, they will but drive it in the deeper.

There are some who when they are sick, afflicted, or aggrieved, avoid complaining or appearing tender, thinking thereby that they only show their lack of courage and generosity; but they desire greatly that others should lament over them, and employ various means to induce them to do so, and would fain be counted patient and brave as well as afflicted. They are patient, but theirs is a false patience, which in truth is only a refined ambition and vanity. "Their glorying is not of God," says the Apostle. A truly patient man neither complains himself nor wishes others to complain for him; he speaks honestly, simply, and truly of his trial without complaining, bemoaning, or exaggeration; and if he is pitied he receives pity with patience likewise, unless it is bestowed on some evil which does not exist. In such case he merely replies that he has not that trial, and so rests calmly in truth and patience, bearing his trial without murmur.

In the contradictions which will disturb your devotional practices (and such you will assuredly find) remember the words of our Blessed Lord. "A woman when she is in travail hath sorrow, because her hour is come; but when she hath brought forth the child she remembereth no more the anguish, for joy that a man is born into the world." You have conceived in your heart the Holy Child Jesus, and before He is born you must bear the pangs of travail. But be of good courage, for when they are passed, the joy that such a man is born into the world will abide with you. And for you He is born, when He is formed in your heart, and in your works by imitation of His life.

When you are sick offer to Christ our Lord all your pains, your suffering, and your languor, and beseech Him to unite them to those He bore for you. Obey your physician, and take your medicine, your food, or your remedies for the love of God, remembering how He tasted gall for the love of man: let your desire for recovery be in order to serve Him. Be willing to languish in obedience to His Will, and prepare to die when He calls you, that you may be with him and praise Him forever. Remember that whilst the bee makes its honey it often feeds upon bitter juices, and we have no better opportunity of making acts of patience and meekness, than whilst we are eating the bread of bitterness, and living in the midst of sufferings. And as no honey is so good as that made from the thyme, which is a lowly and bitter herb, so that virtue, which is practiced in low and despicable sufferings, is the most precious.

Consider within you how Jesus Christ was crucified: naked, blasphemed, calumniated, forsaken, overwhelmed with every kind of injury, sadness, and toil; and reflect that your sufferings can in noways be likened to His, either in kind or degree, and that you can never bear anything for Him compared to what He has borne for you.

Reflect also upon the sufferings which the martyrs endured, and how many there are who bear far greater trials than yours, and say, "Surely my labors are consolations, my pangs are as roses when compared to those who, without help, succor, or alleviation, overwhelmed with far greater misfortunes, live in perpetual death."

CHAPTER FOUR

External Humility

———————————•———————————

"**B**ORROW . . . empty vessels not a few," said Eliseus to the poor widow, "and pour oil into them" (*4 Kings* 4), and before we can receive the grace of God into our hearts they must be thoroughly empty of all self-glory. The kestrel has a peculiar property of frightening away birds of prey with its looks and cries, for which reason the dove seeks it beyond all other birds, and lives fearlessly in its neighborhood; and so humility repulses Satan and preserves in us the gifts and graces of the Holy Spirit. For this reason all the Saints, and especially the King of Saints and His Mother, ever honored and cherished this virtue above all others.

We call vainglory that which we seek for ourselves, either for that which is not in us, or being in us, is not our own, or being in us and our own, is not worthy to be glorified in. Noble birth, the favor of the great, popular esteem, are not in ourselves, they come either from our forefathers or from the opinion of others. Some are proud and conceited because they have a fine horse, a plume in their hat, or are magnificently attired, but who cannot perceive the absurdity of this, since if anyone has reason to be proud it surely is the horse, the ostrich, or the tailor! And how very contemptible it is to rest our hope of esteem in a horse, a feather, or a garment! Another thinks of his well-trimmed beard and mustache, or his well-curled hair, his delicate hands, or of his accomplishment in dancing, music, and so on, but is it not very contemptible to try to enhance his worth or his reputation through such foolish and frivolous things? Others, who have acquired a little science, demand the respect and honor of the world on that account, as if all must needs come to learn of them and bow before them. Such men we call pedants. Others pride themselves on their personal beauty, and think that everyone is admiring them: all of them in their turn are utterly silly, foolish, and impertinent, and their glory in such empty things we call vain, absurd, and frivolous.

You may judge of real worth as of real balm, which is tried in water, and if it sinks, and remains at the bottom, it is known to be precious and costly; and so in order to know whether a man is really wise, learned, generous, and noble, observe whether his gifts make him humble, modest and submissive. If so they are genuine, but if they float to the surface and would fain display themselves, be sure that in proportion as they make a show, so are they less worthy. Those pearls which are formed or fed in the wind and thunder leave only a pearly shell without any substance; and so those virtues and attractive qualities which have their root and support in pride, self-sufficiency, and vanity, have but the outward show of excellence, and are without sap, marrow, or solidity.

Honor, rank, and dignity are like the saffron, which flourishes and increases most when it is trodden underfoot. All the value of beauty is gone when its possessor is self-conscious; to be pleasing it should be forgotten; and science becomes contemptible when it is puffed up and degenerates into pedantry.

If we are punctilious about rank, title, and precedence, we both lay our claims open to investigation and contradiction, and render them vile and despicable. For that honor which means something when willingly offered, becomes contemptible when it is sought after, demanded, or exacted. When the peacock displays his gorgeous plumes, he lays bare also all his deformities; and those flowers which are beautiful in their native soil, soon wither if we handle them. And as they who inhale the mandragora from afar off, and for a brief space, find it very delicious; but those who inhale it near, and for long, become drowsy and ill: so worldly honors are acceptable to him who receives them indifferently without resting in them or seeking them eagerly, but they become very dangerous and hurtful to him who clings to and takes delight in them.

The desire and pursuit of virtue tend to render us virtuous, but the desire and pursuit of honors tend to make us odious and despicable. A really great mind will not waste itself on such empty goods as rank, honor, and form. It has higher pursuits, and leaves these for the weak and vain. He who can procure pearls will not be satisfied with shells, and those who aim at virtue do not trouble themselves about honors. Of course each man may enter into, and remain in, his own sphere without lack of humility, so long as he does it with indifference, and without effort. Just as vessels coming from Peru laden with gold and silver bring also a number of monkeys and parrots which cost nothing, and add but little to their freight, so those who aspire to be virtuous, may well accept their rightful rank and honors, but always without bestowing much care or thought on them, and without being involved in cares, vexations, disputes, and anxieties in consequence. I am not alluding here to those invested with public dignities, nor to special and important occasions, in which everyone is bound to maintain a fitting dignity with prudence and discretion, combined with charity and courtesy.

CHAPTER FIVE

Inward Humility

———————●———————

BUT you, Philothea, would have me lead you further in the practice of humility, for that of which I have been speaking is rather wisdom than humility. There are some who neither will nor dare consider and dwell upon the individual grace which God has conferred upon them for fear of vainglory and self-conceit, but they are mistaken. For if indeed, as the Angelical Doctor tells us, the sure way of attaining to the love of God is to dwell upon His mercies, the more we appreciate them, the more we shall love Him; and as everyone is more alive to private than to public benefits, they should more especially consider them. Assuredly nothing can so humble us before the compassion of God as the abundance of His mercies; nothing so humble us before His justice as the abundance of our misdeeds. Let us reflect upon all He has done for us, and all we have done against Him; and as we count over our sins in detail, even so let us count over His mercies.

We need not fear to be puffed up with the knowledge of what He has done for us, if we keep well before us the truth that whatever good there may be in us, is not of us. Though a mule is laden with the precious and perfumed treasures of a prince, is it not still a clumsy, filthy beast? "What hast thou that thou didst not receive? And if thou didst receive it, why dost thou glory, as if thou hadst not received it?"

(*1 Cor.* 4:7). On the contrary, a lively consciousness of mercies received makes us humble, for such knowledge gives birth to gratitude. But if in the consideration of God's grace any vanity were to slip in, we should find an infallible remedy in the remembrance of our ingratitude, our imperfections, our weakness; and if we reflect on what we have done without God, we shall require no further proof that what we do when He is with us is not of ourselves or of our own strength; we shall rejoice in it certainly, and rejoice because we have done it, but we shall give all the glory of it to God, who is its author.

Thus the Blessed Virgin declared what great things God had done in her, but only in order to humble herself and exalt Him. "My soul," she says, "doth magnify the Lord. . . . Because He that is mighty hath done great things to me." (*Luke* 1:46-49).

Sometimes we profess that we are nought, that we are weakness itself, and the very offscouring of the earth. But we should be ill-pleased to be taken at our word, and generally esteemed according to what we say. On the contrary, we pretend to fly and hide ourselves, in order to be followed and searched after. We pretend that we should be amongst the humble, and take the lower place, but it is in order the better to go up higher. True humility does not affect to be humble, and makes few lowly speeches, for she not only desires to hide other virtues, but, above all, to hide herself; and if it were lawful for her to lie, or deceive or offend others, she would appear outwardly proud and haughty, so as to conceal her real self, and live unknown and in concealment. My advice, therefore, is, that you do not abound in expressions of humility, or, at least, let a deep inward feeling agree with whatever you say outwardly. Never cast down your eyes without humbling your heart, and do not pretend that you wish to be among the last, unless you truly desire it in your heart. This I hold for so universal a rule, that I make no exception to it, only sometimes ordinary courtesy may require us to concede the superiority to those who evidently have no claim to it, and in that there is neither deception nor false humility, for in such a case the concession of superiority is a beginning of honor, and since we cannot give it them altogether, it is well to give what we can. I should say the same with regard to certain expressions of honor and respect which may not appear strictly true, but which really are true if he who utters them has in his heart a sincere intention to honor and respect him to whom he addresses them; for, although the words themselves may be exaggerated, yet there is no harm in following the conventional rules of society in using them. Still, I should wish that our words were always as far as possible in conformity with our feelings, that so we might be actuated in all, and through all, by cordial sincerity and candor.

A really humble man would rather let another say that he is contemptible and worth nothing, than say so himself. At any rate, when he knows that such things are said, he does not contradict them, but consents willingly; he believes it himself, and is content that others should share his opinion. There are many who say that they leave mental prayer to perfect men, they themselves are not capable of it; others that they dare not communicate frequently, for they feel themselves unworthy. Some say that they fear to disgrace religion if they pretend to it, by reason of their frailty and sinfulness; or they refuse to devote their talents to the service of God and their neighbor, because they say that, knowing their weakness, they fear lest they be puffed up if they do any good thing, and so in doing good to others, they injure themselves. All these excuses are deceptive, not only false humility but evil, inasmuch as they seek tacitly and secretly to find fault with the things of God, or at least to cover their own self-love, indolence, and evil disposition under the cloak of humility. "Ask thee a sign of the Lord thy God, either unto the depth of hell, or unto the height above," said the prophet to Achaz. But Achaz said, "I will not ask, and I will not tempt the Lord." (*Is.* 7:12). Oh, wicked man, he feigns a deep reverence for God, and under pretense of humility refuses to seek the grace proffered by His divine mercy! Could he not perceive that to refuse God's favors is mere pride? That His gifts must be gratefully received, and that true humility lies in obeying Him and following His Will to our utmost? And His Will is that we be perfect, uniting ourselves to Him, and imitating Him to the utmost of our capacity. The proud man who trusts in himself may well fear to undertake anything, but the humble are bold in proportion as they feel their own insufficiency; and as they count themselves weak they acquire strength, because all their reliance is in God, who delights to magnify His Omnipotence in our weakness, and to exalt His mercy upon our misery. We may then humbly and devoutly presume to undertake all that may be judged proper for our advancement by those who guide our souls.

Nothing can be more foolish than to fancy we know what we do *not* know, and no vanity is more contemptible than that which affects knowledge which it does not really possess. For myself, I would neither boast of what I do know, nor pretend to be more ignorant than I am. When charity requires, you should impart freely and gently whatever is necessary for your neighbor's instruction, or may serve to comfort and help him; for although humility conceals her gifts in order to their preservation, she is always ready to produce them when charity requires it, thereby strengthening, enlarging, and perfecting them. In this, humility resembles that tree of Tylos, which at night folds up and conceals its beautiful flowers, opening them again to the rising sun; for which reason the inhabitants of that island say that the flowers sleep at night. So humility enfolds and conceals all our virtues and human perfections, producing them only at the call of charity, which is not an earthly but a heavenly virtue, not a moral but a divine perfection, and the very sun of all the other virtues, over which she should always preside; and therefore such humility as is opposed to charity is undoubtedly spurious.

I would neither affect wisdom nor folly, for if humility forbids me to affect wisdom, simplicity and honesty forbid me to affect folly; and as vanity is opposed to humility, so all artifice, affectation, and pretense are opposed to honesty and simplicity. Nor because certain eminent servants of God have assumed a garb of folly must we think to imitate them, the inducing causes of their actions being so rare and extraordinary that they cannot be any example to us. When David leaped and danced before the Ark of the Lord, it was not in assumed extravagance of demeanor, but simply that his external actions corresponded to the unusual, immeasurable gladness of his heart. Therefore, when Michol, his wife, reproached him with his folly, he was not offended at her contempt, but continuing in his earnest hearty demonstrations of joy, declared himself willing to bear some reproach for God's sake. In like manner, if any despise you, or count you as foolish and contemptible on account of those actions which proceed from a true and hearty devotion, humility will teach you to take pleasure in such honorable contempt, the cause of which is not really in you but in those that reproach you.

CHAPTER SIX

Humility Makes Us Love Our Own Abasement

———•———

A STEP further, Philothea, would I lead you, and bid you in every thing to welcome your own abasement. And if you ask what I mean, I answer that the word in Latin means humility, and humility abasement; so that when the Blessed Virgin says in her song of thanksgiving, that because the Lord has regarded her humility, therefore all generations shall call her blessed, she means that God has looked favorably upon her abasement, her poverty and lowliness, in order to crown her with favors and graces. Yet there is a difference between the virtue of humility and abasement, for the latter is that littleness, meanness, and imperfection which is in us, although we think not of it, but humility consists in really knowing and freely acknowledging our abasement. Now the perfection of this humility is not only to know and acknowledge it, but to take pleasure and delight therein, and that not from lack of spirit or energy, but the more to exalt God's Majesty and to esteem our neighbors better than ourselves.

The better to explain this duty to which I exhort you, I would have you remark that of the ills under which we labor, some are abject and others honorable; now, many are ready to endure these last, but few willingly submit to the former. For instance, take a devout hermit, whose garments are tattered and himself cold and needy; everyone honors him whilst they pity his sufferings; but if a poor mechanic, a needy gentleman endures the same, he is despised and ridiculed, and so his poverty becomes abject. If one bound by vows of obedience receives meekly a sharp rebuke from his superior, or a child from his parent, it is called mortification, obedience, goodness; but if a man or woman of the world bears the same mortification meekly, it is called cowardice and want of spirit, albeit borne for the love of God. This, again, then, is an abject endurance. One person has a sore on his arm, another on his face; the one suffers only from the disease, the other has in addition to endure disgust and aversion and abasement. What I say, then, is, that we must learn not only to love our burden, which is done by the virtue of patience, but also to love its attendant abasement, which is done by the virtue of humility.

Again, some virtues involve abasement, and some involve honor: for the world despises patience, gentleness, simplicity, and oftentimes humility itself; whilst it highly prizes sagacity, valor, and liberality. So, too, different fruits of the same virtue are differently esteemed; thus almsgiving and forgiveness of offenses are alike the result of charity, but whilst everyone honors the first, the world despises the latter action. A young person who resists the example of his or her companions and will not join in the excesses of pleasure, drinking, gaming, dressing, or idle talk, is ridiculed and criticized by the others, and his self-denial is called bigotry, or affectation; now to take such contempt gladly, is to rejoice in abasement. Again, we are deputed to visit the sick. If it be to a poor and miserable man that I am sent, it is an abasement in the eyes of the world, and, therefore, I will welcome it; but if I, on the contrary, am sent to the rich, the abasement is spiritual, for it is neither so worthy nor so meritorious an act; therefore I will still delight in it. You fall in the street, and in addition to the hurt you receive you become an object of ridicule—well, receive it gladly. There are some failings in which there is no harm beyond their abasement; and though humility does not require us to commit them, it does require that having committed them we should not vex ourselves on account of them. Such are little foolish sayings and doings, breaches of etiquette, and similar slips which we are bound in prudence and courtesy to avoid, but if we are guilty of them, then we should patiently accept the consequent abasement and receive it willingly as a practical lesson in humility. I would go further still and say, that if I have been led through anger or wantonness to use unbecoming language, therein offending God and my neighbor, I should assuredly repent heartily, feel a lively regret for the offense, and do my utmost to make amends, but at the same time I would endeavor to welcome the abasement and degradation which are the result of my fault, and if it were possible to separate the two, I would undo the latter, whilst I humbly retained the former.

But although we welcome the humiliation which comes to us from our defects, we must not omit to remedy these as far as may be by all fair and legitimate means; especially when they are of consequence. If I have got disease in my face, I would seek its cure, but not forget the humiliation I have endured. If I have done something which offends no one, I will make no excuse, for although I was wrong, the evil is temporary, and I will not set aside the degradation which is entailed; but if out of carelessness or foolishness I have given cause of offense or scandal to anyone, I will repair my fault with a sincere excuse, for the mischief is lasting, and charity obliges me to undo it. So occasionally charity requires us to remedy this abasement for our neighbor's sake, who might be injured by our loss of reputation; but in such a case, whilst we conceal our degradation from the eyes of others, we must treasure it up in our own heart, and not lose the lesson it teaches.

If you ask me what are the most profitable humiliations, I reply that undoubtedly those will do us most good and serve God best which are accidental or attendant upon our position in life, because these we do not seek for ourselves, but receive them as God sends them, and His choice is always better than ours. But if we must choose, no doubt the greatest are the best, and those are greatest which are most opposed to our natural inclinations, always supposing them suitable to our condition in life, for I say once for all, that our own will and preferences hinder and lessen almost all our virtues. Ah, who can teach us to say with the royal Psalmist, "I have chosen to be an abject in the house of my God, rather than to dwell in the tabernacles of sinners!" (*Ps.* 83:11). None can teach us that holy lesson save Him who, to exalt us, lived and died, the scorn of men, and the outcast of the people. I have said to you many things which will seem hard as you read them, but if you practice them, they will be sweet to you as sugar and honey.

CHAPTER SEVEN

How to Preserve a Good Reputation
Together with the Practice of Humility

———•———

MEN do not receive praise, honor, and glory for ordinary virtues, but for something extraordinary. By praise we seek to induce others to value the merit of someone; by honor we show that we value it ourselves, and glory I hold to be the brilliant reputation ensuing upon collective praise and honor; so that if honors and praises resemble precious stones, the union of many produces, so to say, an enamel of glory. Now, inasmuch as true humility does not allow us to imagine that we excel or ought to be preferred to others, it does not allow us to seek for that praise, honor, and glory which we hold to be the meed of excellence; but it does not militate against the Wise Man's precept to value our good name. (*Prov.* 22:1). For a good reputation does not imply any marked superiority, but simply an ordinary good and respectable life, which humility in no way forbids us to be conscious of—any more than to desire to be held in good repute for the same. Undoubtedly humility might despise even a good name, were it not that thereby charity would be injured, for a good reputation is one of the foundations of society, without which we are not only useless but actually hurtful to the public welfare, and a cause of scandal—therefore charity demands and humility consents that we should seek and studiously preserve a good name.

Again, as the leaves of a tree which in themselves are little worth, are yet very useful not only in adorning it, but in sheltering the tender fruit, so a good reputation, though in itself of little value, becomes precious, not only as an ornament of our lives, but as the guardian of our virtues, especially those which are tender and frail. Our energies are stimulated at once gently and powerfully by the necessity of preserving our reputation, and really being that which we are thought to be. Let us then strictly watch over our virtues, because they are pleasing to God who is the first and chief end of all our actions: and as those who preserve fruits not only prepare them but put them into vessels suitable for their preservation, so whilst divine love is the principal guard of our virtues, we may safely add the further protection of a good reputation.

But we must not be over-eager or over-careful concerning it, for those who are so very sensitive about their reputation are like people who are always taking medicine for every trifling indisposition: they intend to preserve their health, whilst really they ruin it; and those who are so delicate about their reputation, lose it altogether, for this excessive sensitiveness makes them uneasy, touchy, and insupportable to others, provoking the malice of slanderers.

As a general thing, self-control and contempt for calumny and evil reports are more successful remedies than resentment, disputes, and revenge. Calumny dies away under contempt, but irritation seems half to verify it. The crocodile hurts only those who fear it, and neither will calumny hurt any save those who take it to heart.

An excessive fear of losing our good name implies want of reliance in that which is its principal foundation—the truthfulness of a good life. Those towns whose bridges are built of wood are always in dread of dangerous floods, but where the bridges are stone, they fear nothing but very unwonted inundations. So a truly Christian soul can afford to despise the vexations of evil tongues, but weaker men are forever fretted and aggrieved. Certainly he who would fain stand well with everyone, ends with standing well with no one, and he who is willing to be honored by those who are themselves corrupt and dishonorable, deserves to lose his honor.

A good name is like a signboard to indicate where virtue dwells, therefore in all things and everywhere virtue is to be preferred. If then it is said that, because you are of a devout habit, you are a hypocrite, or if having forgiven an injury you are called a coward, take no heed of such things. They are the judgments of foolish, trifling people; and even if you were thus to lose your good name, still you are not justified in forsaking virtue or in turning aside from its paths: for this would be to prefer mere foliage to fruit—that is to say, external gain to inward and spiritual good.

We should be jealous of our good name, but not idolize it; and as we would not offend the eyes of good men, neither must we wish to please those who are bad. The beard is an ornament to men, and long hair to women; if it is all plucked out by the root it will scarcely grow again, but if it be only cut or shaven, it will soon grow again and be yet stronger and thicker; and so if our reputation be cut or even closely shaved by the tongue of slander (which David compares to a sharp razor), we need not be disquieted, it will soon rise again, both more lovely than before, and more substantial. But if we lose our reputation by our vices, our meanness, or our evil deeds, the root is plucked up, and we shall hardly ever recover it. The root of good reputation is goodness and probity, and whilst it remains in us, the honor due to it will ever spring up anew.

We must forsake this idle conversation, this useless pursuit, this frivolous friendship, this foolish inclination if they tarnish our good name, for it is worth more than all such empty gratifications; but if murmurs, vexations, or slanders arise because of our pious practices, our progress in devotion, and our pursuit after our eternal welfare, let us leave such curs to bay the moon! For if indeed they are able to excite any unjust suspicion of our good name, and so cut the hair and shave the beard of reputation, it will soon grow again, and the razor of calumny will only strengthen our good fame as the pruning-hook strengthens the vine, causing its fruit to abound and multiply.

Let us keep our eyes fixed on our Crucified Saviour, and go on in His service in simple-hearted confidence, with discretion and prudence: He will watch over our reputation, and if He permits it to be lost, He will restore it tenfold, or else cause us to advance in that blessed humility, one grain of which weighs more than all worldly honors. If we are unjustly blamed, let us calmly oppose the calumny with truth; but if it perseveres, let us persevere in our humility, for we cannot better protect our reputation than by trusting it wholly in the hands of God. Let us imitate St. Paul and serve God "in good repute and evil repute," so that we may be able to say with David, "For Thy sake have I borne reproach, shame hath covered my face." (*Ps.* 68:8).

There are some exceptions—such as horrible and infamous crimes which no one should endure to have imputed to him falsely; and certain persons on whose good reputation the edification of others depends. In such eases, following the opinion of divines, we must calmly seek reparation of the evil.

CHAPTER EIGHT

Meekness and the Remedies for Anger

———— • ————

THE holy Chrism used in the Church by Apostolic tradition for Confirmation and blessings is composed of olive oil and balm; thus representing, amongst other things, two of the most precious and blessed virtues which were conspicuous in our Saviour, and which He has enjoined on us as the special means of serving and imitating Him. "Learn of Me," He said, "for I am meek and humble of heart." Humility perfects us towards God, mildness or gentleness towards our neighbor. The balm which (as I have before said) always falls to the bottom when mixed with other liquids, represents humility, and the olive oil, which always rises to the top, represents gentleness and mildness which rises above all else, and excels among virtues, being the flower of charity, which St. Bernard pronounces to be perfect when in addition to being patient it is gentle and amiable. But give good heed that this precious oil of mildness and humility be within your heart, for one of the great wiles of the enemy is to lead men to rest content with the external signs of these virtues, and, without searching their inward affections, to think that because their words and looks are gentle, therefore they themselves are humble and mild, whilst in truth they are far otherwise. This is evident when, in spite of their show of gentleness and humility, they start up in wounded pride at the slightest insult or vexatious word. It is said that those who take the medicine called St. Paul's cure, will not, if it be pure, suffer from swelling with the viper's bite; and so if our humility and gentleness are genuine, they will preserve us from the swelling and inflammation which insult is wont to provoke in our hearts. If, then, when we are bitten and stung by our enemies and slanderers, we become proud, swollen, and indignant, it is a sure sign that our humility and meekness are false and artificial, not hearty and genuine.

When the holy Patriarch Joseph dismissed his brethren on their homeward journey, he charged them, "Be not angry in the way." (*Gen.* 45:24). This present life is but the road to a blessed life, let us not be angry on the way one with another; let us go forward with our brethren and companions gently, peacefully, and lovingly. I exhort you earnestly never to give way to anger, and never, under any pretext whatever, let it effect an entrance into your heart. St. James says explicitly that "the anger of man worketh not the justice of God." Undoubtedly, we must oppose what is wrong, and steadfastly check the vices of those under our care, but we must do so quietly and gently. Nothing appeases the elephant when irritated so much as the sight of a lamb, and nothing breaks the force of a cannonade so well as wool. The correction which is administered through passion, although reasonable, will not be as effectual as if reason alone were the instigator; for the reasonable soul is naturally subject to reason, but tyranny only subjects it to passion; and wherever reason is accompanied by passion, it is rendered hateful in proportion, and its just empire is lowered by its unworthy society. The peaceful visit of a prince gratifies and comforts his people, but when he is accompanied by an army although it may be for the public good, these visits are very unacceptable and mischievous, since, however strictly military discipline is observed, it is impossible always to insure that none shall suffer unjustly. So, whilst reason reigns and administers its reproofs, corrections, and chastisements, albeit with strictness and severity, it is loved and approved; but if it is accompanied by anger, wrath, and passion (which St. Augustine styles its soldiers), it becomes more an object of terror than of love, and it will be resisted and disliked. It is better (says St. Augustine, writing to Profuturus) to exclude wholly even the slightest wrath, albeit just and reasonable, for once having entered the heart it is hard to dislodge; especially though it enters in but a mote, it speedily waxes great and becomes a very beam. For if it abides with us, and, contrary to the Apostle's injunction, the sun goes down upon our wrath, and it is turned into hatred, we can no longer set ourselves free, for then it will be fed by a thousand false fancies and delusions; inasmuch as no angry man ever thinks his anger unjust.

It is safer, then, to avoid all anger, rather than to try and guide our anger with discretion and moderation; and if through our frailty and weakness we are sometimes overtaken, it is better to resist it decidedly, than to try and make terms; for if once we yield ever so little, our anger will gain the upper hand, and like the serpent, easily drag his body where once he has inserted his head. Do you ask how to resist anger? As soon as you feel the slightest resentment, gather together your powers, not hastily or impetuously, but gently and seriously. For, as in some law courts, the criers make more noise in their efforts to preserve quiet than would be made by those they seek to still, so, if we are impetuous in our attempts to restrain our anger, we cause greater discomposure in our hearts than before; and once thrown off its balance, the heart is no longer its own master.

Having then sought calmly to control yourself, follow the counsel given by St. Augustine in his old age to the young Bishop Auxilius. "Do," he said, "as it becomes a man to do; if with David thou feelest that thy spirit is vexed within thee, make haste to cry, 'Have mercy on me, O Lord,' that He may stretch forth His right hand to moderate thine anger." When we feel ourselves stirred with passion, we must imitate the Apostles amidst the raging storm and tempest, and call upon God to help us; then He will bid our angry passions to be still, and great shall be our peace. But I would have you remember, that when we pray to be delivered from the anger with which we are struggling, we should pray gently and calmly, without excitement, and so with all the other remedies we may adopt against this evil.

Furthermore, as soon as you are conscious of having committed a hasty action, lose no time in repairing the error by an act of gentleness towards the person with whom you have been irritated. Just as the surest cure for lying is to unsay a falsehood as soon as we are conscious of having told it, so the best cure for anger is to make immediate reparation in meekness; for, as the proverb says, fresh wounds are always the easiest to heal.

Moreover, when you are at peace and without any cause for anger, try to lay in a stock of gentleness and meekness, always speaking and acting both in things great and small as gently as possible. And remember that the Spouse in the Canticle of Canticles had honey not only from her lips, but that it was "under her tongue," that is, in her breast; and she had not only honey but milk. (*Cant.* 4:11). So we must not only use gentle words towards our neighbors, but must be filled with gentleness, that is, our very inmost soul. And we must not be satisfied with the aromatic fragrance of honey, that is, with agreeable and courteous dealings towards strangers, but we must have the milk of charity towards our own household, and not resemble those who are angels abroad and devils at home.

CHAPTER NINE

Gentleness Towards Ourselves

———————•———————

ONE of the forms in which we should practice gentleness regards ourselves, in never growing irritable with ourselves on our imperfections; for, although, in reason we must be vexed and angry with ourselves when we commit faults, yet we ought to guard against a bitter, fretful displeasure, or spiteful anger with ourselves. Some make a great mistake in being angry because they have been angry, hurt because they have been hurt, and vexed because they have been vexed. Thus, whilst they fancy that they are ridding their breast of anger, and that their second passion remedies the first, in truth, they are preparing the way for fresh anger on the first occasion. Besides this, all this indignation and vexation and irritation with ourselves tends to foster pride and springs entirely from self-love, which is displeased at finding that we are not perfect. We should endeavor then to look upon our faults with a calm, collected, firm displeasure. A judge who passes sentence thoughtfully and calmly, punishes vice more effectually than if he is impetuous and hasty, for in the latter case, he does not punish so much according to the crime committed, as according to his own feeling; and so we correct ourselves more effectually by a quiet persevering repentance than by an irritated, hasty, passionate repentance; for such as these are not according to the magnitude of our faults, but according to our impulse.

For instance, a man who especially aims at purity, will be overwhelmed with angry self-reproach for some slight offense against it, whilst he will only laugh at some grievous slander of which he has been guilty. On the contrary, one who specially abhors slander will torment himself in consequence of some slight murmuring, whilst he passed unnoticed a gross act of impurity; and so with other sins: and all this is the consequence of judging conscience by passion instead of by reason.

Believe me, that as the remonstrances of a father will have much greater effect upon his child if they are offered kindly and gently than if they are hot and angry; so when we have erred, if we reprove our heart gently and calmly, rather pitying than reproaching it, and encouraging it to amendment, its repentance will be much deeper and sounder than if we were angry, stormy, and irritable.

For instance, if I particularly desired not to yield to the sin of vanity, and, nevertheless, I fell grievously into it, I would not begin to say to my heart, "Art thou not wretched and abominable, to be carried away by vanity after so many good resolutions? Well mayst thou die of shame, and not presume to lift up thine eyes, blind, insolent, faithless traitor, to thy God," or so forth. I would rather seek to correct it by reasoning and compassion thus—"My poor heart, here we are fallen into the snare, from which we had so often resolved to escape! Come, let us rise up once more and forsake it forever, let us call for God's mercy, and put our trust in it, for it will assist us in standing firmer for the future, so will we return to the path of humility. Let us not be discouraged, but be well on our guard from this time. God will help us and guide us." And by such reproof I would establish a firmly rooted resolution not to fall again into the same fault, taking such steps as seem advisable, and as my director may point out to prevent it.

If anyone does not find that he can sufficiently touch his heart by this gentle correction, he can make use of a harsher, sharper reprehension, in order to bring it to utter confusion. But after using severity and reproach he still should conclude his anger and indignation with a calm, holy confidence in God, imitating that great penitent, who, when his soul was prostrate in affliction, consoled it, saying, "Why art thou sad, O my soul: and why dost thou disquiet me? Hope in God: for I will still give praise to Him: the salvation of my countenance, and my God." (*Ps.* 42).

Therefore when your heart has fallen raise it gently, humbling yourself greatly before God, and acknowledging your fault, but without marveling at your fall; since it is no marvel that infirmity should he infirm, weakness weak, and frailty frail. But nevertheless heartily detest the offense of which you have been guilty in God's sight, and with hearty courage and confidence in His mercy, begin once more to seek that virtue from which you have fallen away.

CHAPTER TEN

We Must Be Careful in Our Business Without Overeagerness or Solicitude

———————— • ————————

THE diligence and care with which we ought to attend to our affairs is very different from solicitude, anxiety, and worry. The angels are careful of our salvation, and seek it with diligence, but they are not subject to anxiety and eager solicitude, for though care and diligence are a part of their charity, nevertheless solicitude and anxiety would be wholly opposed to their bliss; since though care and diligence are compatible with tranquillity and peace of mind, anxiety and over-carefulness are not so, and much less agitation and eagerness.

Be very careful and diligent in all such business as falls to your share, for God who has allotted it to you, would have you do it well. But if possible avoid solicitude—that is to say, do not undertake your affairs with disquietude, anxiety, and worry, and do not hurry and excite yourself about them, for all excitement hinders reason and judgment, and prevents us from doing well that very thing about which we are excited.

When Our Lord rebuked St. Martha, He said, "Martha, Martha, thou art careful and troubled about many things." If she had simply been diligent, she would not have been troubled, but because she was full of care and disquiet, she was hurried and troubled, and for this our Saviour rebuked her. The rivers which flow calmly through our plains, bear great barges and much rich merchandise, and the rain which falls

151

gently on the land, fertilizes it and makes it bear fruit; but when the rivers and torrents overflow their banks, they carry devastation with them, and violent tempestuous rains ravage the meadows and fields. Never was anything done well that was done with haste and impetuosity—the old proverb bids us "make haste slowly." King Solomon says that "he that is hasty with his feet shall stumble." (*Prov.* 19:2). We always do that quickly enough which we do well. The drone makes more noise and is much more eager than the honey bee, but it produces wax only and no honey; and so those who worry themselves with gnawing care, and noisy solicitude, never do much, nor anything well.

Flies do not tease us by their sting but by their numbers; and important affairs do not trouble us so much as innumerable little matters. Try to meet the occupations which come upon you quietly, and perform them with regularity, one after the other; for if you endeavor to do all at once, or in confusion, your spirit will be so overcharged and depressed that it will probably sink under the burden without accomplishing anything.

In all your undertakings rely wholly on God's Providence, through which alone they can succeed; but seek steadily on your part to cooperate with it, and then rest satisfied that if you are trusting all to God, whatever happens will be best for you, whether it seems to your own judgment good or bad.

Imitate a little child which will walk along with one hand clinging to its father, and with the other gathering the wayside fruits. So whilst with one hand you collect and use the good things of this world, always with the other keep hold of your Heavenly Father, frequently turning to Him, in order to learn whether He approves your occupations and proceedings. Above all, beware of letting go your hold on His protection with the intention of gathering more abundantly, for if He is not with you, you cannot move one step without falling to the ground. Therefore, when you are occupied in ordinary business and occupations which do not require your closest attention, think more of God than of them; and if your business is sufficiently important to absorb your whole attention in doing it well, then from time to time look to God, just as the sailor on his homeward voyage looks oftener to the sky than to the waves which carry him. So will God work with you, in you and for you, and your labor will be followed with consolation.

CHAPTER ELEVEN

Obedience

———— • ————

C HARITY alone places us in perfection. But the three great means of attaining to it are obedience, chastity, and poverty. Obedience consecrates our heart, chastity our body, and poverty our worldly means to the love and service of God. These are the three branches of the spiritual cross, and all have their foundation in the fourth, which is humility. . . . Let us try, then, to practice these virtues, each according to his vocation; for if they do not place us in the state of perfection, they will nevertheless give us perfection itself. Moreover, we are all bound to practice these three virtues, although not all to practice them in the same way.

There are two kinds of obedience, one imperative, the other voluntary. By the first, you are bound humbly to obey your ecclesiastical superiors; that is the Pope, your Bishop, your pastor, and such as may be commissioned by them. You are further bound to obey your temporal superiors, that is your sovereign, and the magistrates whom he appoints over the land; and lastly, you owe obedience to your domestic superiors, whether parents, master, or mistress. This is imperative obedience, and no one can be exempt from the duty of obeying his superiors, their authority to govern and command, according to their several conditions, being given them by God. Of necessity, then, you must obey their orders; but if you would seek perfection, follow also their counsels, and even their wishes and inclinations, as far as charity and prudence will permit; obey them when they enjoin what is agreeable, such as to eat, or rest, for, although there seems to be but little merit in obeying such commands, there is blame in disobedience. Obey them in indifferent things, such as, wearing this or that dress, taking this or that road, singing, or keeping silence; such obedience is much to be commended. Obey them in hard, difficult, displeasing things, and that will be perfect obedience. And, last of all, obey meekly without answering back, speedily without delay, cheerfully without fretfulness, and above all, obey in a loving spirit for love of Him who for our sakes became obedient even unto the death of the Cross, and who, says St. Bernard, preferred losing His life to being disobedient.

In order to learn ready obedience to your superiors, give way readily to the will of your equals, yielding when you can harmlessly do so to their opinions, avoiding peevishness and contention; and conform yourself willingly to the wishes of your inferiors whenever it is reasonable to do so, and avoid all unnecessary exercise of imperious authority.

It is a great mistake to fancy that you would obey easily in the religious state, if you find it difficult and vexatious to obey those whom God has already placed over you.

Voluntary obedience is that to which we bind ourselves by our own choice. We do not choose our own sovereign or Bishop, father or mother, but we do choose our confessor and director. And whether we bind ourselves by a vow to obey him, as we are told of St. Teresa, who, besides her solemn vow of obedience to the superior of her Order, bound herself by a simple vow to obey Father Gratian; or simply without any vow place ourselves under obedience to him, this obedience is called voluntary, since it arises from our own choice and will.

We must obey all superiors in those things in which they are especially set over us, obeying our temporal rulers in all political and public matters, our spiritual rulers in all things ecclesiastical, our father, husband, or master in domestic concerns, and our confessor in all appertaining to the guidance of our soul.

Submit the direction of your pious observances to your spiritual father, by which means they will be forwarded, and acquire double grace and excellence; the first of themselves inasmuch as they are pious, the second through the obedience which dictates them and in virtue of which they are performed. Happy are those who are obedient, for God will not suffer them to go astray.

CHAPTER TWELVE

The Necessity of Chastity

———————•———————

CHASTITY is the lily of the virtues. It renders men almost equal to the angels. Nought is beautiful save through purity, and the purity of men is chastity. We call chastity integrity, and its opposite corruption. In short, it is its own peculiar glory to be the white and beautiful virtue of both body and soul.

There are certain bodily pleasures which may not be indulged in save in lawful marriage, the sanctity of which by a just compensation repairs that which is impaired by enjoyment. Even in marriage we must preserve our uprightness of intention, so that if there be any inordinateness in our pleasure, at least our will may be entirely upright.

As the first step to this virtue, beware of admitting any kind of bodily pleasure, which is forbidden and prohibited, as are all those which are enjoyed out of marriage, or within it, if contrary to its rules. As the second step, retrench as far as possible all useless and superfluous delights even though they be lawful and permitted. Thirdly, do not fix your affections on the pleasures which are ordained and permitted, for even if they follow from the end and purpose of holy matrimony, yet you must not attach your heart and mind to them.

In truth everyone greatly needs this virtue. Those who are in widowhood should have a courageous chastity, which can not only despise present and future objects, but can resist the imaginations which may be produced in their minds by the past delights of marriage, which render them all the more liable to the wiles of impurity. Thus St. Augustine admires the purity of his beloved Alypius, who had altogether forgotten and despised carnal lusts, in which nevertheless he had indulged in his youth. And in truth whilst fruits are whole and entire they may be preserved, some in straw, some in sand, others in their own foliage; but once touched, it is nearly impossible to keep them except preserved in honey and sugar. Thus chastity which is as yet no way wounded or hurt may be preserved in many ways, but having once been meddled with, nothing can preserve it except a perfect devotion, which is, as I have often said, the true honey and sugar of the mind.

Virgins have need of a very simple and tender chastity, banishing all manner of curious thoughts from their hearts, and despising all impure pleasures with absolute contempt. Therefore pure souls should beware of ever doubting that chastity is incomparably better than all which is incompatible with it; for, as St. Jerome says, Satan violently urges virgin souls to long for carnal pleasures, representing them as infinitely more agreeable and delicious than they are. This temptation, says this holy Father, disturbs them greatly, while they count that as very sweet of which they are ignorant. For as the moth, beholding the flame, hovers curiously around it, to discover whether it is as pleasant as it is beautiful, and urged by its desire ceases not until it loses itself in its first attempt; even so youth often allows itself to be so possessed by the false and foolish esteem it entertains for these delights, that after sundry inquisitive thoughts, it finally ruins and loses itself therein, being thus even more foolish than the moth, for it has some reason for believing that the fire which is so beautiful will also be pleasant, but the others know that what they seek is utterly impure, and yet still overvalue the foolish, brutal delight.

As to those who are married, it is quite true (although the mass of men cannot perceive it) that they stand greatly in need of chastity, for in them it lies not in total abstinence from carnal pleasures, but in self-control amidst pleasures. And just as to my mind there is more difficulty in the precept, "Be ye angry and sin not," than in "Be not angry," and that it is easier to avoid anger than to regulate it; so it is easier wholly to abstain from carnal lusts than to be moderate amid them. Undoubtedly the holy freedom of marriage has a special power to extinguish the fire of concupiscence, but the weakness of those who enjoy it easily passes from that which is permitted to that which is forbidden; from use to abuse. And as we see many rich men who steal, not from need, but from avarice, so we see many married people exceed their due limits through mere intemperance and lust, notwithstanding the legitimate object at which they might and should stop, their concupiscence resembling a wandering fire which goes singeing here and there, without fixing anywhere. It is always dangerous to take violent drugs, for if you take too much, or if they are not duly prepared, you will receive great damage thereby. Marriage has been blessed and instituted in part as a remedy against concupiscence, and it is doubtless an excellent remedy, but it is also a very violent, and consequently a dangerous, remedy, unless used with discretion.

Further, the various casualties of human life, besides long illnesses, often separate husbands and wives. Therefore, they need two kinds of chastity, one for absolute abstinence when thus separated, the other for moderation when they are together as usual. St. Catherine of Siena beheld amongst the damned several souls grievously tormented for having violated the sanctity of marriage, which befell them, she said, not through the magnitude of their sin, for murderers and blasphemers are greater sinners, but because their conscience gave no heed to the sin, and consequently continued long in it.

Thus you see that all manner of persons stand in need of chastity— "Follow peace with all men," says the Apostle, "and holiness, without which no man shall see God." And by holiness he means chastity, according to both St. Jerome and St. Chrysostom. No, assuredly, without purity no man will see God, and none who is not of a clean heart shall inhabit His holy tabernacle. Our Saviour Himself has said that all dogs and impure persons shall be banished thence; and "Blessed are the clean of heart, for they shall see God."

CHAPTER THIRTEEN

Rules for the Preservation of Chastity

———————●———————

B E EXTREMELY prompt in turning away from all that leads and lures to impurity, for this evil works insensibly, and by small beginnings progresses to great mischief. It is always easier to avoid than to cure this.

Human bodies resemble glasses, which cannot be carried together so as to touch, without the risk of breaking one another; and when sound and good fruits press upon each other, they are damaged. Even water in a vessel, however pure, cannot long preserve its freshness, if it is touched by any animal substance. Never permit anyone to trifle with you, either from folly or vanity, for although chastity may be preserved amidst such actions, which are rather light than malicious, still the flower and freshness of chastity suffer some hurt and damage; but all impure contact is the utter ruin of chastity.

Chastity has its origin in the heart, but its substance is in the body; wherefore it is lost by means of the external senses of the body, and by the thoughts and desires of the heart. It is impurity to behold, to hear, to speak of, to breathe, to touch impure things, if the heart takes delight therein. St. Paul says, "Let not fornication be so much as named amongst you." The bee not only refuses to touch what is carrion, but hates and avoids all bad odors arising thence; and the bride in the

Canticles is described as dropping myrrh from her hands, which is a preservative against corruption. Her lips are bordered with vermilion, indicating the modesty of her words, her eyes are doves' eyes, by reason of their clearness, her ears carry earrings of gold, the emblem of purity, her nose is as the cedars of Libanus—an incorruptible wood; and such should the devout soul be, chaste, pure, and modest in hands, lips, ears, eyes, and the whole heart.

Do not associate with immodest persons, above all if they are impudent, as for the most part is the case; for just as the stag causes the sweet almond-tree to become bitter by licking it, so these infected, stinking souls can scarcely speak to anyone, either of one sex or the other, without injuring their purity: venom is in their eyes, and their breath is like that of the basilisk.

On the contrary, associate with chaste and virtuous persons; read and often think on sacred things, for the Word of God is chaste, and renders those who take delight therein chaste also; wherefore David compares it to the topaz, which has the property of deadening the ardor of concupiscence.

Abide ever nigh to Jesus Christ crucified, spiritually in meditation, and actually in the Holy Communion. For as whatever lies upon the herb called *Agnus castus* becomes chaste and pure, so if you rest your heart upon Our Lord, who is the true chaste and Immaculate Lamb, you will speedily find that your heart and soul will be purified from all stains and lusts.

CHAPTER FOURTEEN

Poverty of Spirit in the Midst of Wealth

———————•———————

"BLESSED are the poor in spirit, for theirs is the kingdom of Heaven." (*Matt.* 5:3).

Woe, then, to those who are rich in spirit, for their portion will be Hell. He is rich in spirit whose heart is in his riches, and whose riches fill his heart. He is poor in spirit who has not riches in his heart, nor his heart in riches. The halcyon builds its nest in the shape of a ball, leaving only one little opening, at the top, and so strong and impenetrable is it, that when the waves of the sea surround it no water ever enters, but always rising on the waves the birds remain open and in the midst of the sea as lords over it. Even so should your heart be open only to Heaven and impenetrable to riches and earthly things; if you possess them preserve your heart from loving them; let it rise above them, and be poor in the midst of wealth, and master of its riches. Beware of losing the spirit of holiness in the good things of the world, but let your hearts always be the superior, not in them but above them.

There is a difference between possessing poison and being poisoned. Apothecaries keep poisons for various uses, but they are not poisoned, because the poison is but in their shops, not in themselves; and so you may possess riches without being poisoned by them, that is, if you have them in your house or in your purse and not in your heart, being rich in substance, but poor in spirit. It is a great happiness for a Christian to be actually rich but poor in spirit, for thus he can use wealth and its advantages in this world and yet have the merit of poverty as regards the next.

No man will own that he is avaricious; everyone repudiates this despicable narrowness of heart. Men excuse themselves on the plea of providing for their children, or on that of prudence and forethought; they never have too much, but always find some good reason for seeking more; and even the greatest misers not only will not confess their avarice, but in their consciences they do not believe themselves to be avaricious; for it is as a burning fever, which as it grows stronger is the less noticed by its victim. Moses beheld how fire from heaven burnt a bush without consuming it, but the profane fire of avarice consumes and devours the miser without burning him, for amidst the fiercest lusts he fans himself with an imaginary and delicious breeze, and believes that insatiable thirst is but natural and rightful.

If you desire, eagerly and anxiously, that which you have not, though you may say that you do not seek to acquire it unjustly, you are still really avaricious. If a man longs anxiously and earnestly to drink, albeit he desires water only, he gives undeniable proof that he is feverish.

I doubt if it is possible to desire to possess honestly that which another possesses, for by this desire we must involve the other's loss. If he possess a thing justly, has he not a better right in justice to keep it than we have to wish for it? And why should we interfere with his convenience by wishing for it? At least if the desire is not unjust it is uncharitable, for we should not like anyone to desire (even honestly) that which we honestly wish to keep for ourselves. Such was the sin of Achab, who wished honestly to possess himself of Naboth's vineyard, whilst in his turn Naboth wished with greater justice to retain it. Achab indulged the wish for a long time eagerly and anxiously, and thus displeased God. Do not give way to the wish for that which is another's until he on his part wishes to part with it; then his desire will render you not only just, but charitable. I would not forbid you to increase your means and possessions, as long as you do it not only with justice, but with gentleness and charity.

But if you are very strongly attached to what you do possess, if you are absorbed in your possessions, and they fill your heart, engrossing your thoughts, and filling you with anxious fears lest you lose them, believe me you are still somewhat feverish; for fever patients drink the water that is given them with an eagerness and relish not usual to those who are in perfect health. You cannot take great delight in anything without its engrossing your heart more or less. If you love any of your possessions, and find that your heart is grievously afflicted, be sure that you loved them dearly, for nothing so well tells our love for what we lose, as our grief for its loss. Therefore do not let your desires for that which you have not assume a definite shape, and do not fix your heart on that which you have; do not be overpowered by such losses as you may meet with, and then you may venture to think that although you are rich in fact, you are not in spirit, but that being poor in spirit, you are blessed, for the Kingdom of Heaven is yours.

How to Practice Real Poverty, While Being Actually Rich

———— • ————

THE painter Parrhasius, by an ingenious invention, represented the Athenians as of a fickle, contradictory disposition, at once passionate, unjust, inconstant, covetous, compassionate, merciful, proud, vainglorious, humble, bullying, and cowardly, and all that in one. And I would combine riches and poverty in your heart, a great care and a great contempt for things temporal.

You should be much more watchful than men of the world are, in order to turn your possessions to good use. Are not the gardeners of kings and princes more particular and diligent in the cultivation and embellishment of the gardens committed to their charge than they would be were these their own, and that because they belong to those kings and princes, whom they would fain please by their assiduous services? Our possessions are not our own; God has given them to us that we may cultivate them, and it is His Will that we should render them useful and fruitful. By our care thereof we render to Him an acceptable service.

And this care must be greater and more real than that which men of the world employ; for they labor only for self-love, but we for the love of God. Now as self-love is violent, turbulent, and restless, so our cares in its behalf will be troubled, anxious, and uneasy; and as the love of

God is gentle, peaceful, and tranquil, so our cares springing from that source, although for worldly goods, will be gentle, mild, and without uneasiness. Let us take such care as this of our possessions and of their increase on lawful occasions, according to our station; for this service God demands of us for His love's sake.

Take care, however, that you are not deceived by self-love, which sometimes counterfeits the love of God so successfully as to deceive you. To prevent this, and also for fear lest your care for worldly goods should grow into avarice, in addition to what I have said in the preceding chapter, it is well constantly to practice real practical poverty, in the midst of the riches and advantages with which God has endowed you.

Always dispose of a part of your means by giving freely alms to the poor, for you impoverish yourself by that which you give, and the more it is the more you are impoverished. Undoubtedly God will restore it to you in this world as well as in the next, for nothing brings such prosperity as almsgiving, but meanwhile you will be the poorer for what you give. Oh, the holiness and richness of making oneself poor by almsgiving!

Love poverty and the poor; for by this love you will become truly poor yourself, since we become like to that which we love, as says Holy Scripture. Love brings those who share it into an equality. "Who is weak, and I am not weak?" says St. Paul. (*2 Cor.* 11:29). He might have continued, "Who is poor, and I am not poor?" For love made him like to those he loved. If, then, you sincerely love the poor, you will truly share their poverty, and be poor with them.

If you love the poor, go frequently among them, take pleasure in bringing them around you, and in visiting and in conversing willingly with them; and mingle with them in the church, the street, and elsewhere. Be poor in speech towards them, speaking with them as their friend, but let your hands be rich, imparting to them freely of your abundance.

Would you go still further? Then do not stop at being poor with the poor, but make yourself still poorer than they. The servant is less than his master, do you become the servant of the poor; go and tend their sickbeds with your own hands, feed them, serve them, minister to them. Such service is more noble than royalty! How nobly did St. Louis, one of the greatest of monarchs, follow this counsel! frequently helping to serve the poor at the table which he provided for them, and daily causing the poor to share his own table; and many times he ate what remained of their food with an incomparable love. When he visited the hospitals (as was his frequent custom) he generally ministered to those who suffered under the most revolting diseases, those afflicted with leprosy, cancer, and similar diseases; and serving them on his knees and with bared head, acknowledging in their persons the Saviour of the world, and cherishing them with the tender love of a mother for her child.

St. Elizabeth of Hungary mingled freely amongst the poor, and sometimes wearing a peasant's dress would say to her ladies that were she poor she would always wear such. Were not these sovereigns poor amidst their riches, and rich in their poverty?

Blessed are they who are thus poor, for theirs is the Kingdom of Heaven. To them the King of kings and of poor men will say in the day of judgment, "I was hungry, and you gave me to eat; I was . . . naked, and you covered me: come . . . possess you the kingdom prepared for you from the foundation of the world." (*Matt.* 25:34-36).

There is no one who is not liable occasionally to suffer some need or inconvenience. A guest arrives whom we would fain receive with honor, and we are unable to do so; the attire we need is not to be had just when we want it; all the wine in our cellar is spoilt; or accidentally when traveling we cannot obtain accommodation such as we are accustomed to. However rich we are it is easy to find wants, and then as regards our deficiencies we are poor. You should always hail such little trials gladly, welcome them heartily, and endure them cheerfully.

Or if circumstances arise which impoverish you either greatly or in a less degree, such as storms, fire, floods, blight, bad harvests, robbery, or injustice, then is the time to practice poverty, submitting to such losses with meekness, and adapting yourself with patience and resolution to such involuntary poverty. Esau and Jacob both approached their father with hairy hands, but the hair on Jacob's hands was not his own, and could be plucked off without hurting him, whilst that on Esau's hands grew from his natural skin, and whoever endeavored to pull it off would have hurt him; he would have cried out and defended himself. If we are much attached to our worldly goods, and lose part of them by means of the weather, the thief, or by injustice, how full of grief, complaint, and impatience we are! But if our principal reason for caring for them is that God has given them to us, and not on our own account, their loss will not deprive us of composure or tranquillity. Such is the difference in the clothing of men and beasts, for the garments of the latter adhere to their flesh, and those of men can be put on or laid aside as they will.

CHAPTER SIXTEEN

The Practice of Spiritual Riches
amidst Real Poverty

———————— • ————————

IF YOU are really poor, then above all be poor in spirit, and make a virtue of necessity by using that precious stone poverty to the best advantage. We do not see its glory in this world, and yet it is of the greatest beauty and value.

Have patience; you are in good company. Our Lord, our Blessed Lady, the Apostles, and numberless saints, were poor, and despised the riches which they might have enjoyed. How many, great in this world, have in spite of opposition sought to embrace holy poverty in cloisters and hospitals? St. Alexius, St. Paul, St. Paulina, St. Angela, and many others, sought her earnestly, whilst to you she vouchsafes to come and offer herself. You have found her without search and without trouble; embrace her as the beloved of Jesus Christ, who was born, lived, and died in poverty, which was His companion during His whole life.

Your poverty has two great privileges which may profit you greatly; first, that it was God's Will and not your choice that you should be poor. What we receive entirely from the Will of God is always acceptable to Him, if we do but accept it heartily and for love of His Holy Will. Suffering is greatly purified by a whole-hearted acquiescence in God's Will.

The second privilege is that it is real poverty. Poverty which is praised, caressed, esteemed, and succored is not genuine poverty; it partakes of the nature of riches, and at any rate it is far removed from real poverty. But when it is despised, rejected, reproached, and forsaken, then it is real poverty. And such is usually poverty in the world; for men who are poor not voluntarily but of necessity are not thought much of, and for that very reason their poverty is more truly poor than that of professed religious, although the latter poverty has a special and great charm by reason of the vow and of the motive.

Do not, then, complain of your poverty, for we complain only of that which displeases us; and if poverty displeases you, you are no longer poor in spirit, for your heart would fain be otherwise; neither be troubled because you have less resistance than you need, for therein lies the excellence of poverty. To wish to be poor without suffering any inconvenience is to be very ambitious, for then you aim at the honor of poverty and the convenience of wealth.

Do not be ashamed of being poor, or of seeking charitable alms; receive what is given you in humility and bear refusals with meekness. Remember how our Blessed Lady traveled into Egypt with her dear Son, and how much contempt, poverty, and sufferings they endured. If you do the like, you will be very rich in your poverty.

CHAPTER SEVENTEEN

Friendship—First, of
Bad and Frivolous Friendships

———— • ————

L OVE is the chief amongst the passions of the soul. It is king of
all the heart's impulses; it draws all things to itself, and makes us
like to what we love. Therefore give good heed that you love nothing
wicked, else you will become altogether wicked yourself: and friendship
is the most dangerous of all love, because other affections may exist
without mutual communication, but friendship being entirely founded
upon this, it can scarcely exist without at the same time involving participation in the qualities of him towards whom it is exercised.

All love is not friendship; for we may love without being loved,
and then love but not friendship exists, for friendship is mutual love,
and unless it is mutual, it is not friendship. Again, it must not only
be mutual, but the parties who love must be aware of their reciprocal affection, otherwise it will still only be love, not friendship. And,
further, there must exist between them some communication as the
groundwork of friendship.

Friendship varies according to the variety of these communications, and they vary according to the benefits interchanged; if these
are vain and false, then the friendship is vain and false; if they are true,
then the friendship will be true; and the more excellent those qualities
exchanged, the higher will the friendship be. For as that honey is the

best which is gathered from the choicest flowers, so that love which is founded on the choicest communication of good gifts will be the purest. And as there is found in Heraclea of Pontus a poisonous honey which, being gathered from the aconite which abounds there, stupefies those who eat it, so that friendship which has its foundation in false and vicious communications is itself wicked and false.

Friendship arising from the mere gratification of the senses is utterly gross and unworthy of that name, as is that arising from vain and superficial merits which also depend upon the senses only. By sensual gratification I mean that chiefly and directly connected with the external senses, such as the pleasure of beholding beauty, listening to a pleasant voice, and similar things; and by superficial vain merits I mean certain qualities and accomplishments which foolish men call virtues and perfections. How many girls, women, and young people do not hesitate to say such an one is very amiable, and has great merit, because he dances well and is skillful in all games, or dresses, or sings, or talks well, or is very handsome. Amongst charlatans the greatest buffoon is the best man!

Now all this concerns the senses only, and friendship arising from such sources must be sensual, vain, and frivolous, deserving rather to be called foolery than friendship. Such are the friendships of young men which are based on personal appearance, dress, fashion, idle conversation, and are fit only for the age when virtue and judgment are as yet unformed and in the bud; accordingly such friendships are but of passing duration, and melt away like snow before the sun.

CHAPTER EIGHTEEN

Flirtations

———————— • ————————

WHEN these foolish friendships exist between persons of different sex without intention of marriage, they are called flirtations. For being mere abortions, or rather shadows of friendship, by reason of their excessive vanity and imperfection, we can call them neither love nor friendship. But by their means the hearts of many are taken captive, and entwined with one another in vain and foolish affection, having no root but the frivolous intercourse and despicable attractions of which I spoke before. And although these foolish love-passages usually end in carnal pleasures and vile lusts, such is not the original intention of those who practice them, else they would no longer be flirtations, but manifest impurities. Often years may elapse before those who are attached by this folly commit anything contrary to actual chastity, only steeping their hearts in wishes, desires, sighs, coquetries, and other similar follies and vanities, and this upon various pretexts.

There are some who have no other aim than the indulgence of their hearts in inspiring and being inspired with love, therein following their amorous inclinations, and considering nothing in the choice of their loves but their taste and natural instinct; so that on meeting an attractive object they do not examine into its inward life or deportment, but begin a train of follies, entangling themselves in a net, whence afterwards it will be hard to escape. Others let themselves be led by vanity, esteeming it a glorious thing to take captive and bind hearts in the bonds of love. And these make their choice through vainglory, preparing their snares, and laying their nets in spacious, exalted, rare, and illustrious quarters. Others are led by their amorous inclinations and vanity at once, for although their hearts be naturally inclined to love, they still seek to turn it to the advantage of their vainglory. All such friendships are bad, foolish, and vain, tending to sin; bad because they distract the heart and its affections from God, and from those to whom love is due; foolish, because they have neither reason nor foundation; vain, because neither profit, honor, nor satisfaction ensues. On the contrary, they waste time, tarnish honor, and give no satisfaction but that of an eager search and hope after they know not what; for it is a universal rule with these contemptible, weak minds that there is always some undefined wish which can neither be defined nor relieved, but is forever burdening their hearts with distrust, jealousy, and uneasiness. St. Gregory Nazianzen, writing against vain women, speaks admirably on this subject. He addresses women, but his words apply equally to men: "The natural beauty suffices thy husband, but if it is bestowed on several men, as a net spread out to catch many birds, what will become of it? Thou wilt be pleased with him who is pleased with thy beauty; thou wilt return glance for glance, look for look; then will ensue smiles, and light words of love—stealthily indulged at first, but soon you will grow bolder, and go on to open liberties. Beware, O my tongue, of saying what will follow—this much, however, I will say—whatever young men or women do amid these vain indulgences will be dangerous. The chain of trifles holds together; one link involving another, as iron is drawn by the magnet, leading many after it." Oh, how wisely does this great Bishop speak! What are you trying to do? To inspire love? Well—but it is impossible to impart without likewise receiving it. The player is trapped in his own game. The herb approxis kindles into flame as soon as it approaches fire, and it is the same with our hearts—as soon as they behold a soul inflamed with love for them, they burn for it. I will go some way, you say, but not far. Alas, you deceive yourself, this love-fire is more active and penetrating than you think; for you imagine that you receive but a spark, and you will be amazed to find that in a moment it has seized your heart, reduced your resolutions to ashes, and your reputation to smoke!

The wise man asks, "Who will pity the charmer who is bitten by a serpent?" I say with him: "Foolish man, do you pretend to charm love as you will? You would play with it, but it will sting and bite you cruelly, and everyone will mock you who sought to charm it, and with false courage attempted to take a viper into your breast, and so have spoilt and lost both your honor and your soul." Oh, how great an error to stake the treasure of your soul on so frivolous a game! Truly God asks man only for his soul, his soul only for the will, the will only for love. Alas, we have not nearly as much love at command as we require! I mean that we need infinitely more to love God worthily, and yet, wretched as we are, we squander it on vain frivolities, as though we had enough and to spare! Surely that great God who demands our entire love in gratitude for our creation, preservation, and redemption, will demand a strict account of all these idle amusements. If we have to give a rigid account of every idle word, how will it be with our foolish, hurtful friendships? The walnut tree injures the vine and the soil where it grows, as owing to its great size, it absorbs the nourishment of the earth, which thus becomes insufficient for the support of the other plants; its thick foliage overshadows them entirely, while persons who pass by, being attracted by the fruit, tread and crush the ground around it. Thus, foolish flirtations have a similar evil effect on the soul—they occupy and absorb it so that it can perform no good work; and the leaves—that is, idle amusements, conversations, and triflings—engross all its leisure. And finally they invite many temptations, distractions, suspicions, and other evil consequences, trampling down and spoiling the heart. In short, these flirtations not only banish heavenly love, but even the fear of God; they enervate the mind, tarnish the reputation, and though apparently the evil is but trifling, it is a very plague-spot in the heart.

CHAPTER NINETEEN

True Friendship

———————— • ————————

I WOULD bid you love everyone with the love of charity, but have no friendship save with those who can interchange virtuous love with you, since the more your friendship stands on the foundation of virtue, the more perfect will it be. If your bond of union be the pursuit of science, it is a commendable friendship; still more if it be prudence, discretion, decision, and justice. But if your bond of intercourse be charity, devotion, and Christian perfection, then indeed will your friendship be precious; precious because it has its origin in God, because it is maintained in God, and because it will endure forever in Him. What a good thing it is to love on earth as we shall love in Heaven, and to learn to cherish one another here as we shall do forever there. I am not now speaking of the mere love which charity excites towards all men, but of the spiritual friendship by which two or more souls participate in each other's devotion and spiritual affections making them of one mind. Such may well say, "Behold how good and joyful a thing it is to dwell together in unity." Yes, truly, for the precious balm of devotion distills from one soul to another in continual interchange, so we may indeed say that "there the Lord hath commanded blessing, and life forevermore." (*Ps.* 132). Surely all other friendships are but empty shadows as compared to this, and their links are but as chains of glass compared to the great bond of holy devotion which is all pure gold. Do not form any other friendships. I say *form,* because you must neither forsake nor despise those friendships to which nature and duty call you amongst relations, connections, benefactors, and neighbors; I am speaking only of those which you select yourself.

Some will tell you that it is better to have no especial friendships or attachments, that they engross the heart, distract the mind, and foster jealousies; but such are mistaken. They have read in the works of saints and devout writers that individual attachments and excessive friendships are hurtful in the religious life, and imagine it to be the same with the rest of the world, but that is not so. In a well-regulated convent, the general end of all is true devotion, and such individual communication is unnecessary, lest it tend to partiality; but it is needful for those who are in the world, and seek after virtue, to bind themselves together in a holy and sacred friendship, by means of which they encourage, stimulate, and forward one another in doing good. Just as those who journey in the plain do not need assistance one from another, but those who are on steep and slippery paths support each other for security's sake, so those who are professed religious do not require private friendships; but those who are in the world need them, to aid and succor one another in the many evils and dangers which they encounter. In the world all have not the like spirit, all do not seek the same end, and therefore it becomes necessary to turn aside and form congenial friendships, which of course involve partialities, but they are such as do no harm, and cause no division except between the good and the bad, the sheep and the goats, the bees and the drones.

Do we not read in Holy Scripture that our Blessed Lord entertained an especial and tender friendship for St. John, Lazarus, Martha, and Mary Magdalen? Just as we know that St. Peter cherished St. Mark and St. Petronilla, as St. Paul did Timothy and St. Thecla. St. Gregory Nazianzen repeatedly dwells upon his fervent friendship with the great St. Basil, of which he says, "It seemed as though we had but one soul animating two bodies: and if we may not believe those who affirm that all things are contained in all things, yet of us two you may believe that we were both in each of us, and one in the other; we both had but one aim, to cultivate virtue, and to suit the deeds of our life to our future hopes, thus departing from this mortal earth even before death." St. Augustine also mentions that St. Ambrose had no common love for St. Monica on account of her rare and excellent virtues, and that she in return cherished him as an Angel of God.

But it is too obvious a point to require further proof. St. Jerome, St. Augustine, St. Gregory, St. Bernard, and all the most eminent servants of God, have entertained very special friendships without in any way injuring their perfection. St. Paul when finding fault with the Gentiles calls them men without natural affection, that is, incapable of friendship; and St. Thomas, like all good philosophers, acknowledges friendship to be a virtue. He speaks of individual friendship, for he says that it cannot be extended in perfection to many. Thus, perfection does not lie in rejecting all friendships, but in entertaining none that are not pure, holy, and sacred.

CHAPTER TWENTY

The Difference between
True and False Friendships

———————•———————

TAKE notice that the Heraclitan honey, which is so poisonous, resembles that which is wholesome: there is great danger of mistaking the one for the other, or of eating them together, and the goodness of the one would not counteract the ill effects of the other. You must beware that you be not deceived in your friendships under any pretext whatever, for Satan often deludes those who love. They begin with holy love, but without care it will be sullied by frivolous, sensual, and even carnal affections; there is danger even in pure spiritual love, but deception is more difficult in it, for its purity and clearness directly show the stains that Satan would fain have on it, for which reason he sets to work all the more subtly.

You may distinguish holy and virtuous friendship from that of the world in the same way that the Heraclitan honey is distinguished from that which is good. The former is sweeter to the taste than the latter, owing to the aconite which is in it; and worldly friendship generally offers many sweet words, flattering and passionate speeches, and praises of beauty, elegance, and sensual qualities; but holy friendship speaks a simple, honest language, and only praises the goodness and grace of God, which is its firm foundation. And as that poisonous honey produces giddiness in those who eat it, so false friendship produces giddiness of the mind, causing those who share it to totter in their purity and devotion, and leading them to affected, wanton, and immoderate looks, sensual caresses, inordinate sighs, little complaints of not being loved, slight furtive and enticing glances, gallantries, kisses, and unusual familiarities and favors, the certain and indubitable presages of an approaching ruin of chastity. But holy friendship has no looks but what are simple and modest, no caresses but those that are pure and sincere, no sighs but for Heaven, no familiarities but those of the soul, no complaints but that God is not loved, the infallible signs of purity.

The Heraclitan honey confuses the sight, and worldly friendship confuses the judgment, and makes people imagine they do well whilst really they are in sin, and induces them to accept all their false excuses and pretexts as substantial reasons. They fear light and love darkness, but holy friendship has a clear light, and does not seek to hide itself, appearing willingly before good men. Lastly, the Heraclitan honey leaves a bitter taste in the mouth, and so worldly friendship turns to evil, to anger, impurity, jealousy, confusion, irritation; but true friendship is always pure, courteous, and loving, and only changes to a yet more perfect and holy union, which is a lively representation of that blessed love which we shall enjoy in Heaven.

When we see a man dress himself out and draw near to flatter and wheedle, and whisper in the ears of a woman with no pretension to lawful marriage, without doubt it is in order to incite her to impurity; and a virtuous woman will close her ears to the voice of the charmer who seeks to enchant her: but if she hearken to him, what an ominous sign it is of the future loss of her heart!

Young people who indulge in looks and caresses, or speak words in which they would be unwilling to be surprised by their fathers, mothers, husbands, wives, or confessors, bear witness that their conduct is not that of honor and conscience. Our Lady was troubled on seeing an angel in human form because she was alone, and he praised her greatly although his praise was heavenly. O Saviour of the world!

Purity fears an angel in the form of a man; why then does not purity fear a man even in angelic form, when he pours forth praises sensual and human?

CHAPTER TWENTY-ONE

Counsels and Remedies against Evil Friendships

———————— • ————————

WHAT is the remedy against all these unholy, unblessed friendships? As soon as you feel any inclination towards them, speedily turn away, hasten to the Cross of Christ, and let His crown of thorns surround your heart, that those "little foxes" may not come near. (*Cant.* 1:15). Do not parley with the enemy. Do not say, "I will hearken to him, but not obey him, I will open my ears, but close my heart to him." Rather be strict in such things; the heart and the ears are closely connected, and as it is impossible to stop a torrent in its course down the mountain side, so is it to defend the heart from that which we admit to our ears. The goat, according to Alcmaeon, breathes through its ears instead of its nostrils. This Aristotle denies. I know not how this is, but I do know that our heart draws its breath through the ears, receiving thereby the thoughts of others, which it exhales again by the mouth. Be watchful, therefore, against hearkening to foolish words, else your heart will be infested, and do not fear to be uncivil or rude in rejecting all such.

Remember that your heart is dedicated to God, and your love sacrificed to Him. It is sacrilege to take one particle from Him; rather renew your offering by countless resolutions and protestations, taking shelter therein as a stag at bay. Call upon God, He will succor you, and

His love will protect yours, so that it may be wholly His.

And if you are already taken in the net of such hollow friendships, hasten into the presence of God, acknowledge before Him your weakness and vanity, and then, with the greatest firmness that you can, abandon all these follies, abjure the vain profession that you have made, renounce the promises received, and by a great and determined act of the will arrest your heart in its progress, and resolve never again to enter on so dangerous a path. If you can depart from the object of such love I greatly approve of it. For as it is said that he who is bitten by a serpent cannot be easily cured in the presence of those who have been themselves wounded by the same bite, so the person who has been stung by love will be healed with difficulty in the sight of the other victim of the same passion. The young man of whom St. Ambrose speaks in his second volume on Penance, having made a long voyage, returned entirely freed from the impure loves in which he had previously indulged. He was so changed that when his partner in sin met him and said, "Dost thou not know me, I am still myself?" he replied, "But I am no longer myself." Absence had brought about this happy change. And St. Augustine tells us that he hastened from Tagaste to Carthage in order to overcome his exceeding grief at the loss of his friend.

But what must he do who cannot withdraw himself? Let him absolutely retrench all particular familiarity, all private conversation, amorous looks, smiles, and, in general, all communications and allurements which might nourish this filthy and smoking fire. Or, if he must speak to the other party, let it be to declare by a bold, short, and serious protestation the eternal divorce that he has sworn. I cry aloud to every one who has fallen into these wretched snares: "Cut them, break them, tear them! You must not amuse yourself in unraveling those criminal friendships, you must rend them asunder. Do not untie the knot, burst them or cut them, so that the cords and strings may be worth nothing. We must make no compromise with a love that is contrary to the love of God."

But after I have thus broken the chains of this infamous bondage, there will still remain some feelings: the marks and traces of the iron will still be imprinted on my feet, that is my affections. No, Philothea, they will not, if you have conceived such detestation of the evil as it deserves; for if this is the case you will no longer be stirred by any movement but that of an extreme horror of this infamous love, and of all relating to it; and you will rest free from all other affection towards the object you have abandoned but that of a most pure charity for God's sake. But if, through the imperfection of your repentance, you still feel certain evil inclinations, procure for your soul a mental solitude as I have taught you before; retire into it as much as you can, and renounce all your evil inclinations by ejaculations of the spirit a thousand times repeated. Reject them with all your strength; occupy yourself more than usual with holy books; confess and communicate more frequently; reveal with humility and simplicity the suggestions and temptations which trouble you to your director if you can, or at least to some faithful and prudent soul. And doubt not that God will deliver you from these passions if you continue faithfully in these good exercises.

Do you say that it is ungrateful thus to break off a friendship? Welcome that ingratitude which is pleasing to God! But it is not ungrateful; on the contrary, we serve our friend as well as ourself, for the danger was mutual, and, if not now, ere long he too will join your song of thanksgiving, and say, "O Lord, thou hast broken my bonds asunder. I will offer unto thee the sacrifice of praise, and will call upon the name of the Lord." (*Ps.* 115).

CHAPTER TWENTY-TWO

Further Counsels Concerning Friendship

———————— • ————————

FRIENDSHIP requires an abundant communion or interchange, without which it can neither begin nor continue. But together with the communion of friendship other communications are wont to glide from heart to heart by a mutual expression and infusion of affections, inclinations, and impressions. This happens chiefly when we esteem highly him whom we love; for then we open our whole heart to the object of our friendship, and readily receive his inclinations and impressions, whether they be good or had. Assuredly the bees which gather Heraclitan honey seek honey only, but they insensibly suck the poison of the aconite when they feed upon it. In this respect therefore give good heed to the teaching we have received from our Blessed Lord, and from holy men of old. Let us be wise money-changers, that is to say, let us beware that we do not receive bad money with that which is good, nor spurious gold instead of pure gold! Discriminate between what is worthless and precious, for scarcely anyone is without his faults. Why should you be infected with your friend's faults and failings along with his love? Unquestionably you should love him despite his imperfections; but neither love nor follow them, for friendship requires the communication of what is good, not of what is bad. As those who take gravel from the Tagus, after they have separated the gold which is in it from the sand, take it away, leaving the sand behind, so in friendship men should reject the sand of imperfections, and not allow it to sift into their hearts.

St. Gregory Nazianzen mentions that some of those who loved and admired St. Basil went so far as to imitate even his bodily imperfections, his slow absent manner, the shape of his beard, and his peculiar gait; and we often see that husbands and wives, parents and children, or friends who love each other very dearly, either out of complaisance or imitation acquire sundry little habits and peculiarities in their mutual intercourse. But it should not be so, for everyone has plenty of individual failings without assuming those of another, and friendship, far from requiring us to put on one another's faults, would rather oblige us to strive mutually to overcome all such failings. We must doubtless bear patiently with our friend's faults, but not encourage him in them, still less adopt them ourselves.

In this I allude only to *imperfections;* as to *sins,* we must neither encourage nor tolerate them in our friend. It is a poor and unworthy friendship which can see a friend perishing and not succor him; see him dying of a cancer and not have courage to make the sharp incision which would save him. True and living friendship cannot exist amid sin. The salamander is said to extinguish the fire in which it lies, and sin destroys that friendship where it effects an entrance: if the sin be but accidental, it will be put to flight by a friendly correction; but if it be rooted and permanent, then friendship will perish, for it can exist only where virtue is. Still less should friendship ever lead us into sin. Our friend becomes an enemy if he would cause us to sin, and deserves to be cast off if he strive to cause his friend to perish; and that is sure to be a false friendship which is entertained towards a vicious man or is nourished in sin. If we love a vicious person, our friendship too will be evil; for since it cannot be founded on true virtue, it must rest in some false good or mere sensual attraction.

The connection between men of business concerning temporal matters is but a shadow of real friendship, since its object is not personal attachment, but the love of gain.

We may take two precepts as the pillars of our Christian life: first, that of the wise man—"He that feareth God shall likewise have good friendship" (*Ecclus.* 6:17); secondly, that of St. James—"The friendship of the world is the enemy of God."

CHAPTER TWENTY-THREE

The Practice of External Mortification

———————————•———————————

IT IS said that if you inscribe any word on an almond kernel, and then replacing it in its husk plant it, all the fruit of the future tree will be marked with the same word. I cannot approve of those who in reforming a man would begin with external things—his face, his hair, or his dress. On the contrary, we must begin from within. "Turn ye to Me with your whole heart," is God's call; "My son, give Me your heart." For the heart is the mainspring of our actions; and so the Divine Bridegroom says, "Put Me as a seal upon thy heart, as a seal upon thy arm," for truly whoever has Jesus Christ in his heart will soon show it in all his outward actions. Wherefore I would have you above all things inscribe and engrave on your heart that blessed Name, being persuaded that if you do so, all the actions of your future life (which spring from your heart as the tree from its kernel) will be stamped with that saving Name of Jesus. And inasmuch as He will be in your heart, He will also be in all your gestures, in your eyes, your mouth, your hands, and all your members; so that you may say with St. Paul, "I live, yet not I, but Christ liveth in me." (*Gal.* 2:20). In short, whoever commands a man's heart, commands him wholly. But this same heart, by which we would begin, requires to be trained in its outward demeanor, in order that it may not only display holy devotion, but be wise and discreet. To which end I will give you several counsels. If you are able to fast, you will do well to observe some abstinence beyond what is enjoined by the Church, for in addition to the ordinary benefits of fasting, namely, lifting up the mind, subduing the flesh, strengthening virtue, and earning an eternal recompense, it is a great matter to be able to command our tastes and inclinations, and to keep the body and its appetites subject to the law of the spirit: and even if we do not fast to any great extent, Satan is the more afraid of those who, he is aware, know how to fast. The early Christians practiced abstinence, especially on Wednesday, Friday, and Saturday. Do you fast on such of those days as may be dictated by your own devotion and by your director.

I am inclined to say as St. Jerome said to the good lady Leta, "I disapprove of long and immoderate fasting, especially for the young." I have learnt by experience that when the young colt wearies of his road, he tries to quit it; that is to say, that when young people are enfeebled by excessive fasting, they are easily led into self-indulgence and luxury. The stag runs badly both when it is too fat and when it is too thin, and we are exposed to temptation when the body is overindulged and when it is over-subdued; for as the one makes it easy and indolent, so the other makes it low and despondent; and just as we cannot control it when it is over-fed, neither can it serve us when it is under-fed. Lack of discretion in discipline, fasting, and bodily mortification, sometimes renders the best years of a man's life nearly useless as regards the service of charity, as was the case with St. Bernard, who repented of his excessive austerity: and those who have begun with over-strictness are compelled at last to become over-lax. Would it not have been better to keep steadily to such a well-ordered system as was suitable to their engagements and circumstances?

Fasting and labor weary and exhaust the flesh. If your labor is necessary or serviceable to the glory of God, I should select for you the discipline of labor in preference to that of fasting. It is in this spirit that the Church dispenses those who are engaged in useful service for

God and their neighbors, even from her prescribed fasts. One finds his labor in fasting, another in nursing the sick, visiting prisoners, hearing Confessions, preaching, comforting the afflicted, in prayer and similar exercises. And these labors are of more avail than that, for whilst they subdue the flesh, they bring forth more excellent fruit. Besides this, it is better to preserve more than sufficient bodily strength than unnecessarily to waste it. It may at any time be subdued, but it cannot always be restored.

We should do well to remember our Blessed Lord's command to His disciples, "Eat such things as are set before you." (*Luke* 10:8). I think that there is more profit in eating whatsoever is offered you, whether it suits your taste or not, than in always choosing the worst. For although the latter practice appears more austere, the former is more submissive, for by it you not only renounce your tastes but your choice, and there is considerable mortification in entirely subduing all tastes and subjecting them wholly to circumstances; besides which, this kind of mortification makes no display, gives no offense, and is especially suitable for one living in society, for nothing more strongly indicates a luxurious, gluttonous habit, than rejecting one dish for another, examining everything, never being satisfied with anything. I think more of St. Bernard's drinking oil instead of wine or water than if he had intentionally drunk wormwood; for it was a proof that he did not think about what he drank. It is in this indifference as to what we eat and drink that we shall follow the spirit of that precept, "Eat such things as are set before you." Of course I do not include such food as is unwholesome or injurious to the body, for instance hot stimulants, etc., and there are occasions in which nature requires to be aided and strengthened for the better furtherance of God's service: a continued, habitual temperance is far better than occasional, rigid abstinence alternating with great relaxation.

The discipline, taken in moderation, has a wonderful power of awakening the appetite for devotion. The hair shirt mortifies the flesh exceedingly, but the use of it, generally speaking, is not proper for either married persons or those of weak constitutions, or for such as have great pains to bear. However, on special days of penance, it may be used with the advice of a discreet confessor.

Every one should take that just proportion of sleep in the night, which he requires for being usefully awake in the day. Holy Scripture, the example of the Saints and our natural reason, all commend the morning as the best and most profitable part of the day. Our Blessed Lord Himself is called the Rising Sun and His Mother the Morning Star. I recommend you, therefore, to go to rest early at night, so that you may be awake and rise early in the morning, which is the pleasantest and the least cumbered time of the day; the very birds call us to awaken to the praise of God; and early rising is profitable both for health and holiness.

Balaam went on his ass to meet Balak, but inasmuch as his motive was not honest, the Angel of the Lord stood in his way with a drawn sword. Three times the ass, seeing the Angel, turned aside, and Balaam smote her with his staff; but the third time having fallen down beneath him, the Lord opened her mouth, and she said, "What have I done unto thee? Why strikest thou me, lo, now this third time?" and then Balaam's eyes were opened and he saw the Angel, who asked him, "Wherefore hast thou smitten thine ass these three times? . . . unless the ass had turned out of the way, giving place to me who stood against thee, I had slain thee and she should have lived." Then he answered and said, "Lord, I have sinned, not knowing that thou didst stand against me." Balaam was at fault, but he punished the ass who was not. It is often so with us: a woman grieves over her sick husband or child, and straightway she begins to fast and mortify herself as David did on a similar occasion. Alas, my daughter, you are smiting the ass, you afflict your body, but it cannot remedy the evil on account of which the sword of God is unsheathed against you! Rather correct your heart which idolizes your husband or indulges your child in sin, preparing it for future pride, vanity, and ambition. Again, a man is conscious that he is often guilty of self-indulgence, and his conscience being stirred with pious fear, reproaches him. Then at once he exclaims against his flesh, and subjects it to the severest mortifications. Well might the flesh cry out with Balaam's ass, "Wherefore smitest thou me?" It is against thee, my soul, that God raises His arm; thou art the criminal, why dost thou lead me into evil? Why dost thou use my eyes, my hands, my lips to unholy purposes? Why dost thou perplex me with unholy thoughts? Do thou cultivate good thoughts, and I shall do good deeds; seek modest society, and I shall not be tempted to impurity; but alas, thou puttest me into the fire and biddest me not burn! Thou fillest mine eyes with smoke and expectest that they should be not inflamed! And in such a case God would say, smite your heart, bruise, wound, subdue it, for it is with it that I am displeased. When we want to cure the itch, it will not suffice to bathe and wash the skin, we must purify and restore health to the blood; and so, in order to cure our faults, it is doubtless well to mortify the flesh, but above all we must purify our affections, and renew our hearts, and it is advisable never to adopt bodily mortifications without the direction of our spiritual guide.

CHAPTER TWENTY-FOUR

Society and Solitude

———————— • ————————

TO SEEK society and to shun it, are alike blamable extremes for those who are living in the world, and it is to such that I am speaking. By shunning it we indicate disdain and contempt for our neighbor, and by seeking it we imply idleness and inactivity. We should love our neighbor as ourself, and it is not a proof of love to shun him; whilst as a sign that we love ourselves we should be content with our own society, that is to be alone. "First think of thyself, and then of others," says St. Bernard. If then you are not called upon to receive or enter society, remain by yourself and hold converse with your own heart. But if you are rightly called on to join in society, then go as in God's sight, and mix with a free and loving heart amongst your fellows. That is bad society which has a bad object in view, or which is composed of evil livers; from indiscreet or profligate persons turn away, as the bee turns from all that is foul and impure. For just as the society of one that has been bitten by a mad dog is dangerous, especially to children and weak people, so is that of ill-regulated and profligate men, especially to those whose piety is as yet tender and weak. Some kinds of society have no end except recreation from more serious occupation, and though we should not exceed in such, still we may lawfully bestow our leisure therein. Another kind we owe to courtesy, such as mutual visits and meeting together out of respect to our neighbors; and with regard to these we should neither be punctilious in their observance, nor discourteous in their neglect, but unobtrusively fulfill our part, so as at once to avoid incivility and distraction.

And lastly, as to the society of virtuous and pious persons, the oftener you seek such, the better. The vine that is planted amidst olive trees bears the richest fruit, and the soul that is constantly associated with holy people must imbibe their good qualities: drones cannot make honey, but the bees make them work. It is a great advantage to associate with the truly devout. At all times let simplicity, candor, gentleness, and modesty prevail in your conversation. There are some persons who weary everyone by the affectation of all their looks and actions; and as all the world would be annoyed by a man who would never walk without counting his steps, or speak without singing, so society is extremely troubled by those whose deportment is always artificial and all their proceedings measured, for there is always a certain degree of presumption in such people. As a general rule, we should preserve a quiet cheerfulness of manner. St. Romuald and St. Anthony have been much praised because throughout all their austerities their manner and countenance were always cheerful, pleasing, and courteous. "Rejoice with them that rejoice," and again I would say with the Apostle, "Rejoice in the Lord always; again, I say, rejoice. Let your modesty be known to all men." (*Phil.* 4:4). In order to rejoice in the Lord, the cause of your joy must not only be lawful but good, for there are some lawful things which yet are not fitting; and that your moderation may be known, avoid presumption, which is always reprehensible. Nothing can be more contemptible than practical jokes, or jests which annoy and give pain to others. I have before shown how you may retire into solitude within yourself, even in the largest society; and besides this you should seek some solitary place, not in the desert like St. Mary of Egypt, St. Paul, St. Anthony, Arsenius, and the other solitary Fathers, but retiring into your own room, or your garden, or wherever you can; there gather together your mind and heart, and refresh your soul with pious meditation and holy thoughts, or by sacred study, imitating the Bishop of Nazianzen, who speaking of himself says, "I was walking with myself at sunset by the seashore, for thus I am accustomed to seek relaxation and relief from my ordinary cares." And then he goes on to narrate his pious reflections which I repeated to you before. And St. Augustine records of St. Ambrose that, entering into his apartment (for the entrance was open to all), he found him reading, and having waited some time for fear of disturbing him, he went away in silence, thinking that the brief space which that holy pastor could devote to refreshing and invigorating his mind amidst the many cares and occupations ought not to be intruded on.

CHAPTER TWENTY-FIVE

Propriety in Dress

———— ● ————

S T. PAUL desires Christian women (and he undoubtedly includes men) to adorn themselves in decent apparel with modesty and sobriety. (*1 Tim.* 2:9). Now propriety in dress and its appearances consists in material, fashion, and cleanliness. As to the latter, it should be invariable; and as far as possible you should avoid all dirt or untidiness. Outward purity is as it were a type of that which is within; and God Himself specially required personal cleanliness of those who ministered at His altars, and took the chief part in devotion. As to the material and fashion of clothes, propriety in these respects depends upon various circumstances, such as time, age, rank, those with whom you associate; and it varies with different occasions. Most people dress better on festival days according to the season, and in penitential seasons, such as Lent, just the reverse. So at a wedding we wear marriage garments and at a funeral the garb of mourning, and when going into the presence of princes we dress differently from what we do at home. The wife may adorn herself to please her husband, and it is lawful for maidens to desire to be pleasing in the eyes of their friends. But everyone despises old age when it would affect to adorn itself; such trifling can be tolerated only in youth.

Study to be neat, and let nothing about you be slovenly or disorderly.

It is an affront to those with whom you associate to be unsuitably dressed, but avoid all conceits, vanities, finery, and affectation. Adhere as far as possible to modesty and simplicity, which, doubtless, are the best ornaments of beauty, and the best atonement for its deficiency. St. Peter admonishes women not to adorn themselves, with plaiting the hair and putting on of apparel (*1 Peter* 3:3), and such follies in men are altogether disgusting. We are apt to suppose that vain women are but weak in virtue, at any rate it is smothered in their ornaments and finery. They excuse themselves, saying that they see no harm; but I say, as I have said before, that the devil rejoices in such things. I would have my spiritual children always suitably attired, but without show or affectation. Theirs should be the incorruptible ornament of a meek and quiet spirit. (*1 Peter* 3:4). St. Louis summed up all in saying that every one should dress according to his station, so that wise men may not say, you are too fine, nor the young, you are too homely. But if the latter are not content with what is suitable, you must adhere to the counsel of the wise.

CHAPTER TWENTY-SIX

Conversation: And First, of Conversation Concerning God

———— • ————

PHYSICIANS are wont to judge of a man's state of health by examining his tongue, and our words are a faithful index to the state of our soul. The Saviour Himself has said, "By thy words thou shalt be justified, and by thy words thou shalt be condemned." (*Matt.* 12:37). Our hand is quickly raised to the spot where we are wounded, and our tongue turns as quickly to the subject we delight in. If, then, you have a hearty love of God, you will frequently speak of Him with your family, your friends, and neighbors; for "the mouth of the just shall meditate wisdom: and his tongue shall speak of judgment." (*Ps.* 36:30). The bee produces nothing but honey from its little proboscis, and your tongue will always be sweetened by His Name, and will know no greater joy than to overflow with His praise and benediction. Thus it is told of St. Francis that when he spoke the Holy Name of the Lord, his mouth seemed to be filled with the sweetest of delicacies. But when you speak of God, remember of whom it is you speak. And let it be with reverence and devotion, not pompously or as it were preaching, but with the spirit of gentleness, charity, and humility, and as far as you can let your lips drop as the honeycomb (*Cant.* 4:11), with the fragrance of devotion and heavenly things; now into the ear of one, now another, silently beseeching God to grant that this heavenly dew may reach the hearts of those who hearken.

But this holy work must be done softly and meekly; not as a matter of teaching, but naturally; for it is wonderful how gentleness and a prepossessing manner tend to attract and win the hearts of men.

Never, then, talk of God or of holy things as a mere formal matter of conversation, but always with devotion and thought, avoiding a peculiar vanity which we find in some professors of religion, who at all times and seasons introduce sacred and fervent expressions as a matter of course, and without thought, and then imagine that they themselves are what their words would indicate, which is far from being the case.

CHAPTER TWENTY-SEVEN

Modesty in Conversation, and Becoming Reverence

———•———

S T. JAMES says, "if any man offend not in word, the same is a perfect man. He is able also with a bridle to lead about the whole
body." (*James* 3:2). Beware of ever using any impure expressions, for
even if you have no bad intention, those who hear you may receive
them differently. Impure words fall on a weak heart like oil on cloth,
spreading all around, and may fill it with evil thoughts and defile it. As
bodily poison enters in by the mouth, so that of the heart enters by the
ear, and the tongue that utters it is a murderer; even if the venom does
not take effect owing to the heart being furnished with an antidote,
still the malice of the tongue is the same. Neither let anyone give as an
excuse that he spoke without thought, for our Blessed Lord, who seeth
all thoughts, has said, "Out of the abundance of the heart the mouth
speaketh." Even if we intended no harm, the Evil One did, and he is
sure to use our lawless words as a weapon against the heart of someone.
It is said that they who eat the plant called Angelica always have a sweet,
pleasant breath; and those whose hearts are full of modesty and purity
(which is heavenly virtue) are always pure, modest, and courteous in
their language. As to unholy, indecent things the Apostle will not so
much as have them named among us, telling us that "evil communications corrupt good manners."

If unholy words are used secretly and with deliberate intention, they are infinitely more poisonous; for just as in proportion to its sharpness and point a dart enters easily into the body, so the more pointed a bad word, the further it penetrates the heart. Those who fancy that it is clever to introduce such things in society, do not know its aim, which should be like that of a hive of bees, gathered together to make honey, that is for pleasant and virtuous intercourse; and not like a nest of wasps which will feed upon anything however unclean. If any foolish person speaks to you in unbecoming language, show that your ears are offended, either by turning away from him, or by whatever means may be most discreet at the time.

A spirit of mockery is one of the worst imperfections of the mind, and displeases God greatly, so that He has often punished it most severely. Nothing is more hurtful to charity, and still more to devotion, than contempt and derision of our neighbor, and such is inevitably found in mockery. For this reason it has been said that mockery is the greatest insult a man can offer his neighbor, inasmuch as in other offenses he does not altogether cease to respect the person whom he offends, but in this he despises and contemns him.

But as to a play upon words, one with another, in all modesty and good-humor, such as the Greeks called Eutrapelia, there is no harm in it, but it affords an innocent way of deriving amusement from our trifling vexations and disturbances; only we must beware that such trifling does not degenerate into mockery. The latter causes laughter at the expense of our neighbor, but this fun and merriment arise only from modest freedom and ease.

CHAPTER TWENTY-EIGHT

Rash Judgment

———•———

"JUDGE not, that ye be not judged," were our Saviour's words; "Condemn not, and ye shall not be condemned"; and St. Paul says, "Judge not before the time until the Lord come, who both will bring to light the hidden things of darkness, and will make manifest the counsels of the hearts." (*1 Cor.* 4:5). Rash judgments are most displeasing to God, and the judgments of men are rash, because men are not one another's judges, but therein usurp the office of Our Lord. They are rash also, inasmuch as the chief guilt of sin depends upon the intention and thought of the heart, which is as the hidden things of darkness to us; and they are rash because everyone has enough to do in judging himself, without presuming to judge his neighbor. It is just as necessary to judge ourselves as to refrain from judging others; for as our Blessed Lord forbids the latter, St. Paul enjoins the former, saying, "If we would judge ourselves, we should not be judged." (*1 Cor.* 11:31). But too often we reverse these precepts, and continually do that which is forbidden, judging our neighbor, whilst that which is enjoined us, namely, judging ourselves, we do but rarely.

We must seek the motives of rash judgments in order to cure them. There are some whose dispositions are naturally bitter, unkindly, and harsh, and who accordingly are bitter and harsh in all their dealings, who, to use the words of the Prophet, "turn judgment into bitterness, and the fruit of justice into wormwood" (*Amos* 6:12), always judging harshly of their neighbor. Such as these greatly need the treatment of a good spiritual physician, for inasmuch as this asperity is natural to them, it is very difficult to overcome; and although it is rather an imperfection than a sin, it is still dangerous from its tendency to rash judgment and evil-speaking. Others judge harshly not out of bitterness, but from pride, imagining that they exalt their own merit by depreciating that of others: arrogant and presumptuous minds, who admire themselves, and are so exalted in their own estimation that all besides appear low and contemptible to them. It was the Pharisee that said, "I am not as other men are." (*Luke* 18:11). Some again have not this open pride, but they view the faults of others with some complacency in order to enhance their (as they imagine) opposite virtues. This complacency is so secret and imperceptible that it requires a keen sight to discover it, and those who are subject to it are unconsciously so, unless it is shown to them. Others there are who readily judge their neighbors to be guilty of the vices to which they themselves are addicted, or similar ones, in order to excuse and flatter themselves and quiet their consciences with the vain thought that the multitude of criminals diminishes their own guilt. Others give way to rash judgments out of indulgence to their philosophical theories, which would fain search into men's characters and ways; and if unfortunately they are occasionally right in their judgment, it encourages them so that it is hard to wean them away from the habit.

Others judge by feeling, always thinking well of those they like, and ill of those they dislike, except in the one case of *jealousy,* where excessive love leads a man to think ill of its object. This jealousy is an impure, imperfect, disturbed, sickly love, which will for a single look or smile condemn those it loves as faithless. Again, fear, ambition, and similar weaknesses of the mind, often tend to excite suspicion and rash judgment.

What is the remedy? Those who drink the juice of the Ethiopian herb Ophiusa, imagine that on all sides they behold serpents and such horrible sights; and those who have imbibed pride, envy, ambition, and hatred, see nothing but what to them appears bad and hateful. Accordingly, as the former to be cured must drink palm wine, so the latter should drink deeply of the holy wine of charity, which will purge them from the corrupt humors which result in distorted judgments. Far from seeking out what is evil, charity dreads encountering it; and when she does meet it she hides her face, and strives not to see it. She shuts her eyes at the first sound of its approach, and then with holy simplicity believes that it was not sin itself, but only the shadow of sin. If she is forced to recognize it, then she makes haste to turn away, and tries to forget it. Charity is the great cure of all evils, but of this above all. All things look yellow to him who has the jaundice. It is said that the cure for this complaint must be applied to the soles of the feet. Now this sin of rash judgment is a spiritual jaundice, which makes all things appear evil in the eyes of him who labors under it; and he who would be healed, must apply the remedy not to his eyes, that is his intellect, but to his affections, which are as the feet of his soul. If your heart is gentle, your judgment will be gentle; if it is charitable, your judgment will be so too. I will give you three striking examples. Isaac said that Rebecca was his sister, but when Abimelech saw him caressing her he judged immediately that she was his wife. A malicious person might have supposed some less honorable connection, but Abimelech put the most charitable construction on what he saw. (*Gen.* 26). So should we always judge as favorably as possible of our neighbor, and if an action bears a hundred interpretations, we must adopt only the worthiest.

The Blessed Virgin was with child, and St. Joseph knew it, but he also knew that she was holy, pure, and angelic, and could not imagine her to be guilty of sin; therefore he left her to the judgment of God. Why did he thus? Scripture expressly says because "he was a just man." (*Matt.* 1:19). The just man, when he can find no excuse for the action or intention of one whom hitherto he has esteemed, still refuses to condemn him, but rather leaves the judgment to God.

Our crucified Saviour, being unable to excuse the sin of those who crucified Him, at least lessened the intensity by asserting their ignorance. (*Luke* 23:34). If we cannot excuse sin, at least let us bespeak compassion for it attributing it to the least aggravated cause that we can, as to ignorance or infirmity.

Are we then never to judge our neighbor? No, never, for it is God who judges criminals when brought to justice. It is true that He makes use of the voice of magistrates as His channel; they are His interpreters, and should judge only according to His judgments, as being His oracles; but if they give judgment according to their own passions, then indeed they judge, and will themselves be judged, since it is forbidden to men, *as men,* to judge one another.

We do not of necessity judge a matter because we see or know it, for the Scriptural sense of the word implies some uncertainty, small or great, real or apparent, to be overcome. Therefore Holy Scripture says that those who believe not are condemned or judged already, because there is no doubt of their damnation. It is not always wrong to doubt our neighbors. We are forbidden to judge, not to doubt; but still we should not indulge doubt or suspicion without great caution, and only insofar as these are based on reason and argument, otherwise our doubts and suspicions are rash. If some suspicious person had seen Jacob embracing Rachel beside the well (*Gen.* 29), or Rebecca receiving bracelets and earrings from Eliezer, who was a stranger (*Gen.* 24), he would, doubtless, have looked on them with suspicion, and that without cause, for it is a rash suspicion which thinks ill of actions in themselves indifferent, unless circumstances give cause for mistrust.

All those, then, who watch carefully over their consciences, are little given to pass rash judgments. As the bee retires to her hive in cloudy or foggy weather, so pious persons do not expend their thoughts on doubtful matters, nor upon the questionable proceedings of their neighbors, but rather avoid such, and employ themselves in good resolutions for their own amendment.

It is the sign of an idle mind to take delight in examining the lives of others, always excepting such as are responsible for men's souls whether in public or private, for it concerns their conscience to watch over and examine that of others. Let them fulfill their charge in all loving-kindness, but all the more examine and judge themselves.

CHAPTER TWENTY-NINE

Detraction

———————————•———————————

RASH judgments lead to disquiet, contempt for others, pride and self-complacency, and a hundred other evils, amongst which slander stands prominent, the very pest of society. Oh, for a live coal from off God's altar wherewith to touch the lips of men, that their iniquity might be taken away, and their sin purged, even as the Seraphim purified the mouth of the Prophet Isaias! (*Is.* 6:6, 7).

Whoever unjustly deprives his neighbor of his good name is guilty of sin, and is further bound to make reparation, according to his slander: no man can enter Heaven with another's goods, and of all worldly goods none is equal to a good reputation. Slander is a kind of murder, for we have three lives—the spiritual life, which consists of the grace of God, the corporal life, which is in the soul, and the civil life, which consists of our reputations. Sin destroys the first, death the second, and slander the third; but the slanderer is guilty of a triple murder with his tongue. He destroys his own soul and that of his hearer by a spiritual homicide, and deprives the object of his slander of civil existence. St. Bernard says that Satan has hold both of the slanderer and of him who hearkens to slander, for that he has the tongue of one and the ear of the other. David, speaking of slanderers, says: "They have sharpened their tongues like serpents." (*Ps.* 139:4). Aristotle says that the serpent's

tongue is forked, having two points; and such is the tongue of the slanderer, who with one stroke wounds and poisons the ear of his listener
and the reputation of him whom he slanders.

I beseech you, therefore, never to speak ill of anyone, either directly
or indirectly. Beware of falsely imputing crimes and sins to your neighbor, of disclosing his secret faults, of exaggerating those which are obvious, of interpreting good actions ill, of denying the good which you
know to be in any, or of maliciously concealing it or lessening it, for all
these things grievously offend God: above all of falsely accusing another
or denying the truth to his prejudice, which involves the double sin of
falsehood and injury.

The most refined and venomous slanderers are those who pretend
to mean well, or craftily insinuate their poison by means of jests and
banter. "I really love him very much," one will say, "and altogether he is
a good man, but in truth he was wrong to commit that breach of trust,"
or "that woman is highly virtuous, it is a pity that she slipped once,"
and so on. Do you not perceive the artifice? The archer draws his arrow
as near to him as possible, but his object is that it should fly the farther,
and whilst these men seem willing to retain their slander within themselves, they really launch it but the more fiercely. Slander in the shape of
a jest is worse than all, for as hemlock is not in itself a quick poison and
an antidote may easily be found, yet when taken in wine it is incurable;
and so slander, which by itself would go in at one ear and out at the
other, remains in the mind of the listeners when it is dressed up in some
clever or witty saying. "The venom of asps is under their lips," David
says. (*Ps.* 139:4). The sting of the asp is scarcely perceptible, and only
excites a trifling sensation, but let the system once receive the poison,
and there is no longer any cure.

Do not publish that such a man is a drunkard, a thief, or impure
because you have once known him guilty of such a thing, one act does
not justify the name. The sun stood still once at Josue's command, and
another time it was darkened on account of our Saviour's death, yet
no one would say that it was either dark or motionless. Noah and Lot

were both drunk once, yet neither was a drunkard; neither was St. Paul bloodthirsty because he had once shed blood, nor a blasphemer because he had once blasphemed. Before a man deserves the epithet of vicious he must be advanced in, or accustomed to, vice, therefore it is unfair to call a man passionate or a thief, because he has on some occasion been angry or dishonest. Even if a man has long been vicious, we run the risk of falsehood in calling him so. Simon the leper called Magdalen a sinner because she was formerly one, but he told a lie, for she was no longer a sinner but a holy penitent, and our Saviour Himself undertook her defense.

The proud Pharisee esteemed the publican as a great sinner, as unjust, an adulterer or extortioner; but he was strangely mistaken, for at that very time the publican was justified. Surely if God's goodness is so great that in one instant we can obtain pardon and grace, how can we tell that he who was a sinner yesterday is the same today? Yesterday must not judge today, nor today yesterday; it is the last day which will give the final verdict.

Thus we can never pronounce a man to be wicked without danger of falsehood. If we must needs speak, we must say that he has been guilty of such an evil deed, at such a time he misconducted himself, or he is now doing so; but we should not condemn today because of yesterday, nor yesterday because of today, still less tomorrow.

But whilst you give good heed to speak no evil concerning your neighbor, beware of falling into the opposite extreme, as some do, who, seeking to avoid slander, praise vice. If you come in the way of a downright slanderer, do not defend him by calling him frank and honest-spoken; do not miscall dangerous freedoms by the name of simplicity and easiness, or call disobedience zeal, or arrogance self-respect; do not fly from slander into flattery and indulgence of vice, but call evil evil without hesitation, and blame that which is blamable. By this means you will glorify God. I would add certain conditions:

When you blame the vices of another, consider whether it is profitable or useful to those who hear to do so. Thus to dwell upon profligacy before the young is dangerous; it is safer simply to condemn everything of the sort, avoiding details. Again, if you chance to be the leading person in society when such subjects are named, and your silence would give you an appearance of approving vice, then you should speak; if on the contrary you are an insignificant member of the company, do not assume the censorship. Above all, you must be exceedingly exact in what you say; your tongue when you speak of your neighbor is as a knife in the hand of the surgeon who is going to cut between the nerves and tendons. Your stroke must be accurate, and neither deeper nor slighter than what is needed; and whilst you blame the sin, always spare the sinner as much as possible.

We may speak freely of notorious and infamous sinners, but still with charity and compassion, avoiding arrogance and presumption, and not rejoicing in another's ill, which is the sure sign of an evil, cruel heart. Of the enemies of God and His Church we must needs speak openly, since in charity we are bound to give the alarm whenever the wolf is found amongst the sheep.

Everyone thinks himself at liberty to judge and censure princes, and to decry whole nations according to his inclinations. Do not indulge this failing; it is displeasing to God, and may involve you in numberless disputes.

When you hear ill of anyone, refute the accusation if you can in justice do so; if not, apologize for the accused on account of his intentions; and if even that fails, deal compassionately with him, remembering yourself and calling to the mind of others that those who are preserved from sin owe it only to the grace of God; and thus gently check the conversation, and if you can, mention something else favorable to the accused.

CHAPTER THIRTY

Further Counsels Concerning Conversation

———•———

L ET your speech be gentle, frank, sincere, clear, simple, and truthful.
Avoid all duplicity, artifice, and affectation; for although it is not
expedient to tell everything which is true, it is at no time allowable to
tell what is not. Never permit yourself to tell a lie in the way of excuse
or otherwise, remembering that God is a God of truth. If you accidentally say what is untrue, and it is possible at once to correct yourself by
explanation or reparation, do so. A sincere excuse is of far more avail
and more powerful than a lie.

Although there may be occasions in which we may prudently and
discreetly cover and keep back the truth, we should not do so except in
matters of importance where it is necessary for the glory and service of
God. In truth all artifice is dangerous, for the Holy Spirit will not dwell
with the double-minded. No art is so valuable as simplicity.

Worldly prudence and carnal wisdom appertain to the children of
this world, but the children of God go on in a straightforward course,
and their hearts are steady and confident. Lying, duplicity, and dissimulation are the sure signs of a low, groveling mind.

In the fourth book of his *Confessions*, St. Augustine had said that
his soul and that of his friend made but one soul, that after his friend's
death his life was abhorrent to him, since he had but half a life, and

yet for the same reason he feared to die, and to cause his friend to die wholly. Later in life he thought these expressions too affected and artificial, and struck them out. Remark well how susceptible this great man was to affectation in words! Unquestionably, faithful, straightforward, sincere speech is a great ornament to the life of a Christian. David says, "I said, I will take heed to my ways, that I sin not with my tongue" (*Ps.* 38:2); and "Set a watch, O Lord, before my mouth, and a door round about my lips." (*Ps.* 140:3).

The royal St. Louis gave it as a counsel never to contradict anyone, unless there was some harm or sin in consenting; and thus to avoid altercation and dispute. But when it is necessary to contradict some one, or give an opposite opinion, it should be done gently and skillfully, so as not to irritate our neighbors; and besides, we gain nothing by lack of mildness. The short speech so much commended by the ancients does not so much mean that we should use few words, as that we should not use many that are unprofitable, for in conversation, quality matters more than quantity. I would have you avoid extremes, for there seems to be a lack of confidence or some degree of contempt in being always constrained and strictly refusing to join in familiar conversation; whilst a perpetual chatter and gossip, which gives no one else time or opportunity to speak, is trifling and vexatious.

St. Louis condemned private discussion or conversation in general society, especially at meal times. "If anyone has something good to say," he remarked, "let him give all present the benefit of it; but let him be silent on private and important subjects."

CHAPTER THIRTY-ONE

Amusements: First, of Those Which Are Lawful

———————•———————

WE MUST needs sometimes relax the mind, and give the body some recreation. Cassian relates that one day a sportsman found St. John the Evangelist amusing himself by stroking a partridge which sat upon his wrist. The man inquired how so great a person could spend his time in so humble an amusement, to which St. John replied by asking why he did not always keep his bow strung. "For fear," the hunter answered, "lest if it were always bent it should lose its power when it is wanted." "Then do not mind," rejoined the Apostle, "if I sometimes relax the strict application of my mind to seek some recreation, so that I may return with more energy to contemplation." It is a failing to be so harsh and rigid that we will not allow ourselves or others to indulge in any recreation. Air and exercise, cheerful games, music, field-sports, and the like, are such innocent amusements that they only require to be used with ordinary discretion, which confines all things to their fitting time, place, and degree.

Those games which serve to exercise mental or bodily activity or skill, such as bowls, chess, etc., are praiseworthy amusements in themselves. You must, of course, guard against excess either in the time they occupy, or the importance given them; for if you devote too much time, they cease to be recreations and become occupations; you do not refresh the mind or body—on the contrary, you overpower and stun both. After playing for five or six hours at chess, the mind is tired and exhausted, and a long time spent in any active game instead of invigorating the body wearies it. If the interest of the game is too deep, it produces over-anxiety; moreover, it is not well to attach great importance to such things as dexterity and skill in any mere game. Especially avoid attaching yourself to them, for however allowable such things are as amusements, they become evils as soon as they absorb the heart. I do not mean that you may not lawfully take pleasure in your amusement, otherwise it would not be a recreation, but you must not be devoted to it, or eager and absorbed in it.

CHAPTER THIRTY-TWO

Forbidden Games

———•———

D ICE, cards, and similar games, in which success depends mainly on chance, are not only dangerous amusements like dancing, but actually and naturally bad and blamable. For this reason they are forbidden both by civil and ecclesiastical law. Do you ask where the great harm is? The winner in such games does not win on his deserts but according to chance, and the luck which often falls to those who have exercised neither skill nor industry; and this is contrary to reason. You will answer that this is taken for granted and understood, and thus, you are not dealing unfairly. But it does not alter the fact; your understanding and your game are alike unreasonable, for gain, which should be the reward of industry, becomes the reward of luck, which can deserve no reward since it is no way dependent upon us.

And although these games are called recreations, they are in truth most absorbing occupations. Is it not an occupation to keep the mind stretched to a close and continual attention, disturbed by incessant disquiet, apprehension, and excitement? Is any business more dreary, somber, and melancholy than that of a gamester? If you do but talk or laugh or cough, you distract him. Furthermore, the only gratification in play is to win, and is not that an unrighteous gratification, which can only be obtained by the losses and harm of another? Surely such pleasure is an unrighteous one.

The great king, St. Louis, hearing that his brother, the Comte d'Anjou, and Walter de Nemours were gambling, rose from his sick bed, and went with faltering steps to their apartment, where he rebuked them sharply, throwing their dice and part of their money out of the window into the sea. And the holy and chaste damsel, Sara, speaking in prayer to God of her innocence, said, "Thou knowest, O Lord, that . . . never have I joined myself with them that play." (*Tob.* 3:16-17).

CHAPTER THIRTY-THREE

Balls and Recreations
Which Are Lawful but Dangerous

———————•———————

B ALLS and dances are in themselves matters of indifference, but the ordinary attendant circumstances have a tendency to evil, and consequently are perilous. They take place at night, and the darkness and obscurity add to the dangers of amusements in their own nature so susceptible of evil. Moreover, the long watching which they involve entails the loss of the following mornings, and thereby the service of God is neglected. It is surely a folly to reverse day and night, light and darkness, and follow idle vanities instead of good works. Those who go to a ball carry vanity with them; and vanity has a great tendency to excite bad passions and blamable affections.

I would say to you of balls what physicians say of mushrooms—the best are but unwholesome food; and I say the best balls are but indifferent. If, however, you must eat mushrooms, let them be well prepared. If you cannot well avoid mixing in such pursuits, go in a careful ,watchful spirit, with modesty, dignity, and pure intentions. Eat but little and seldom, says the physician, of this unwholesome food, for however they are cooked they are hurtful in any quantity. Then go seldom, and beware that you do not become over-fond of the amusement.

Pliny says that mushrooms being porous and spongy easily imbibe any infection, so that if they are near a serpent they acquire its venom:

so balls and similar assemblies usually attract all that is least commendable; while envy, disputes, vexations, and imprudent attachments abound there, and find a more than usually easy access into the heart. Such idle recreations are generally dangerous, inasmuch as they dissipate the spirit of devotion, weaken our energies, cool our charity, and arouse many evil inclinations in the heart; therefore they should be entered upon with great caution.

It is said that after eating mushrooms you should always drink some good wine—and after mixing in such amusements you should arouse some good and holy reflections which may counteract any dangerous impression made on your mind by the vain pleasure you have enjoyed. Suitable reflections would be:

1. Whilst you were at this ball, there were souls in torment owing to sins committed or instigated under similar circumstances.

2. And at the same time holy and pious men were serving God, singing His praise and contemplating His beauty. How much better was their time spent than yours?

3. Whilst you were dancing, some souls departed this life in bitter anguish, and thousands of men and women were wandering in the streets or lying on their beds of suffering, enduring the pains of fever and other diseases. They know no rest; will you not pity them, and remember that the day will come when you must suffer as they do now, whilst others will be dancing as you have done?

4. Our Blessed Lord, His Mother, the Saints and angels, were watching you, and surely they pitied and lamented over you, seeing your heart occupied and pleased with such unsatisfying trifles.

5. Whilst you are thus engaged, time slips on and death draws nigh. He mocks you, and calls you to join his dance, in which the music is the groaning for past sin, and in which you will make but one step from life to death: this is the true pastime of men, since in it they pass in an instant from time to eternity, either of good or ill.—God will inspire you with many similar reflections if you live in His fear.

CHAPTER THIRTY-FOUR

When We May Play or Dance

———— • ————

L AWFUL games and dances should be matter of recreation only, not of interest, occupying but a short time, and that rarely. If they are habitual, they will become an occupation. You ask when we may indulge in them? The seasons for such ordinary diversions are more frequent, those for others very rare, inasmuch as they are more blamable and dangerous. But you may enjoy them under the safeguards I have mentioned, when discretion and prudence dictate that you should comply with the wishes of that society in which you find yourself. Courtesy and kindness, the companions of charity, sometimes render unimportant things good, and those which are dangerous allowable: they even neutralize the mischief in some things that are bad, so that games of chance, which of themselves are blamable, are not so when we play them from some good motive. Thus St. Charles Borromeo relaxed, when amongst the Swiss, in certain matters concerning which he was otherwise strict; and St. Ignatius Loyola accepted an invitation to play. St. Elizabeth of Hungary joined in dancing and other sports without prejudice to her devotion, which was so deeply rooted in her soul that just as the rocks around the lake of Rieti grow beneath the dashing of the waves, her holiness waxed greater amidst the pomps and vanities to which her rank exposed her. Great fires flame all the more when the wind blows, but a little fire will be altogether extinguished unless it be sheltered.

CHAPTER THIRTY-FIVE

We Must Be Faithful in
Things Great and Small

───────── • ─────────

THE Bridegroom in the Song of Songs says that his spouse has ravished his heart with one of her eyes and one hair of her neck. (*Cant.* 4:9). Of all the human body, no part is so preeminent whether for its mechanism or its power as the eye; none less important than the hair. Therefore the Divine Bridegroom implies that He accepts not only the great deeds of devout persons, but also the lowest and least; and that to serve Him well we must pay great attention alike to great and mighty things, and to those which are small and lowly, since through both alike we may lose or win His love.

Be ready, then, to suffer heavy afflictions, if need be, martyrdom itself, for Christ's sake; determine to give to Him all that is dearest to you when He pleases to take it—father, mother, brother, husband, wife, child, the sight of your eyes, and your life itself; to all such submission your heart should be disposed. But as meanwhile Divine Providence does not try you with such severe and heavy afflictions, and does not require your eyes, give Him at least your hair; that is to say, meekly endure all little evils, trifling inconveniences, and unimportant losses, which happen daily; for by using these little opportunities with a good and loving purpose you will overcome your heart and have it entirely under control. All such trifles, as the daily chances of life—this headache, toothache, or fever, the perversity of a husband or wife, the breaking of a mirror, this slight, the loss of a ring, handkerchief, or glove, the little inconvenience of going early to bed and rising early to pray and communicate, the little shame at being publicly noticed in certain religious observances—all these and similar trifling annoyances will (if they be taken and received cheerfully) please that Divine Goodness which has promised to the faithful an ocean of bliss in return for a cup of cold water; and inasmuch as these opportunities are perpetually occurring, their right use affords an abundant means of laying up spiritual treasures.

In reading in the life of St. Catherine of Siena of all her visions and raptures, her sacred wisdom and her discourses, I should not doubt that with the eye of contemplation she had ravished the heart of her Heavenly Bridegroom. But at the same time I delighted to find her attending to the lowly household cares in her father's house, turning the spit, lighting the fire, cooking and baking, with a heart full of love and yearning towards God. Nor do I value the humble meditations which occupied her whilst engaged in such lowly offices less than the ecstasies and raptures which she so often enjoyed, and which were perhaps granted as the reward of her humility and self-abnegation. In her heart she considered that ministering to her father she was like Martha ministering to Our Lord; her mother she likened to the Blessed Virgin, and her brothers to the Apostles, thus spiritually serving the heavenly household, and finding great sweetness in her humble duties, because in them she knew she performed the will of God.

Hence I would have you learn how important it is that all our actions, however trifling, be offered to His Divine Majesty. And to this end imitate that virtuous woman who is described by King Solomon (*Prov.* 31), who, whilst she stretched out her hands to great and honorable things, did not neglect her spindle and distaff. Apply yourself to great things in prayer and meditation, in the Sacraments, in telling of the love of God, and spreading His knowledge in all hearts, and in all such important works as befit your vocation. But do not neglect your spindle and distaff, that is to say, practice those lowly, unobstrusive virtues which spring like flowers from the foot of the Cross, such as visiting the poor, ministering to the sick, household cares and the labors involved therein, and then you will never be idle; meanwhile, intersperse all such occupations with pious reflections after the example of St. Catherine.

Great occasions of serving God but rarely offer themselves; small occasions perpetually occur, and Christ Himself has said: "He that is faithful in that which is least, is faithful also in that which is greater." (*Luke* 16:10). If, then, you do all in the name of God, you will do all well, whether you eat or whether you drink, whether you sleep or repose from labor, whether you are engaged in honorable or menial offices. If you conduct them rightly you may greatly advance your salvation, doing all things because such is the will of God.

CHAPTER THIRTY-SIX

The Necessity of a Just and Reasonable Mind

———————— • ————————

REASON is the essential distinction of man, and yet it is rare to find really reasonable men; the more so as self-love hinders reason, and leads us into numberless trifling but dangerous acts of injustice, which, like the little foxes spoken of in the Canticles, spoil the vines (*Cant.* 2:15); for because they are trifling we do not heed them, and being numerous they do great mischief. Let us see some instances.

We accuse our neighbors in little things, but we excuse ourselves in great things. We seek to buy cheap and sell dear. We demand justice towards others, but towards ourselves mercy and indulgence. We would have none find fault with our words, but we are sensitive and captious to the words of others. We would fain make our neighbor give up any property we want and are willing to pay for; is it not more just that he should retain it and leave us our money? We are displeased with him because he will not study our conveniences; has he not rather reason to complain of us for striving to inconvenience him?

If we are addicted to some particular duty, we neglect the rest and only pursue that which suits our taste. If one of our dependants is unattractive or displeasing to us, we are never satisfied with anything he does, but are perpetually finding fault and worrying him; and on the contrary we have an ever-ready excuse for one that we like. Some parents have an aversion for a virtuous child on account of some bodily defect, whilst they show undue preference to one who is attractive and vicious. So we esteem the rich above the poor, albeit the latter are virtuous and of good character. We are even guided in our preference by fine clothes; we are particular in exacting our own rights, and expect others to be more yielding with regard to theirs; we maintain our own rank punctiliously, but would have others be humble and condescending; we are ready to complain of our neighbor, but we would have no one complain of us. We think much of what we do for others, and little of what they do for us. In short, we resemble the Paphlagonian partridge which has two hearts, for towards ourselves we have a gentle, liberal, courteous heart, but towards our neighbor one that is hard, rigorous, and severe. We have one measure whereby to weigh all that appertains to ourselves as advantageously as possible, and another for our neighbor as disadvantageous as may be. Now Holy Scripture says that deceitful lips speak with a double heart (*Ps.* 11:3), and that to have two weights—the one heavy, for receiving, the other light, for giving—is an abomination to the Lord.

Always be impartial and just in your deeds. Put yourself into your neighbor's place, and him in yours, and then you will judge fairly. When you buy, act as though you were the seller, and when you sell act as though you were the buyer, and you will buy and sell with justice. These acts of injustice seem small, because they do not demand restitution, as we only seek our own advantage to the utmost limit of honesty; but, nevertheless, they require correction, for after all they are but cheating tricks, and offend against reason and charity, and no one ever lost anything by generosity, honor, and courtesy, which are the fruits of a noble, upright, straightforward heart. Frequently, therefore, examine your heart, whether it is so disposed towards your neighbor, as you would have his disposed towards you, were you to change places; for this is the true test. Trajan's intimates blamed him for rendering the imperial majesty, as they considered, too accessible. "How then?" he replied. "Should I not seek to be such towards private individuals as I should wish the Emperor to be were I a private individual myself?"

CHAPTER THIRTY-SEVEN

Desires

———— • ————

EVERYONE knows that we must avoid evil desires, for by their indulgence we become evil likewise; but I would urge you not to desire those things which are dangerous to the soul, such as balls and similar perilous amusements, honors, etc., offices, visions, and raptures. In all such things there is great risk of vanity and delusion. Do not indulge in longings after events which as yet are far distant, for they only distract and weary the heart, often disturbing it seriously. If a young man earnestly desires some office which is at present unattainable, to what end is his longing? If a married woman wishes to follow the religious life, where is the use of her wish? Or if I would fain buy my neighbor's land, he being unwilling to part with it, do I not waste my time in wishing? If when I am ill I give way to the wish to minister or preach, visit other sick persons or perform the duties of the healthy, are not my wishes fruitless, since it is not in my power to execute them? And meanwhile these useless wishes impede others which I ought to have—the wish to be very patient, very resigned, obedient, mortified, and gentle under my sufferings, which is what for the time being God requires of me. But we often, in our own unreasonable wishes, resemble women in delicate condition, who ask for cherries in winter, and grapes in spring.

No person who has an appointed duty or vocation should indulge in wishing for some manner of life different from that which is suitable to it and its indispensable conditions; for such indulgence disturbs the mind, and enfeebles it in the performance of its necessary duties. If I wish for a Carthusian solitude, I waste my time and allow this desire to take the place of that which ought to occupy me, namely, to perform my present duty faithfully. I would not even admit of longings after a better intellect, or sounder judgment, for such longings are vain and drive out those which everyone should have to cultivate what he has, such as it is. Nor would I encourage a desire for the means of serving God which He has denied us, but rather faithfully make use of those we have. Of course, I am speaking of such desires as occupy the heart, for there is no harm in common wishes if they do not become habitual. Do not wish for crosses unless you have borne those well which have already been offered to you; it is a mistake to wish for martyrdom whilst we have not courage to endure a sharp word. The enemy of souls often seeks to distract us with desires for distant trials, which will never offer themselves, in order to distract our mind from those present circumstances whence, however trifling, we might derive real benefit. In fancy we fight against African monsters, whilst practically, for lack of thought, we allow the worms on our daily path to destroy us.

Never seek temptations, it is presumptuous and rash so to do; but prepare your heart to await them with courage and to defend itself when they do come.

Variety and superfluity of food always overload the digestion, and if it is weakly, ruin it. Do not overload your soul with desires, neither with worldly ones, which are injurious, nor even spiritual ones, which will hinder you. When the soul is cleansed and set free from evil tempers, it experiences a great hunger after spiritual things, and eagerly desires all manner of pious exercises in mortification, penitence, charity and prayer. Such an appetite is a good sign, but take care that you are able to digest all that you would eat. With the help of your spiritual father select from amongst all such practices those which are suitable to you, and for the present follow, and make the most of them; in this case God will supply you with others in due season, and thus you will not waste time in fruitless wishes. I do not bid you to put aside all good desires, but only to regulate them; to execute those which are practicable at the present moment, and lay up those which are impracticable in store for a fitting season; and this I say alike of spiritual and temporal desires, for by this means alone we can go on calmly and without distraction.

CHAPTER THIRTY-EIGHT

Advice to Married Persons

———— • ————

"THIS (marriage) is a great sacrament: but I speak in Christ and in the Church." (*Eph.* 5:32). It is honorable to all, in all, and in everything, that is, in all its parts. To all, for the unmarried should esteem it in humility; in all, for it is as holy to the poor as to the rich; in everything, for its institution, its end, its purpose, its form, and its matter, are all holy. It is the orchard of Christianity, which fills the world with the Faithful in order to fill up the number of the elect in Heaven, and it greatly concerns the public welfare that the sanctity of marriage, which is the source of all its well-being, be preserved inviolate.

Would that our Blessed Saviour were always invited to all marriage-feasts, as to that of Cana. (*John* 2). Then the wine of consolation and benediction would never be lacking. For the reason this is so scarce is that Adonis is invited instead of Jesus Christ, and Venus instead of His Blessed Mother. He that would have his lambs fair and mottled as Jacob's were, must, like him, set fair rods of divers colors before the sheep when they meet to couple; and he that would have success in marriage, ought in his espousals to set before himself the sanctity and dignity of this holy Sacrament; but, instead of this, there are a thousand disorderly diversions, feastings, and words. No wonder, then, that unhappiness follows.

Above all, I exhort married persons to have that mutual love which is so earnestly enjoined by the Holy Ghost in the Scriptures. It is little to have natural love, for a pair of turtle doves has the same; or mere human love, for in that the heathen were not lacking; but I say with St. Paul: "Husbands, love your wives, as Christ also loved the Church. . . . Let women be subject to their husbands, as to the Lord." (*Eph.* 5:22, 25).

It was God who brought Eve to Adam and gave her to him as his wife, and it is God, my friends, who with His invisible hand bound the knot which unites you and gave you to one another; therefore give good heed that you cherish a love which is holy, sacred, and divine.

The first result of such love is the indissoluble union of your hearts. If two pieces of wood are carefully glued together, their union will be so close that it is easier to break them in some fresh place than where they were joined; and God so unites man and wife, that it is easier to sever soul and body than those two. And this union is less that of the body, than of the heart, its affections and love.

The second result of this love is inviolable fidelity. Of old a man's seal was always engraved on a ring which he wore on his finger, as is frequently testified in Holy Scripture; and this is the meaning of the marriage ceremony. The Church, through her priest, blesses a ring, and giving it to the man thereby seals his heart with this Sacrament, so that it may never be given to any other woman, as long as this one lives. Then the bridegroom places the ring on the hand of his bride, that she in like manner may know that her heart must never be given to any other man than to him whom Christ has given her.

The third end of marriage is the birth and bringing up of children. And surely it is a great honor to be permitted to increase the number of souls whom God will save, and who will serve Him through all eternity; your part being to bring forth those bodies, into which He will infuse an immortal soul. Therefore do you, husbands, preserve a tender, constant, and heartfelt love for your wives; the woman was taken from that side which was nearest Adam's heart, that she might be the more heartily and tenderly loved. The weakness and infirmities of your wife, whether mental or bodily, should not excite your contempt, but rather a tender loving compassion; since God has created woman to be dependent on you, and to add to your honor and esteem, and although she is given to be your companion, you are still her head and her superior. And do you, wives, love the husbands God has given you, tenderly, heartily, but with a respectful love and full of reverence; for it is God's Will to make them the superior and more vigorous sex, and He has ordained that woman should be dependent upon man, bone of his bone, flesh of his flesh, taking her from his ribs and beneath his arm, to show that she is to be subject to the hand of her husband. And Holy Scripture forcibly inculcates this subjection, at the same time making it light to bear, not only bidding you bear the yoke in love, but also bidding husbands to use their power gently and lovingly. St. Peter says, "Ye husbands, likewise dwelling with them according to knowledge, giving honor to the female as to the weaker vessel." (*1 Peter* 3:7).

But whilst I exhort you to cultivate this reciprocal love, you must take care that it turns not to jealousy; for as the worm often breeds in the ripest and most delicate apple, so jealousy arises in the most ardent hearts, spoiling and corrupting love, little by little giving rise to dissension, confusion, and separation. Assuredly, jealousy can find no place where affection is mutually founded on solid virtue, for it is a sure sign of coarse, sensual love arising from a feeble, inconstant, insufficient, mistrusting virtue. It is a vain imagination that love is exalted by jealousy. It may testify that love is great, but not that it is good, pure, and perfect; since the perfection of love presupposes confidence in the virtue of what we love, whereas jealousy presupposes lack of confidence.

And if you, husbands, would have faithful wives, set them the example, be yourselves faithful and pure. And you, wives, be very cautious, and permit no trifling around you. At all times women have been wont to wear pearls at their ears. Pliny assigns as a reason the pleasure that they take in their jingle one against the other. But I, when I remember how God's chosen servant Isaac sent earrings as the first pledge of his love to Rebecca, am inclined to believe rather that the mystical signification is that the first tribute to a husband, and that which a wife should watchfully preserve for him, is her ear, that no sound or language may enter therein, but the sweet music of pure and modest words, which are the pearls of great price of the Gospel; one should always remember that poison enters the soul by the ears, as it enters the body by the mouth.

Love and fidelity always engender confidence; and for this reason saints in the married state have used mutual caresses—caresses truly loving but chaste, tender but sincere. So Isaac and Rebecca, the most chaste married couple of the olden time, by their mutual conduct, at once edified Abimelech and made him to know that they were man and wife. The great St. Louis, equally rigorous towards himself and tender in his love for his wife, was almost blamed for his softness in caressing her, although, in truth, he merited rather praise for knowing how to adapt his brave and martial spirit to these endearments which tend to keep up and nourish the mutual love and affection of husband and wife.

Before the birth of St. Augustine his mother, St. Monica, dedicated him to Christianity and to the glory of God, as he himself tells us, a good lesson to Christian women how they should dedicate to the Divine Majesty the fruit of their womb, for God, who freely accepts the willing obligations of a humble heart, usually causes such dedications to fructify, as in the case of Samuel, St. Thomas Aquinas, St. Andrew of Fiesole, and many others.

The mother of St. Bernard (worthy mother of such a son!) was wont, as soon as her children were born, to offer them to Jesus Christ, thenceforth loving them with reverence as a holy trust given her by God, who so blessed her offering that all the seven were holy. And as soon as children are born into the world and are capable of exercising reason, both parents should carefully seek to impress their hearts with the love of God. This had been the earnest aim of the good Queen Blanche with regard to her son St. Louis, to whom she often said, "I would far rather, dear child, see you dead than guilty of one mortal sin"; words which were so deeply engraved in the heart of that pious prince that he declared no day of his life did he pass without remembering them, and striving to live in accordance with their principles. We speak of races and generations as "houses," and the Jews spoke of their children as "making houses," in which sense it is said that because the Egyptian midwives feared God, "He built them houses" (*Exod.* 1:21), and, therefore, we may learn that men do not found a good "house" by heaping up worldly goods, but by training their children virtuously, and in the fear of God. And to this end no labor should be spared, for children are the crown of their parents. Thus St. Monica so earnestly strove against the evil tendencies of her son that, following him over land and sea she travailed with him through her tears, while working his conversion, still more than she had already done in the flesh.

St. Paul bids women take charge of their household, and many consider that their devotion is more effectual therein than that of their husbands, who are less constantly at home. So Solomon in his Proverbs attributes all household prosperity to the virtuous woman whom he there describes. (*Prov.* 31).

We read in Genesis that Rebecca being barren, Isaac entreated the Lord for her, and his prayer was granted. (*Gen.* 25:21). There is no union so precious and so fruitful between husband and wife as that of holy devotion, in which they should mutually lead and sustain each other. There are some fruits, such as the quince, which are uneatable except when preserved, owing to their bitterness and others, such as the apricot and cherry, which are so delicate that they cannot be kept except they are preserved. So wives should endeavor to soften their husbands with the sugar of devotion, for without it man is but a rough, harsh being; and husbands should encourage their wives in devotion, for without it a woman is weak and frail. St. Paul says that "the unbelieving husband is sanctified by the believing wife, and the unbelieving wife is sanctified by the believing husband." (*1 Cor.* 7:14). Because in the close union of matrimony one may guide the other to virtue. But that is a truly blessed state in which the faithful husband and wife sanctify one another in the sincere fear of the Lord.

This mutual support should be such as never to admit of anger, dissension, or hasty words. Bees cannot dwell where an echo or other loud noise prevails, neither will the Holy Spirit abide in that house which is disturbed by strife, altercation, and noisy discussions.

St. Gregory Nazianzen records that in his time it was the custom to celebrate the anniversary of a wedding. It would be a valuable custom if, instead of worldly feasting and gayety, husbands and wives were to dedicate that day to Confession and Communion, and more than ordinarily fervent prayer; commending their married life to God, and renewing their resolutions of sanctifying it by mutual faithfulness and love, thus, through Christ, taking breath, as it were, in the midst of the cares attending their vocation.

CHAPTER THIRTY-NINE

Further Instructions to the Same

————————•————————

THE marriage bed ought to be undefiled, as the Apostle says (*Heb.* 13.4), that is to say, free from uncleanness and other unlawful deeds. Holy marriage was instituted in the Garden of Paradise, where, as yet, there had never been any disorder of concupiscence, nor anything unbecoming.

There is some resemblance between sexual pleasures and those taken in eating—for both relate to the body; but the former, by reason of their coarse vehemence, are called simply carnal. I shall explain, therefore, what I cannot say of the one by what I shall say of the other.

1. Eating is ordained for our preservation; as, then, eating merely to nourish and preserve a person is a good thing, holy and commanded, so that which is requisite in marriage for the bringing children into the world and multiplying the people, is a good thing and very holy, for it is the principal end of marriage.

2. To eat, not for the preservation of life, but to keep up that mutual intercourse and condescension which we owe to one another, is a thing in itself both lawful and just. So the mutual and lawful compliance of the parties united in holy matrimony is called by St. Paul a debt, a debt, moreover, of so grave a nature that he allows neither of the parties to exempt themselves from it without the voluntary consent of the other;

not even for exercises of devotion, as I have already explained in the chapter on Holy Communion. How much less, then, may they do so through a capricious pretense of virtue, or through anger or disdain.

3.   As those who eat to maintain a mutual intercourse of friendship with others, ought to eat cheerfully and endeavor to show an appetite for their food; so too this debt should be always paid as faithfully and freely as if it were in hopes of having children, although on some occasions there might be no such expectation.

4.   To eat for neither of these reasons, but merely to content the appetite, may be tolerated, but does not deserve praise; for the simple pleasure of the sensual appetite is not sufficient to render an action praiseworthy.

5.   To eat in excess is a thing more or less blamable as the excess is great or little.

6.   One may exceed in eating not only as to quantity, but also as to time and manner of eating. Honey, which is so good and wholesome a food for bees, may sometimes nevertheless become hurtful to them, as when in spring they eat too much of it and become sick and die. In like manner this intercourse, so holy, just, and commendable in itself, and so profitable to the commonwealth, is nevertheless in certain cases dangerous to those who exercise it; for it frequently weakens the soul with venial sin, as in cases of mere and simple excess; and sometimes it kills it with mortal sin, as when the *order* divinely ordained is violated and perverted. For since the bringing of children into the world is the principal end of marriage, to do anything in order to prevent the accomplishment of this end is always mortal sin. Let that, then, which is holy be done holily, even though on account of some accident or circumstance, the end hoped for cannot at that time be brought about; for even in this case it is still just and lawful, so it be done lawfully; no accident whatsoever being able to prejudice the law which the principal end of marriage has imposed.

It is a certain mark of a mean, contemptible spirit to think on eating and food before mealtime; and still more to amuse oneself afterwards with the pleasure which we took in eating, keeping it alive with our words and imagination, and wallowing in the recollection of the sensual satisfaction which we had in swallowing down those morsels; this is the case with those who before their dinner have their minds fixed on the spit, and after dinner on the dishes—men fit to be scullions in a kitchen, who, as St. Paul says, make a god of their belly.

Persons of honor never think of eating but when they sit down to table, and after dinner wash their hands and their mouth that they may neither keep the taste nor the scent of what they have been eating.

Let this serve as a lesson to married people not to keep their affections engaged in those corporal pleasures which, according to their vocation, they have exercised; but when they are past, to wash their heart and affection, and purify themselves from them as soon as possible, that they may the more freely and readily practice other actions more pure and elevated. In this advice consists the perfect practice of the excellent doctrine which St. Paul gives to the Corinthians. "The time is short," said he; "it remains that those who have wives be as if they had none" (*1 Cor.* 7:29); that is, according to St. Gregory, so to live with them as not to be diverted from spiritual exercises. And this, of course, applies as well to the wife as to the husband. "Let those who use the world," says the same Apostle, "be as though they used it not." (*1 Cor.* 7:31). Let each, then, use this world according to his calling, not entangling his heart in it, but keeping himself as free and prompt to serve God as if he used it not. It is the great evil of man, says St. Augustine, to desire to enjoy the things which he ought only to use, and to wish to use those which he ought only to enjoy. We ought to enjoy spiritual things, and merely use those which are corporal; for when we set ourselves to enjoy the latter instead of merely using them, our soul is changed, and from being rational becomes brutal and animal. I have now said all that I wish to say, and have sufficiently implied, without saying it, that which I was unwilling to say.

CHAPTER FORTY

The Widowed

———————————•———————————

S T. PAUL instructs all prelates in the person of St. Timothy, saying, "Honor widows that are widows indeed." Now, to be a "widow indeed" these things are requisite:

1. That the widow be such, not only in body, but in heart; that is, that she have an inviolable resolution to continue in the state of holy widowhood. For those widows who only await the opportunity of marrying again, are separated from men only in bodily presence, but are united to them by the wish of the heart. If the true widow in confirmation of her widowhood, will offer her body and her chastity to God by a vow, she will add a great ornament to her widowhood, and greatly strengthen her resolution; for reflecting that after her vow she can no longer forsake her chastity without forsaking Paradise, she will be so jealous of her design, that she will not permit the least thought of marriage to settle in her heart; but this holy vow will place a strong barrier between her soul and all things contrary to her resolution. St. Augustine strongly recommends this vow to the Christian widow, and the ancient and learned Origen goes further, for he counsels married women to vow and dedicate themselves to widowed chastity, in case their husbands should die before them; so that amidst the sensual pleasures of their marriage they may still enjoy the merit of a

chaste widowhood by means of this anticipated promise. Such a vow renders the deeds which follow it more acceptable to God, strengthens our courage to perform them, and not only gives to God those works which are the fruit of our good will, but also dedicates to Him the will itself, which is the tree of our good actions. By simple chastity we lend our body to God, still retaining the liberty to submit it to sensual pleasures; but by the vow of chastity we give it Him as an absolute irrevocable gift, without reserving any power to recall it, thus happily rendering ourselves His slave, whose service is better than all royalty. And as I greatly approve the counsel of those two great men, so would I have those souls who are so happy as to wish to follow it, to do so prudently, holily, and entirely, after due examination of their own strength, and invocation of divine guidance, and under the counsel of some wise and pious director; and then it will be fruitfully done.

2. Further, this renunciation of a second marriage must be done in purity and simplicity, so as to center all affections more wholly in God, and unite the heart from all sides to that of His Divine Majesty: for if the wish to enrich her children or any other worldly aim induces a widow to remain such, she will have her measure of praise, but not before God, since nothing is praiseworthy in His sight but what is done for Him.

Moreover, the widow who would be truly such must be separate and voluntarily deprived of all profane delights. St. Paul says that, "she who liveth in pleasure, is dead whilst she liveth." To resolve to remain in widowhood, and yet to take delight in flattering attentions and caresses, to frequent balls and festivities, to dress with care and studied elegance, this is to be living indeed in the body, but dead in the soul. What, pray, does it signify whether the sign of Adonis' dwelling be made under a plume of white feathers or under a veil of crape? Indeed sometimes vanity gains most by black, which does but enhance the whiteness of that which it surrounds; and the widow who has already tried the means by which women can best please men, has command of the most perilous wiles. Therefore she who lives in foolish pleasures, is dead while she lives, and in truth is but an idol of widowhood.

"The time of pruning is come: the voice of the turtle is heard in our land" (*Cant.* 2:12), that cutting off of worldly superfluities which is required of all who would live piously: but above all, it is necessary for the true widow, who, like a chaste dove, is yet freshly weeping, lamenting, and groaning over the loss of her husband. When Noemi returned from Moab to Bethlehem, and those of her own city asked, "Is this Noemi?" she answered, "Call me not Noemi (which means gracious and beautiful), call me Mara, for the Almighty hath quite filled me with bitterness," because her husband was dead. And so the devout widow never desires to be called or counted beautiful or gracious, being satisfied to be what God would have her—that is, humble and lowly in His eyes.

Those lamps which are fed with aromatic oil yield the most grateful odor when their flame is extinguished; and so those widows whose married love has been pure, spread abroad the greatest perfume of virtue and chastity where their light, that is their husband, is extinguished by death. It is no great thing to love a husband while he lives, but to love him so much as after his death to refuse all other, is a degree of love only appertaining to true widows. To hope in God whilst sustained by a husband is not so rare; but to hope in Him when destitute of that prop is highly praiseworthy. Wherefore, the perfection of those virtues practiced in marriage are best seen in widowhood.

The widow who has children needing her care and guidance, especially in what concerns their vocation in life and the welfare of their souls, neither can nor ought to abandon them; for St. Paul clearly says that they are bound to take this care of them that they may grow up like their parents, and that whoso does not provide for his own is worse than an infidel; but if the children are in such a position as not to need guidance, then the widow should gather together all her thoughts and affections, and apply them purely to her advancement in the love of God. Unless some imperative cause forces a widow to involve herself in external embarrassments, such as a lawsuit, I should counsel her wholly to abstain from such, and to follow that method of conducting her affairs which will be most peaceful and tranquil, even if it be not the most fruitful. For truly the fruits of such worry must be very great to be compared to the blessing of holy tranquillity; besides, all these and similar disturbing entanglements tend to confuse the mind, and open the way to the enemies of chastity, since, in order to please those whose favor is needed, she must assume indevout manners, unpleasing in God's sight.

Prayer should be the widow's continual exercise, for as she must no longer have love for any save God, neither should she have any words save for Him. And as iron is hindered by the diamond from following the magnet, but approaches it in proportion as the diamond is removed, so the widow's heart which could not rise thoroughly towards God, nor follow His divine attraction wholly during her husband's life, should after his death run hastily after the odor of celestial perfumes, saying with the bride, "O Lord, now that I am mine own, receive me as Thine"; "Draw me: we will run after Thee to the odor of Thy ointments." (*Cant.* 1:3).

The virtues best befitting a holy widow are perfect modesty, renunciation of honors, rank, large assemblies, titles, and all such vanities. Let her serve the poor and the sick, console the afflicted, lead maidens towards a devout life, and set a perfect example of virtue to all young wives. Necessity and simplicity are the ornaments of their attire, humility and chastity of their deeds, purity and cheerfulness of their words, modesty and meekness of their eyes; and Jesus Christ crucified is the sole love of their heart.

In short, a true widow is in the Church as a little spring violet, which while it is hidden amid the large leaves of its lowliness, spreads around unequaled sweetness through devotion, and by its subdued color denotes mortification: it grows in open, uncultivated spots, not seeking the contact of the world, that it may the rather preserve the freshness of heart against the heat which longing after wealth, honor, or love, would arouse. "More blessed shall she be," says the Apostle, "if she so remain." (*1 Cor.* 7:40).

I could say much more on this subject, but I shall say all in advising the widow who is jealous of preserving her widowhood, to study with attention the beautiful epistles which St. Jerome wrote to Furia and Salvia, and all those other women who were so happy as to be the spiritual daughters of such a father; for nothing can be added to what he there says except this—that the true widow should never blame or censure those who enter into second or even third and fourth marriages, for sometimes God thus orders events for the advancement of His glory. And one must always keep in mind that which the Fathers taught, that neither widowhood nor virginity have any merit in Heaven, except that which is assigned to them by humility.

CHAPTER FORTY-ONE

A Word to the Unmarried

———— • ————

I F YOU intend at some future time to marry, preserve with jealousy your first love for your husband. It is a poor fraud to offer a worn, troubled heart, instead of one that is pure and intact. But if you are happily called to a virginal and spiritual marriage, then most watchfully keep your whole heart for that Divine Spouse who, as He is purity itself, can love nothing impure, and to whom we owe the first-fruits of everything, but chiefly of love. You will find much useful counsel in the Epistles of St. Jerome; and inasmuch as your condition involves obedience, seek a guide under whose direction you can with greater holiness dedicate your soul and body to the Divine Majesty.

PART FOURTH

—————•—————

Some Needful Remedies
Against Ordinary Temptations

CHAPTER ONE

We Must Not Give Heed to "What Will the World Say?"

———————————•———————————

A S SOON as the men of the world perceive that you seek the devout life, they will launch forth all their raillery and slander against you; the most ill-natured will pronounce your altered ways to be hypocrisy, affectation, or bigotry; they will assert that the world having slighted you, rejected by it, you turn to God; and your friends will overwhelm you with a torrent of what they hold to be prudent and charitable remonstrances. They will tell you that you will grow morbid and melancholy, that you will lose your position in the world, will be considered insupportable, will become old before your time, that your domestic affairs will suffer, that in the world we must do as the world does, that we can surely be saved without such extravagancies and a thousand similar commonplaces. But all this is foolish, idle gossip, and those who talk thus do not really care either for your health or your fortunes. "If you had been of the world," said our Saviour, "the world would love its own: but because you are not of the world, but I have chosen you out of the world, therefore the world hateth you." (*John* 15:19). We have often seen both men and women pass the whole night, or even several nights running, at cards or chess. What passion can be more wearying, more sad and melancholy than that? Yet no one has a word to say against it, and their friends are not disturbed;

but if we devote an hour to meditation, or rise earlier than usual to prepare for Holy Communion, straightway everybody cries out for the doctor to cure us of the jaundice or of hypochondria. We may spend thirty nights in dancing, and no one will object, but if we do but keep watch on Christmas Eve, there is a great outcry the day following! Who cannot perceive that the world is an unjust judge, partial and indulgent to its own children, but harsh and rigorous towards the children of God.

We can never stand well with the world except by coming to an open breach with it; to satisfy it is impossible, it is too exacting. "John the Baptist came neither eating bread nor drinking wine," saith our Lord, "and you say be hath a devil. The Son of Man is come eating and drinking, and you say, Behold a man that is a glutton and a drinker of wine, a friend of publicans and sinners." (*Luke* 7:33). So it is, if out of compliance we yield, and laugh, play and dance with the world, it will be scandalized; and if we do not, it will accuse us of hypocrisy and gloom. If we wear fine clothes it will impute to us some secret design, and if we are ill-dressed, it will call us mean; it will call our gayety dissolute, and our mortification gloomy; and thus, ever beholding us with an evil eye, nothing that we can do will please it. It will exaggerate our failings, and publish our faults; our venial sins will be construed into mortal sins, sins of infirmity into sins of intention; and whilst, as St. Paul says, "charity is kind," the world is ill-natured. Charity " thinketh no evil," but the world always thinks evil; and if it cannot find fault with our actions, it will attack our motives. Whether the sheep be black or white, have horns or have none, the wolf will devour them all the same if he can.

Whatever we do, the world will find fault; if we spend a long time at Confession, it will ask what we can have to say. If we take but a short time, it will say that we do not tell everything; it will spy out all we do, and from one little hasty word it will pronounce our temper unbearable; it will denounce our prudence as avarice, our gentleness as folly; but as to the children of the world their passions will pass as the fruit of a generous spirit, their avarice as forethought, their lusts as honorable. Spiders invariably spoil the bees' labor.

Never heed this blind world, then; let it cry out as it will, like a bat that would disturb the birds of day. Let us be firm in our plans, unchanging in our resolutions; perseverance will show whether we are in earnest in offering ourselves to God and leading a devout life. Comets and planets are pretty nearly alike in their brightness, but the comets, which are but wandering lights, soon disappear, whilst the planets shine with perpetual brilliancy. So hypocrisy and true virtue have a considerable external resemblance, but they are easily distinguished, since hypocrisy does not endure, but soon vanishes like the rising smoke, whilst true virtue abides firm and constant. There is no small advantage to the confirmation of our rising devotion, in encountering opprobrium and calumny; for by their means we are saved from the dangers of pride and vanity, which are like the midwives of Egypt whom Pharaoh commanded to kill all the male Israelites so soon as they were born. We are crucified to the world, and the world should be crucified to us. It counts us as fools, let us count its votaries as madmen.

CHAPTER TWO

We Must Be of Good Courage

———————•———————

HOWEVER much our eyes may admire and seek the light, they will be dazzled by it after having been long in darkness; and before we become familiar with the inhabitants of a strange land, we shall find subjects of astonishment, however courteous and agreeable they may be. It is very probable that you will have sundry inward struggles in the course of your altered life; and that having taken a thorough farewell of the follies and inanities of the world, you will have some sad and discouraging feelings: if so, only be patient, they will come to nothing, they are but the result of novelty, and once conquered, you will receive endless consolations.

Perhaps at first you will be sorry to lose the glory which you earned in your vanity from the frivolous men of the world; but would you exchange for that the eternal glory which God will surely give you? Those idle pleasures and amusements in which your past years were spent will arise before you, tempting your heart to return to them; but have you courage to forfeit an eternity of bliss for such deceitful trifles? Believe me, with perseverance you will not fail to receive such deeply delicious and heartfelt satisfactions, that you will own the world offers you only gall as compared with this honey, and that one day of devotion is worth more than a thousand years of worldly gratification.

But as you gaze upon the steep mountain of Christian perfection: "Alas!" you exclaim, "how shall I ever ascend it?" Be of good cheer; when the young bees begin to take their form they are called nymphs, and are unable to fly to the neighboring flowers or hills and valleys in search of honey, but by degrees, being fed with the honey provided for them, these little nymphs acquire wings and grow strong enough to fly everywhere in quest of honey. We are as yet but nymphs in devotion, and cannot mount up as we would, for we would fain attain to the summit of Christian perfection; but we are gradually being formed by our desires and resolutions. Our wings are beginning to grow, and so one day we may hope to be perfected and mount upwards. Meanwhile let us feed upon the honey of those pious instructions left to us by holy men of old, and let us beseech God to give us the wings of the dove, so that we may not only fly in this present life, but also find our rest in the eternity of that which is to come.

CHAPTER THREE

The Nature of Temptation, and the Difference Between Feeling It and Yielding to It

———————•———————

REPRESENT to yourself a young princess fondly cherished by her husband, against whose virtue some vile person should make an attempt, sending to her a messenger bearing his hateful overtures. First of all, the messenger would lay his master's propositions before the princess; secondly, she would either give or refuse him audience; and thirdly, she would either consent or reject him. So when Satan, the world, and the flesh behold a soul espoused to the Son of God, they ply her with suggestions and temptations by which, firstly, sin is set before her; secondly, she either takes pleasure in it or the reverse; and thirdly, she either consents or turns away: which in fact are the three degrees by which we fall into sin—temptation, delectation, and consent. And although these three steps may not be so obvious in every ordinary sin, they are palpably evident in great and heinous sins.

Even supposing that temptation to some particular sin were to last our whole life, it would not render us odious in the sight of God so long as we neither took pleasure therein, nor yielded our consent; and that because in temptation we are not active, but passive; and whereas we take no delight therein, neither can we partake of any guilt. St. Paul was grievously tormented by the messenger of Satan, a thorn in his flesh (*2 Cor.* 12:7), but far from being displeasing to God, He was the rather glorified therein. The holy Angela of Foligno was so torn with carnal temptations that we cannot hear of them unmoved; and so grievous were the temptations which assailed St. Francis and St. Benedict, that the one cast himself amidst thorns, and the other into snow in order to allay them; nevertheless they lost nothing of the grace of God thereby, but rather grew in it exceedingly. You must, then, be brave amidst temptations, and never imagine yourself to be conquered so long as they are displeasing to you; keeping clearly in mind the difference between feeling them and consenting to them: this means that you may feel them whilst they displease you, but you cannot consent to them except they please you, since taking pleasure therein is the ordinary step towards consent. So then the enemies of our salvation may offer us as many lures and snares as they will, may even be watching to effect an entrance into our hearts, may make what overtures they please, but so long as we have the resolution to take no pleasure therein we shall no more offend God than the princess, whom I brought forward as an example, would offend her husband whilst she took no delight in the propositions she received. There is, however, one difference between the princess and our soul; the former when she has heard the vile proposition can banish the messenger and hear no more of it; but the soul is not always able to banish temptation, although she is always able to refuse consent; therefore, however long our temptation endures, so long as we detest it we shall be uninjured.

But as to the satisfaction which may ensue upon temptation, inasmuch as our soul has two natures, one inferior the other superior, and the former will not always obey the latter but takes its own course; so sometimes the inferior takes pleasure in temptation without the consent and contrary to the will of the superior. This is that contest and war to which St. Paul alludes when he says that "the flesh lusteth against the spirit" (*Gal.* 5:17), and that he sees a law in his members fighting against the law of his mind. (*Rom.* 7:23).

Did you ever observe a large fire heaped up with cinders? If some ten or twelve hours afterwards you seek the fire, you will barely find a lingering spark in the center of the hearth, and that with difficulty; but since you can discover it, there is undoubtedly some fire left, and it will suffice to rekindle the extinguished fuel. So is it with charity (which is our spiritual life) amidst great and pressing temptations. Temptation exercising its attraction on the inferior nature, as it were, buries the soul in ashes, and seemingly extinguishes the love of God; for it is nowhere to be seen, save in the center and depth of the heart, and even there it is hard to find. Nevertheless, there it is, since, although our whole soul and body are disturbed, we still persevere in the resolution not to consent to sin or to temptation; and that attraction which gratifies the outward man, displeases the inner man; and although it surrounds our will, it has not effected an entrance into it. We see that this attraction is involuntary, and therefore not sinful.

CHAPTER FOUR

Illustration of This Principle

———————•———————

I T IS so important for you to understand this rightly, that I will further furnish you with an example. The whole history of the combat which St. Catherine of Siena endured is most admirable. The substance is as follows:—The devil being permitted by God vehemently to assault her purity so long as he touched her not, filled her heart with all manner of unholy suggestions, and, together with his associates, exposed her to all manner of assaults, which, although they were external, so penetrated her heart, that, according to her own confession, all save her most refined and pure superior will was agitated by the storm. This lasted some time, until at last, beholding her Saviour, she exclaimed, "O my Saviour! Where wert Thou when my heart was so filled with darkness and base thoughts?" To which He replied, "My daughter, I was within thy heart." "How couldst Thou be there," she asked, " when it was so foully tenanted? Dost Thou come into that which is impure?" But He inquired, "Tell me, did these unholy thoughts fill thy heart with pleasure or sadness, with delight or with bitterness?" "With exceeding sadness and bitterness," she made answer. Then He replied, "Who filled thy heart with such sadness except Myself, who was hidden within thy soul? Believe Me, my daughter, had I not been there, these thoughts which assailed thy will, but could not master it, would have conquered and effected their entrance; thou wouldst freely have received them, and thus thy soul had perished; but inasmuch as I was within, I filled thy heart with displeasure and resistance, so that it resisted the temptation to the utmost of its power. Therefore thy sufferings were worthy, and have greatly added to thy virtue and to thy strength!"

Here you see how this fire was heaped over with temptation and attraction, even within her heart and around her will, which yet by our Saviour's aid resisted with bitterness, repugnance, and detestation the suggestion of evil, refusing all consent to sin. O grievous trial, when a soul that loves God knows not whether He is within it or not, or whether or not that divine love for which it combats is wholly extinguished within; but the choicest flower of perfection in heavenly love is when the lover suffers and combats for love, without knowing whether he possesses that love for which and by which he fights.

CHAPTER FIVE

Encouragement for the Tempted Soul

———•———

THESE grievous assaults and powerful temptations are never permitted by God save to those whom He purposes to exalt in His pure and excellent love. Nevertheless they are not on this account certain to attain thereto, for sometimes those who have bravely withstood such violent attacks, do not continue faithful to the divine goodness, but are overcome by little temptations. Therefore should you ever be afflicted by grievous temptations, be sure that God grants you a special favor by which He intimates that He would raise you up before His face; but still be very humble and fearful, not feeling confident that you can overcome trifling temptations because you have overcome greater, except by continual faithfulness to Him.

Whatever temptations, then, assault you, and whatever attraction ensues, so long as your will refuses consent to either, be not afraid, God is not displeased. When a man has swooned, and gives no sign of life, we place our hand upon his heart, and if we find the slightest action there, we decide that he lives, and by the help of some cordial or stimulant, he may be restored to consciousness. Thus sometimes through violent temptations our soul seems to have lost all her strength, and, as in a swoon, to be without spiritual life or motion; but if we would know the truth, we must feel the heart. If the heart and will retain their spiritual

259

action; that is to say, if they persevere in refusing to consent and follow temptation and attraction, the spirit of resistance abides in our heart, and we may be certain that charity, the life of the soul, is yet in us, and that Jesus Christ our Saviour is there, although silently and hidden; so that by continual prayer, participation in the Sacraments, and trust in God, we shall regain our strength, and enjoy a vigorous and blessed life.

CHAPTER SIX

How Temptations and Attraction May Become Sinful

———————•———————

THE princess of whom we spoke could not prevent the vile overtures made to her, since they were offered without her consent; but if, on the other hand, she had in any way sought to attract them, undoubtedly she would be guilty; and however she might draw back, she would still deserve blame and punishment. Thus sometimes mere temptation becomes a sin, if we have brought it upon ourselves. For instance, I know that if I play I easily lose my temper and use bad language, and that play is a temptation to me. In such case I sin whenever I play, and am guilty of whatever temptations may injure me in so doing.

Whenever it is possible to avoid the attraction which accompanies temptation, we sin in encountering it in proportion to the pleasure it gives us, or the consent which we give, be it great or little, for a short or long while. If the princess hearkens at all to the unholy overtures made her, she is to blame; but if, having heard them, she takes pleasure therein, dwelling with satisfaction on them although she would not actually consent to the evil, she still gives the spiritual consent of her heart by her satisfaction. There is impurity in allowing either heart or body to consent to what is impure; and impurity consists so entirely in the consent of the heart, that without it the consent of the body cannot be sin.

If then you are tempted to sin, reflect whether you have voluntarily brought it on yourself; and when the temptation is in itself sinful, whether you have cast yourself into it; that is, whether you might not have avoided the occasion, or have foreseen the temptation. If you have in no way induced it, then it cannot be imputed to you as sin.

When the attraction which follows temptation might have been avoided, and yet has not been so avoided, the measure of sin is according to the duration of its stay, and the degree in which we have accepted it. The woman who although she does not seek idle attentions, yet takes pleasure in them when they are offered, is to blame if those attentions are in themselves pleasing to her. Thus if the man who seeks her plays beautifully on the lute, and she takes delight not in his attentions but in the sweetness and harmony of his music, there is no sin, although she should beware of this delight lest it lead to further delight in the attentions themselves. Or if someone suggests to me an ingenious clever stratagem to avenge me of my enemy, and I give no consent, and take no pleasure in the proposed vengeance, but only in the ingenuity of the stratagem, I am not guilty of sin; although it is dangerous to indulge much in such pleasure lest little by little it lead me to take pleasure in the revenge itself.

Sometimes we are surprised by some lurking attraction quickly following temptation, before we are fairly on our guard; and this cannot exceed a light venial sin, which, however, is aggravated, if, after perceiving the danger, we negligently tamper with the pleasure, hesitating whether to receive or reject it; still more if, having perceived it we remain in it for some time by a true negligence, without any sort of purpose to reject it. But if voluntarily and with deliberation we resolve to take pleasure in such delectation, such deliberate resolution is a grievous sin, supposing that the object of delectation is mortally sinful. It is a great sin in a woman to give heed to unholy love, even although she has no intention of ever yielding to it.

CHAPTER SEVEN

Remedies for Great Temptations

————————•————————

WHENEVER you feel the approach of temptation, imitate a little child who sees a wolf or bear in the plain. He instantly flies into his father's or mother's arms, or at all events calls on them for help and succor. Do you in like manner fly to God, seeking His mercy and help: such is the remedy taught us by Our Lord Himself, "Pray that ye enter not into temptation." (*Matt.* 26:41). If, nevertheless, the temptation continues or increases, hasten in spirit to embrace the holy Cross, as though you beheld Jesus Christ crucified before you; then promise not to yield, and ask His aid to preserve you, and continue to do so whilst the temptation lasts.

But whilst thus protesting and struggling turn your thoughts away from your temptation, and call to mind your Saviour; for if you dwell upon the temptation, it may shake your courage, specially if it be of a violent nature. Divert your mind by some useful, praiseworthy work, for as this enters and occupies your heart, it will banish temptations and evil thoughts. The chief remedy against all temptations, great and small, is to unfold the heart, and lay all its suggestions, inclinations, and feelings before our director; for you may observe that the first pledge which Satan seeks to gain from the soul he seduces, is that of silence. And he who tries secretly to lead a woman into sin, cautions her against informing her father of his overtures; but God would ever have us, on the contrary, make our temptations known to our superiors and guides.

If after all this our temptation still continues to weary and persecute us, we have no further remedy except to persevere in protesting that we will not consent. For just as a maiden cannot be married so long as she refuses her consent, in like manner the soul, however troubled, cannot be injured whilst it refuses its consent.

Do not dispute with the enemy, and give him no answer save one, that with which our Blessed Lord answered and confounded him, "Begone, Satan: for it is written, the Lord thy God shalt thou adore, and Him only shalt thou serve." (*Matt.* 4:10). And just as a faithful wife will neither look at nor hearken to him that would lead her astray, but hastily places her heart under her husband's protection, and without parleying with danger, renews her vows of fidelity to him; so the devout soul, when she is assailed with temptation, must not dally with it by dispute or answer, but simply turn to Jesus Christ her spouse, and renew her protestations of faithfulness to Him, and that she will be ever solely His.

CHAPTER EIGHT

The Importance of Resisting Small Temptations

———•———

ALTHOUGH we must struggle with invincible fortitude against great temptations, and the victories obtained over such are most useful, yet on the whole we gain more by struggling against the lesser temptations which assault us. For although the greater are of a more important nature, the number of lesser temptations is so much more considerable, that the victory over them is worthy to be measured against that over those which are greater but rarer. Doubtless bears and wolves are more dangerous than flies, but they do not cause us so much annoyance and irritation, and consequently do not try our patience as much. It is an easy thing to abstain from murder, but it is very difficult to avoid those angry outbursts which are incessantly aroused within us. It is an easy thing to abstain from adultery, but it is not so easy to be wholly and ceaselessly pure in word, look, thought, and deed; an easy matter not to steal what belongs to another, but harder never to long after and covet it; easy not to bear legal false witness, but hard never to tell lies in our ordinary conversation; easy never to be drunk, but hard to be always perfectly temperate; easy never to desire any man's death, but hard never to desire what will injure him; easy to avoid open defamation, hard not to indulge in disdain. In short, these lesser temptations—anger, suspicion, jealousy, envy, levity, folly, vanity, deception, affectation, artifice, impure thoughts—are the continual trials of the most fervent and devout persons; wherefore we must prepare to resist them with the utmost care and diligence, assured that in proportion to our victories over these petty foes will be the number of jewels in that crown of glory which God makes ready for us in Paradise. Therefore, whilst we are prepared to contend bravely and well against great temptations whensoever they assail us, let us in the meanwhile be diligent in resisting these lesser, more trifling attacks.

CHAPTER NINE

How to Remedy Such Temptations

THESE trifling temptations of vanity, suspicion, vexation, jealousy, envy, levity, and similar failings, which are ever hovering before our eyes like flies and gnats, now stinging one cheek, now the other, inasmuch as it is impossible to be wholly free from their importunity, will be most effectually combated by our not allowing them to torment us; for although they annoy us, they cannot do us any real harm so long as we are firm in our resolution to serve God. Treat such assaults, then, with contempt, and do not even condescend to inquire what they mean, but let them hum and buzz about your ears as they will, and attend to them no more than you would to flies; and even if they sting you, do not let them remain in your heart, be content with simply driving them away; neither fighting with them, nor parleying with them, but merely making contrary acts—above all, acts of the love of God. I would not have you persevere in making these acts in opposition to the prevailing temptation, for that would resemble a contest; but after having made an act in direct opposition, if you have had time to ascertain the nature of the temptation, merely turn your heart towards Jesus Christ crucified, and making an act of love to Him, kiss His sacred feet. This is the best way of overcoming the enemy, whether in little or great temptations; for as the love of God includes the perfection of all virtues (and that more excellently than the virtues themselves), so is it a sovereign remedy against all vices; and if your mind is accustomed to seek that refuge in all temptations, it will not need to contemplate and examine them, but as soon as it is disturbed it will turn to its shelter, which, furthermore, is so obnoxious to the Evil One that when he perceives that his temptations only provoke us the more to that divine love, he will cease to attack us.

Such is my advice with regard to these trifling and frequent temptations, which if dealt with individually would waste our time and weaken our strength.

CHAPTER TEN

How to Arm the Heart against Temptation

———————————————●———————————————

FROM time to time examine what passions predominate in your soul, and having ascertained them, let your way of life be altogether opposed to them in thought, word, and deed. For instance, if you know that you have a tendency to vanity, often reflect on the misery of our present life, how these vanities will weigh upon your conscience on your deathbed, how unworthy they are of a noble heart, that they are but a childish trifling, and so forth. Often speak in opposition to your vanity, and despise it, however reluctantly, thus making yourself, as it were, its enemy; for by dint of opposing anything, we gradually learn to hate it, although we may have begun by loving it. Perform as many acts of abjection and humility as you can, in spite of your reluctance; for by this means you will weaken your vanity and strengthen your humility, so that when temptation arises your inclination will be less favorable to it, and you will have more power to resist it. If you are disposed to avarice, often reflect on the folly of this sin, which makes us the slave of that which is destined only to be our servant: remember that when death comes you must forsake all, and leave your riches in the hands of those who will squander them, or abuse them to their own ruin and damnation, and so forth. Condemn avarice, and be warm in praises of the opposing virtue; exert yourself to be generous in almsgiving and charity, and in occasionally forbearing to seize occasions of gain.

If you are inclined to trifle with the affections, either exciting or being excited with love, reflect how dangerous an amusement this is, both to yourself and others: how unworthy a thing it is thus to trifle with and profane the noblest affections of the soul, and how it leads to excessive levity of mind; cultivate purity and simplicity of heart, and conform your actions to such a temper, avoiding all affectations and flirtations.

Finally, in time of peace, that is when you are not under the pressure of those temptations to which you are most subject, carefully practice the opposite virtue; and if occasions do not present themselves, go out of your way to seek them: and thus you will strengthen your heart against future temptation.

CHAPTER ELEVEN

Anxiety

———————•———————

ANXIETY, or disquietude, is not merely a temptation itself, but it is a source from which and by which several other temptations arise. Sadness is that mental pain which is caused by the involuntary evils which affect us; whether they be external, such as poverty, sickness, and contempt; or whether they be inward, such as ignorance, dryness, aversion, and temptation. Thus when the soul is conscious of some such evil, she is dissatisfied because of it, and this produces sadness; forthwith she desires to be free from it, and seeks the means thereto; and so far she is right, for it is natural in us all to desire that which is good and avoid that which we hold to be evil.

If the soul seeks means of deliverance for the love of God, she will seek them with patience, gentleness, humility and calmness, rather awaiting such deliverance from the goodness and providence of God than from her own exertions, industry, or diligence. But if it is through self-love that she seeks deliverance, she will be eager and restless in the search of means thereto, as though it depended more on herself than on God. I do not say that she considers this to be so, but that she acts as though it were. Consequently, if she does not speedily find what she desires, she becomes impatient and greatly disturbed. This, instead of diminishing the original evil, makes it worse, and the soul is distressed and grieved beyond measure, her courage and strength failing, so that she believes her trouble to be irremediable. Thus you see how an uneasiness which in the beginning is justifiable, engenders disquietude, which in its turn brings on an increase of anxiety which is highly dangerous.

Anxiety is the soul's greatest enemy, sin only excepted. Just as internal disturbance and seditions ruin a commonwealth, and make it unfit for resisting external aggression, so when the heart is anxious and disquieted within itself, it loses the power to preserve those virtues which are already acquired, and also the means of resisting the temptations of Satan, who does not fail (as the saying is) to fish in such troubled water.

Anxiety proceeds from an ill-regulated desire to be delivered from the evil we experience, or to acquire the good to which we aspire; nevertheless, nothing aggravates evil and hinders good so much as anxiety and worry. When birds are taken in a snare or net they cannot escape, because they flutter and make all kinds of disorderly exertions to get free, by means of which they do but entangle themselves the more. Therefore, if you earnestly desire to be delivered from some evil, or to attain to some good, above all things calm and tranquilize your mind, and compose your judgment and will; then quietly and gently pursue your aim, adopting suitable means with some method. When I say pursue them *quietly*, I do not mean *negligently*, but without hurry, care, or disquietude; otherwise instead of obtaining your end, you will spoil all, and be but the more embarrassed.

"My soul is continually in my hands: and I have not forgotten Thy law," was the exclamation of David. (*Ps.* 118:109). Frequently during the day if you can, but at least night and morning, examine yourself whether your soul is in your hand, or if it has not been snatched thence by some passion or anxiety. Examine whether your heart is under your control, or if it has not escaped thence in pursuit of some ill-regulated emotion of love, hate, envy, lust, fear, vexation, or joy. And if it has strayed, before all things seek it, and softly lead it back into the presence of God; steadying your affections and desires under His guidance and in obedience to His holy Will. Just as those who fear to lose some precious treasure hold it carefully in their hand, so, imitating King David, we should always say, "My God, my soul is troubled, but it is always in my hand, therefore do I not forget Thy law."

However small and insignificant your desires may be, do not allow them to disquiet you, for if you do, they will be followed by greater and more important desires, which will find your heart more disposed to anxiety and disorder. When you feel disposed to worry, commend yourself to God, and resolve in no way to gratify your desire until your anxiety is entirely allayed: unless it concerns something which cannot be deferred, in which case you must gently and quietly restrain the course of your desire, softening and moderating it as much as possible, and, above all, acting not in accordance with your inclination, but with reason.

If you can disclose your anxiety to the guide of your soul, or at least to some pious and trustworthy friend, doubt not that you will be speedily relieved; for sympathy in the sufferings of the heart has the same effect upon the soul as bleeding upon the body of one laboring under grievous fever; it is the most effectual remedy. Thus St. Louis counseled his son, "If thy heart be ill at ease, hasten to open it to thy confessor, or to some pious person, and by means of his comfort thou wilt be enabled easily to bear thine affliction."

CHAPTER TWELVE

Sadness

———————•———————

"THE sorrow that is according to God," saith St. Paul, "worketh penance steadfast unto salvation: but the sorrow of the world worketh death." (*2 Cor.* 7:10). Therefore sorrow may be either good or bad, according to its results upon us. Undoubtedly there are more bad than good results from it; for the good results are but two, namely, penitence and mercy; whilst there are six evil results—anguish, indolence, indignation, jealousy, envy, and impatience; wherefore the Wise Man said, "Sadness hath killed many, and there is no profit in it" (*Ecclus.* 30:25), since from its source spring but two good and six evil rivers. It is only towards the good that the enemy employs sorrow as a temptation, for inasmuch as he seeks to make sinners take delight in their sin, so he seeks to make good works grievous to the good; and as he can only lead the one to evil by making it seem agreeable, so can he only deter the other from what is good by making it seem disagreeable. Satan delights in sadness and melancholy since he himself is sad and melancholy, and will be so to all eternity, a condition which he would have all to share with him.

Unholy sorrow disturbs the soul, disquiets her, arouses vain fears, disgusts her with prayer, overpowers the brain and makes it drowsy, deprives the soul of wisdom, resolution, judgment, and courage, and crushes her strength: in short, it resembles a hard winter, which withers the beauty of the earth and numbs all life, for it deprives the soul of all suppleness, rendering all her faculties of no avail and powerless. If you are ever assailed by this hurtful sadness adopt the following remedies— "Is any among you sad?" asks St. James, "let him pray." (*James* 5:13). Prayer is a sovereign remedy, for it raises the soul to God, who is our only joy and consolation; but in prayer let your emotions and words, whether inward or outward, conduce to trust and love of God; such as, O God of pity, Merciful and Good God, Loving Saviour, God of my heart, my Joy, my Hope, my Beloved Spouse, Beloved of my soul, and such as these.

Vigorously check the inclination to sadness, and although you seem to do everything coldly, sadly, and without fervor, go on all the same; for the enemy would fain enfeeble our good works by sadness, and when he finds that we will not discontinue them, and that they are but the more meritorious through resistance, he will cease to annoy us.

Refresh yourself with spiritual songs, which have often caused the tempter to cease his wiles; as in the case of Saul, whose evil spirit departed from him when David played upon his harp before the king. (*1 Kings* 16:23). It is also useful to be actively employed, and that with as much variety as may be, so as to divert the mind from the cause of its sadness, and to purify and enliven the mind, for sadness is a cold, withering passion.

Also make use of outward acts of fervor, even though you have no delight in them; such as embracing the crucifix, pressing it to your heart, kissing the hands and feet hanging thereon, raising your eyes and your hands to heaven, and calling upon God with words of love and reliance, such as, "My beloved is mine, and I am His." (*Cant.* 2:16). "A bundle of myrrh is my beloved to me . . . a cluster of myrrh my love." (*Cant.* 1:12-13). "My eyes have failed for Thy word, saying: When wilt Thou comfort me?" (*Ps.* 118:82). "O God, Thou art my God; my soul thirsteth for Thee—and it shall be filled." (*Ps.* 62:2-6). "Who shall separate us from the love of Christ?" (*Rom.* 8:35), and so forth. The discipline in moderation is useful in overcoming sadness, because this voluntary external affliction produces internal consolation; and the soul experiencing outward pain is distracted from that which is within; frequent Communion is an excellent remedy, for that heavenly Food strengthens the heart and gladdens the spirit.

Make known to your confessor and guide all the emotions, cares, and suggestions which spring from your sadness, with faithfulness and humility; seek the society of devout persons as much as is practicable; and above all resign yourself into God's hands, disposing yourself to suffer your grievous sadness with patience, as the fitting punishment for your vain joys; and never doubt that when God has sufficiently tried you, He will set you free from this trial.

CHAPTER THIRTEEN

Actual and Spiritual Consolations, and How to Receive Them

———————•———————

GOD maintains this mighty earth in a state of perpetual vicissitude, by which day is ever changing to night, spring to summer, summer to autumn, autumn to winter, and winter to spring; neither do any two days entirely resemble one another; some are cloudy, others rainy, dry, or windy, and this variety gives a great beauty to creation. Even so is man, whom the ancients called an epitome of the world. He never abides in the same condition; his earthly life flows on like the waters, ebbing and flowing with an endless diversity, sometimes raising him with hopes, sometimes lowering him with fears; now inclining him to the right hand with consolations, now to the left with afflictions; nor are any two days or even hours of his life altogether alike.

Now it is necessary that we should strive after a continual and unalterable evenness of spirit in the midst of such unevenness of matter. And although all things around us change and vary, we must ever remain content and unmoved in looking, seeking, and longing after our God. Let the ship take what course you will, let her steer to east or west, north or south, and be borne about by whatsoever wind, never will the needle of her compass cease to point towards the pole. Let everything be overcast and overturned, not only around us, but within us; that is to say, let our soul be sad or joyful, in sweetness or bitterness, in peace or in trouble, in darkness or in light, in temptation or in repose, in satisfaction or disgust, in dryness or consolation, burnt with the sun or refreshed with the dew; however it be, still the needle of our heart, our mind, and our superior will, which is our compass, must ceaselessly and perpetually tend to the love of God its Creator, its Saviour, its only and Sovereign Good. "Whether we live, we live unto the Lord; and whether we die, we die unto the Lord," says the Apostle (*Rom.* 14:8); and again, "Who shall separate us from the love of Christ?" (*Rom.* 8:35). No, nothing shall separate us from that love, neither tribulation nor distress, nor death, nor life, nor present sorrow, nor fear of things to come, nor the devices of evil spirits, nor the height of consolation, nor the depth of affliction, nor softness nor dryness—nothing shall separate us from that holy charity which is rooted and built up in Jesus Christ.

This absolute resolution never to forsake God, or leave His tender love, serves to balance our souls, and preserve them in holy evenness, amidst the unevenness of this life's restless motion. For just as bees, when they are carried about with the wind, cling to stones in order that they may keep their balance, and not be so at the mercy of the storm; so when our soul has heartily and with true purpose embraced the precious love of God, she remains unmoved and faithful amidst the inconstancy and vicissitudes of joys and sorrows, whether spiritual or temporal, external or internal.

But besides this general principle, we require some special rules.

1. I would say, then, that devotion does not consist in that sweetness, consolation, and visible tenderness, which provokes tears and sighs, and gives us a certain agreeable savor and satisfaction in our spiritual exercises. No, this is not the same thing as devotion; for there are many souls which experience these enjoyments and consolations, and nevertheless are vicious, and, consequently, have no true love of God, much less any true devotion.

When Saul was pursuing to the death David, who fled before him into the wilderness of Engaddi, he entered into a cave where David and his men were hidden. David, who could easily have killed him, spared his life, and would not even alarm him; but having let him go forth unmolested, he cried after him in order to prove his own innocence and to show the king that he had been at his mercy. What did not Saul then do, to show how his heart was softened towards David? He called him his son, he lifted up his voice and wept, acknowledging David's goodness, beseeching the Lord to recompense him, foretelling his future greatness, and bespeaking his mercy towards his own posterity. (*1 Kings* 24). What greater love and tenderness of heart could he have displayed? And yet he had not really changed in spirit, but ceased not to persecute David as cruelly as before. So there are some persons who, when they reflect on the goodness of God and the Passion of Christ, are powerfully moved to sighs, tears, prayers, and other devout actions, whence you might suppose that their hearts were seized with a very fervent devotion. But when they are tried, we find, that as the passing rains of a hot summer, though they fall heavily on the earth, do not penetrate it, and bring forth only mushrooms, even so these tears and emotions in a corrupt heart do not penetrate it, and are altogether fruitless, since all the same these unhappy men would not give up one farthing of their unjustly acquired wealth or renounce one of their perverse affections, nor would they endure the slightest suffering in the service of that Saviour over whom they have wept; so that their good impulses were but as spiritual mushrooms, and were not only no true devotion, but too often deep wiles of Satan, who, whilst he amuses souls with such vain consolations, induces them to remain satisfied with such, instead of seeking true and solid devotion, which consists in a constant, resolute, prompt, and active will to execute what we know to be pleasing to God.

A child will cry bitter tears if he sees the lancet prick his mother who is bled; but if at the same time the mother for whom he weeps asks for an apple or a sugar-plum which he has in his hand, he will refuse to give it up. Such are too often our tender impulses of devotion. We behold the lance piercing the Heart of our crucified Lord, and we weep piteously. Alas! Well may we weep over the bitter death and Passion of our Saviour and Redeemer; but why, then, do we not heartily give Him the apple we hold in our hands, and which He demands so earnestly? That is our heart, the only fruit of love which that Blessed Saviour requires of us. Why we do not give up to Him the many low affections, attractions, and pleasures which He would take from us but cannot, because they are the sugar-plums which we prefer to His heavenly grace? Surely this is but the attachment of little children; affectionate indeed, but weak, capricious, and ineffective! And so devotion does not lie in this tenderness, these visible emotions, which sometimes are only the result of a yielding, susceptible disposition, sometimes a deceit of Satan, who would fain keep us thus diverted, and so excites our imagination accordingly.

2. These emotions and affections are, however, at times good and useful, for they excite the soul's appetite, comfort the mind, and add to the earnestness of devotion a holy joy and gladness which renders even our outward actions comely and agreeable. It was such a taste for heavenly things that roused David to cry out, "Oh, how sweet are Thy words to my palate! More than honey to my mouth." (*Ps.* 118:103). And assuredly the smallest religious consolation we receive is in every way superior to the most delectable worldly joys. And just as those who chew the herb Cytisus are so satisfied with its sweetness that they feel neither hunger nor thirst, so those to whom God has given the celestial manna of His inward sweetness and consolations, cannot seek or receive those of the world, or, at all events, cannot take delight or rest their affections in them. Such heavenly consolations are as foretastes of the eternity of bliss which God gives to those souls who seek it. They resemble the sugared bribes we give to children; they are as cordial waters given by God to comfort the soul, and sometimes they are the pledges of everlasting rewards. It is said that Alexander the Great sailing in the open sea first discovered Arabia Felix by means of the fragrance which the winds bore thence, which reinvigorated his courage and that of his companions. Thus do we often inhale fragrance and sweetness in the sea of this mortal life, which doubtless are a foretaste

and presentiment of the delights of that happy celestial country after which we aspire and long.

3. But, you will ask, since there are some sensible consolations which are good and come from God, and yet at the same time there are also some which are useless, dangerous, and even pernicious, arising from natural disposition, or even from Satan himself, how am I to discern one from the other, and distinguish the good from those that are bad or useless? The general rule concerning the passions and emotions of our souls is that we should know them by their fruits; our hearts are as trees, our affections and passions are the branches, and their actions and deeds the fruit. That heart is good which is inspired with good affections, and those affections and emotions are good which result in good and holy actions. If our emotions, tender inspirations, and consolations make us more humble, patient, forbearing, charitable, and compassionate towards our neighbor, more earnest in mortifying our evil inclinations and lusts, more persevering in devout exercise, more docile and pliable towards those whom we are bound to obey; then, doubtless, they come from God. But if such sweetnesses do not make us sweet, if they make us reckless, irritable, punctilious, impatient, obstinate, proud, presumptuous, harsh towards our neighbors, and if, counting ourselves as already holy, we are unwilling to submit to direction and correction—doubtless such as these are false and pernicious consolations. A good tree will bring forth good fruit.

4. If we enjoy much sweetness and consolation, we must humble ourselves profoundly before God, and beware of saying on account of such favors, How good I am! No, for such advantages do not prove us good, nor, as I have said, does devotion consist in them; let us rather say, Oh, how good God is to those who love Him, and to the soul that seeks after Him! He who eats sugar cannot say that his mouth is sweet, but rather that the sugar is sweet; and thus although our spiritual sweetness is good, and God who gives it us is very good, it by no means follows that we who receive it are good. Let us acknowledge that we are as yet but little children, who need to be fed with milk, and that these

sugared delights are given us only out of indulgence to our tender delicacy, which requires bribes and lures to draw it to the love of God. But as a general thing let us receive these graces and favors humbly, prizing them highly, not so much for their own worth, as because God accords them to our hearts, like a mother who coaxes her child, feeding him herself with sugar plums one at a time. If that child has any affection, he will value his mother's coaxing caresses more than the sweetmeats themselves. And thus it is a great thing to enjoy spiritual sweetness, but their crown is the thought that God Himself, with His tender loving hand, puts them into our mouth, our heart, our mind, and our soul. Having received them in all humility, let us give good heed that we use them according to the intention of the giver. Wherefore does God afford us such delights? In order to make us gentle towards all men, and loving towards Himself. The mother caresses her child so that he may kiss her: let us kiss the Saviour who gives us such blessings; and to kiss Him is to obey Him, to keep His commandments, to do His Will, to follow His precepts, in short, to embrace Him tenderly with obedience and faith.

And when we have enjoyed some spiritual consolation, we should take occasion to strive more diligently after humility and good works. Further, from time to time we should renounce all such sweetness and consolations, withdrawing our hearts from them, and protesting that although we accept them humbly, and delight in them because God grants them to us, and because they kindle our love for Him, still it is not such gratifications that we seek, but God and His holy love; not the comfort, but the Comforter; not the sweetness, but the most sweet Saviour; not the delight itself, but Him who is the delight of Heaven and earth; and with such feelings we should dispose ourselves to abide steadfast in His holy love, even though our life long we were to know no consolation; willing always to say, "Lord, it is good to be where Thou art, in glory or in agony," be it on Mount Calvary or on Mount Thabor.

And, lastly, I advise that if you experience any remarkable abundance of such spiritual delights, tears, and consolations, to take counsel concerning them with your director, so that he may teach you how to moderate and apply them; as it is written, "Thou hast found honey, eat what is sufficient for thee." (*Prov.* 25:16).

CHAPTER FOURTEEN

Dryness and Spiritual Barrenness

———————— • ————————

I HAVE given you instructions for the times of consolation; but such pleasant seasons will not always endure. On the contrary, at times you will be so deprived and destitute of all devout feeling that you will imagine your soul to be a desert, fruitless, sterile land, wherein is no path or road leading to God, nor any water-springs of grace which can moisten the dryness that threatens to reduce it to dust. Alas! The soul that experiences this is truly to be pitied, above all, when the distress is pressing; for then, like David, tears are her meat day and night, whilst Satan mocks her with a thousand suggestions, hoping to reduce her to despair, and inquiring, "Where is now thy God? How wilt thou find Him? Who will restore to thee the joy of His holy grace?"

What are you to do then? Take good heed whence the evil arises. We ourselves are often the cause of our own dryness and barrenness. Just as a mother refuses to give sugar to her sick child, so God deprives us of spiritual consolations, if they arouse a vain complacency within us and cause our souls to be spiritually sick. It is well for me, O my God, that Thou humblest me, for before I was afflicted I went astray! Again, if we neglect to profit by the sweetness and delight of God's love whilst He grants it, He will withdraw it as a punishment of our indolence. Those Israelites who did not gather the manna in the morning could no longer find it, for, when the sun waxed hot, it melted. (*Exod.* 16:21).

Sometimes we repose on the bed of sensual delights and perishable consolation, even as the Bride in the Canticles. The Bridegroom of our heart knocks at the door of our soul, and excites us to resume our spiritual activity; but we parley with Him, because we are unwilling to forsake our vain pleasures and false delights. Therefore He withdraws Himself, and when we seek Him, it is hard to find Him: and truly we have deserved that it should be so, since we have been so disloyal and faithless to His love as to refuse it for the love of the world. If you seek the flesh of Egypt, you will not receive the manna of Heaven. Bees detest all artificial scents, and the sweetness of the Holy Spirit cannot be combined with the deceitful pleasures of the world.

Sometimes spiritual dryness and barrenness are produced by the practice of duplicity and prevarication in Confession and communication with your director; for if you lie to the Holy Ghost, what marvel is it that He refuses you His consolations? If you will not be simple and sincere as a little child, you cannot have the sweet reward of childlike simplicity. And so if you have steeped your heart in worldly gratifications, no wonder that spiritual delights have lost their charm. The Blessed Virgin said, "He hath filled the hungry with good things, and the rich He hath sent away empty." Those who are rich in the pleasures of the world, have no taste for such as are spiritual.

If you have carefully preserved the fruit of past consolations, they will, doubtless, be renewed; for to him that hath much shall more be given; but from him that hath not, who through his own fault has lost what was given him, shall be taken away even that which he hath, that is, those favors which were prepared for him. Rain refreshes those plants which are alive, but it destroys all lingering vitality in those which are not, and causes them to perish and decay. For these several causes, then, we lose our spiritual consolations, and sink into dryness and mental sterility.

Carefully examine your conscience, and see whether you discover any such faults; but do so without anxiety or undue painstaking, and having faithfully considered your conduct, if you discover the root of the evil to be in yourself, thank God, for the evil is half cured when you have ascertained the cause. But, if, on the contrary, you do not discover any especial cause for such dryness, do not yield to a more prying research. Without further efforts simply follow these rules—

1. Humble yourself profoundly before God, acknowledging your misery and nothingness. Alas! What am I when left to myself? Nothing better, O Lord, than a dry ground which by its cracks and crevices testifies how it thirsts after the rain of heaven, whilst yet the wind disperses its soil in dust.

2. Call upon God, and ask His gladness. "Restore unto me the joy of Thy salvation." (*Ps.* 50:14). "My Father, if it be possible, let this chalice pass from Me." (*Matt.* 26:39). Depart, O cold unfruitful wind that driest up my soul, and "Come, O south wind, blow through my garden, and let the aromatical spices thereof flow." (*Cant.* 4:16).

3. Go to your confessor, open your soul entirely to him, reveal to him thoroughly all the folds of your heart, and receive his counsels with the utmost simplicity and humility; for God who very highly esteems obedience, often blesses the advice we receive from others, especially from the guides of souls, even when such a result appears but unlikely, just as He caused Naaman to receive healing in the river Jordan, whither Eliseus had sent him, without any human probability of success. (*4 Kings* 5).

4. But after all, no course is so good or so useful amid such dryness and sterility as not to yield to, and be over eager in, the wish for deliverance from them. I do not mean that you may not wish to be delivered, but that you must not passionately desire it, but place yourself at the entire disposal of God's Providence, willing that He should do what He will with you amidst your thorns and your desires. At such seasons say, "O my Father, if it be possible, let this chalice pass from me," but do not fail to add with all your heart, "Not my will, but Thine be done!" And in that repose as tranquilly as possible: for when God beholds in us this holy submission, He will console us with graces and favors, as

when He saw Abraham resolved to sacrifice his son Isaac, He was content with his perfect and entire resignation, and comforted him with a holy vision, and with abundant blessings. Therefore, in all manner of afflictions, whether bodily or spiritual, and in all distraction or loss of fervent devotion, we should say with our whole heart and with the deepest submission, "The Lord gave (my consolations), and the Lord hath taken away: blessed be the name of the Lord." (*Job* 1:21). If we persevere in such humility, He will restore to us His gracious favor, as He did to Job, who ever thus received all his trials.

5. Finally, amidst all our dryness and barrenness, let us be of good courage, and waiting patiently for the return of consolations, let us go on our way. Let us omit no devotional exercise, but rather, if possible, increase our good works; and if we cannot bring fresh fruits to our Beloved, let us at least offer those that are dry; for to Him all are the same, so long as they are offered by a heart wholly resolved to love Him. When the spring is fine, the bees abound more in honey than in young, for they devote themselves rather to gathering honey than to the propagation of their race, but if the spring be cloudy and cold, they increase their young the more, not being able to go forth in search of honey. Thus frequently the soul finds itself in the bright springtime of spiritual consolations, and in her eagerness to enjoy and amass them she slackens in the performance of good works; whilst, on the contrary, in proportion as she finds herself deprived of the pleasures of devotion, so much does she multiply her good works, and abounds in the inward increase of virtue, patience, humility, self-renunciation, resignation, and self-abnegation.

It is then a great mistake, and one to which women are especially liable, to imagine that a tasteless, emotionless, cold service is less acceptable to God; since our actions are like the rose, which is more pleasing when it is fresh, but has a more powerful scent when it is dry. So although those works which we perform with a kindled heart are more agreeable to us, who consider only our own gratification, yet, if they are performed amidst drought and barrenness, they are more costly and fragrant unto God. And that because in seasons of dryness our will makes us serve God as it were by main force, and consequently our service is more vigorous and faithful than in a milder season. There is little merit in serving a prince amidst the pleasures of peace and the delights of a court; but to serve him amidst the hardships of war, amidst trials and persecutions, that is a true sign of faithfulness and constancy.

Blessed Angela of Foligno says that the prayer most acceptable to God is that which is made forcibly and with constraint; that is, which we undertake not from our own taste or inclination, but solely in order to please God, to which we are as it were driven by our will, conquering and doing violence to the repugnance and dryness which we feel. It is the same as regards all other good works, for the more reluctance we feel towards their performance (be it external or internal), so much the more precious and estimable are they in the sight of God. The less self-interest we have in the pursuit of virtue, the greater therein will be the purity and brightness of divine love. The child embraces his mother when she gives him sugar, but it is a greater sign of love if he embrace her when she has given him wormwood or camomile.

CHAPTER FIFTEEN

An Example and Illustration

———————•———————

IN ORDER to illustrate what I have said, I will give you a passage
from the life of St. Bernard as it is related by a wise and learned
writer.

It is a common thing for nearly all who are just beginning to serve
God, and are not as yet accustomed to the withdrawal of His sensible
grace, or to the vicissitudes of the spiritual life, when they lose the
flavor of fervent devotion and the pleasant light which beckons them
forward on the path heavenward, to lose courage suddenly, and sink
into despondency and sadness of heart. And those who are experienced
in this say that it is because human nature cannot remain long hungry,
without any gratification, either heavenly or earthly. And inasmuch as
souls raised above themselves, by the enjoyment of spiritual delights,
easily renounce visible objects; when by God's disposal their spiritual
joy is taken away, and they being likewise bare of temporal joys, and
not being as yet accustomed patiently to wait the return of their true
sun, imagine themselves to be neither in heaven nor on earth, but to
be buried in perpetual darkness; wherefore, they languish and groan,
becoming burdensome and wearisome, above all to themselves. Such
was the case, during the journey of which I speak, with a member of the
company, by name Geoffrey de Péronne, who was but newly dedicated

to the service of God. Geoffrey, becoming suddenly dry and barren of consolation, and absorbed with his inward darkness, began to recur to thoughts of his worldly friends, his relatives, and the worldly goods which he had forsaken. Through such thoughts his temptation grew so strong that he could not hide it, and one of his most intimate companions perceiving it in his countenance, prudently addressed him with tender words, privately asking, "What is this, Geoffrey? Why art thou, contrary to thy wont, thus pensive and sorrowful?" Then he with a heavy sigh made answer, "Alas, my brother, never in my lifetime shall I taste joy again." The other being moved to pity by his words, with fraternal zeal hastened to inform their common father St. Bernard of what had passed. Bernard, perceiving the danger, entered a church hard by in order to pray for him. Meanwhile Geoffrey, overcome with sadness, reclined his head against a stone and fell asleep. But after a little while both arose, one imbued with the grace of prayer, and the other waking from his slumber with so serene and cheerful a countenance that his friend, marveling at so great and sudden a change, could not refrain from gently reproaching him with the words he had so lately uttered, whereupon Geoffrey answered, "If then I told thee that I should never be glad, now I assure thee that I shall never be sorrowful!" Such was the effect of temptation on this pious man: and I would have you thence observe:

1. That God generally gives to those who enter His service some foretaste of heavenly joy, in order to lead them from earthly delights, and to encourage them in the pursuit of divine love.

2. That it is equally this good God who occasionally, in His wisdom, takes from us the milk and honey of consolation, in order that then we may learn to eat the dry but solid bread of a vigorous devotion, practiced amidst the trials of disgust and temptation.

3. That sometimes fierce temptations arise out of these drynesses and sterilities, and that we must steadily resist these temptations; but the dryness we must bear patiently, since God has appointed it for our trial.

4. That we must never lose our courage amidst our inward troubles, nor say with the good Geoffrey, I shall never be happy; for during the night we should await the day, and even so, amidst the brightest spiritual sunshine we should never say, "I shall never be sad"; but, as the Wise Man says, "In the day of good things be not unmindful of evils." (*Ecclus.* 11:27). Hope amidst trials, and fear amidst prosperity, and in both always humble yourself.

5. That our sovereign remedy is to discover our grief to some spiritual friend who is able to console us.

And finally, I would observe that, as in all other things, so here our merciful God and our great enemy have opposite aims; for by these trials God would lead us to get purity of heart, to entire renunciation of our own interest where His service is concerned, and to a perfect setting aside of self. Satan would convert them rather into occasions of discouragement, to make us fall back upon sensual delights, as also to make us wearisome to ourselves and to others, thereby to decry and disgrace the flame of holy devotion; but if you follow the counsels I have given you, you will greatly increase your perfection by the trials you undergo amidst these inward afflictions, of which I would say yet one word more.

Sometimes disinclination, dryness, and barrenness of heart proceed from bodily indisposition, as when owing to an excess in watching, fasting, and labor, we are overcome with lassitude, drowsiness, heaviness, and similar infirmities. Although these depend upon the state of the body, still they hinder the mind, the two being so closely linked together. Now, when such is the case, we should strive to perform sundry acts of virtue with the full strength of the mind and will, for although the soul may seem to be slumbering, overpowered with weariness and exhaustion, yet these mental acts are still highly acceptable to God.

And at such times we may say with the Bride, "I sleep, but my heart waketh." (*Cant.* 5:2). And as I said before, if there is less pleasure in such exertions, there is more merit. But the fitting remedy in such a case is to reinvigorate the body by means of some lawful relaxation and recreation. It was one of St. Francis' rules for his religious, that they should always keep their labors within such bounds as never to overwhelm the fervor of their spirit.

This holy father himself was once assailed and troubled by so deep a melancholy that he could not conceal it in his exterior deportment. If he wished to converse with his monks, he was unable; if he absented himself from them, it did but make him worse; abstinence and bodily mortifications overpowered him, and he found no relief in prayer. For two years he was in this condition, so that he appeared to be wholly forsaken of God; but at last, after he had endured the heavy storm in all humility, our Saviour suddenly restored him to a happy tranquillity. Thus God's chosen servants are subject to such trials, and those less worthy should not greatly marvel if they too are tried.

PART FIFTH

———————•———————

*Counsels and Exercises for the
Renewing of the Soul, and
Her Confirmation in Devotion*

CHAPTER ONE

How We Should Each Year Renew Our Good Intentions by Means of the Following Exercises

———————•———————

THE first point with regard to these exercises is thoroughly to appreciate their importance. Human nature easily loses ground in what is good, through the frailty and evil tendencies of the flesh, which weighs upon the soul and is ever dragging her down, unless she raise herself forcibly by fervent resolution, even as birds would soon fall to the ground if they did not continue in flight by continual effort and the movement of their wings.

To this end you likewise require frequently to repeat and renew your devout purpose of serving God, for fear that, if you do not, you may relapse into your former condition, or rather into a worse one, for it is the peculiarity of spiritual falls that they always cast us down to a lower level than that whereto we had attained towards devotion. However good a clock may be, we still must wind it daily; and, furthermore, at least once a year it will need being taken to pieces, in order that its rust may be removed, those parts which are displaced be put back, and those which are worn, renewed. So he who takes good care of his heart, will wind it up towards God night and morning, as we have already seen. Besides this, he will from time to time examine into his condition, correct and regulate it; and at least once a year he will take it to pieces and examine all its parts in detail, that is to say, all its affections and passions, in order to correct their defects. And as the clockmaker applies a special oil to all the springs, wheels, and movements of the clock, in order that they may work well and be less apt to rust, so the devout Christian, after having thus dissected his heart in order to renew it, should oil it with the Sacraments of Penance and the Eucharist. These will restore your strength which time has impaired, kindle your heart, revive your good resolutions, and cause the virtues of your soul to flourish anew.

The early Christians carefully practiced this good work on the anniversary of our blessed Lord's baptism, when, as St. Gregory Nazianzen relates, they renewed their profession and vows made in that Sacrament. Let us do likewise, preparing with readiness and giving ourselves seriously to the work.

Having then chosen a suitable season, according to the advice of your spiritual father, and having retired more than usual into solitude, either actually or spiritually, take some of the following subjects of meditation and follow them out according to the method I showed you in the second part.

CHAPTER TWO

The Mercy of God in Calling Us to His Service, And Our Consequent Pledge

———————•———————

CONSIDER the points of your pledge. The first is to forsake, reject, detest, and forever renounce all mortal sin. Secondly, to dedicate your soul, heart, and body, with all appertaining thereto to the service and love of God. And thirdly, that if you fall into sin, you should speedily rise again with the help of His grace. Now, are not these good, just, worthy, and noble resolutions? Think well within your soul how holy, reasonable, and excellent such a pledge is.

2. Consider to whom you have given this pledge—to God: and if we are strictly bound by our promises to men, how much more binding are those made to God? "With my whole heart have I sought after Thee," said David, "let me not stray from Thy commandments." (*Ps.* 118:10).

3. Consider before whom you pledged yourself, for it was in the presence of all the heavenly host. The Blessed Virgin, St. Joseph, your Guardian Angel, St. Louis, and the whole company of saints beheld you, and breathed sighs of joy and approval over your words; with indescribable love beholding your heart bowed down at our Saviour's feet and consecrated to His service. Then there was special rejoicing in the heavenly, Jerusalem, and now it will be commemorated afresh if you heartily renew your good resolutions.

4. Consider by what means you pledged yourself, and how good and gracious God then was to you. Were you not allured by the loving wiles of the Holy Spirit? Did not God draw your little barque to this blessed haven by the cords of love and charity? Did He not entice you with His divine sweetness, with the Sacraments, holy reading and prayer Truly, whilst you slept God watched for you, and whilst your heart was filled with peace, He thought upon you with a holy love.

5. Consider the time at which God led you to these important resolutions—it was in the flower of your life. How great a blessing to learn that which at the soonest we know only too late! St. Augustine, being led to the knowledge of the truth when he was 30 years of age, exclaimed, "O ancient beauty! Too late have I known thee. Alas! I saw thee, but I considered thee not." And you may well say, "O sweetness of old time, why have I been so tardy in appreciating thee? Alas! Even yet I do not deserve to know thee!" Wherefore acknowledging how graciously God has led you from your youth, say with David, "Thou hast taught me, O God, from my youth: and till now I will declare Thy wondrous works." (*Ps.* 70:17). Or if you have been called in old age, how great is His mercy, who, after your misuse of the years gone by, has yet called you before your death, and arrested the course of your sin, which, had it continued, must have wrought your eternal misery.

6. Consider the consequences of your calling; you will assuredly find changes for the better from what you were. Is it not a blessing to have the heart to hold converse with God in prayer, to take pleasure in seeking to love Him, to have mastered and quieted many passions which disturbed you, to have avoided many sins and stains of conscience, and to have shared so many blessed Communions, uniting yourself to the Sovereign Fountain of never-ending grace? Oh, how great are these mercies! Weigh them in the scales of the sanctuary—for it is the right hand of the Lord which hath done all this. "The right hand of the Lord hath done mightily," saith David, "the right hand of the Lord hath exalted me: the right hand of the Lord hath wrought strength. I shall not die but live: and shall declare the works of the

Lord" (*Ps.* 117:16, 17)—with my heart, my mouth, and in my deeds.

After these reflections, which it is evident will abundantly supply you with devout affections, you should conclude with an act of thanksgiving, and a fervent prayer to profit by the same closing in humility and confidence in God, reserving the trial of your resolutions till after the second point of this exercise.

CHAPTER THREE

Examination of Our Soul
As to Its Progress in the Devout Life

———————— • ————————

THIS second point is somewhat long, but it is not necessary for you to undertake it all at once, but you may do so at several different times, reviewing your conduct towards God at one time, that towards yourself at another, towards your neighbor at a third, and your passions and feelings at a fourth. It is neither requisite nor expedient for you to perform this exercise kneeling, except the first and last division which comprise your affections. The other points of examination may be profitably followed out whilst you are walking, or still better in bed, if you are able to keep free from drowsiness and keep well awake. But in this case you must read them carefully beforehand. The second point should be gone through in three days and two nights at most, taking such a part of each day and night as you may be able; for if its parts are too widely separated, the exercise loses its force, and will leave but a faint impression on you. After each point in the examination note carefully wherein you have fallen short, where you have been guilty of error, and what have been your principal hindrances, in order that you may confess them, and receive counsel and encouragement. Although it is not necessary that on the days in which you are engaged in this and the ensuing exercises, you should altogether retire into solitude, yet some retirement is profitable, especially towards evening, when you can retire early to bed, and seek the rest both of body and mind which is suitable to reflection; and during the day make frequent aspirations to God, the Blessed Virgin, the angels, and the heavenly Jerusalem; all being done with a heartfelt love for God, and a longing after perfection.

In order to begin this examination rightly, 1) Place yourself in the presence of God. 2) Invoke the Holy Spirit, asking of Him a clear and distinct light, so that you may truly know yourself, even as St. Augustine cried humbly before God, "O Lord, teach me to know Thee, and to know myself"; or, St. Francis, who inquired of God, saying, "Who art Thou, and who am I?" Declare that you do not enquire into your progress in order to take to yourself any merit therein, but giving all to God; neither to glory in it, but to glory in God, and thank Him for such progress. Promise, likewise, that, if as you anticipate, you find that you have advanced but little, or rather have gone backwards, that you will not therefore be disheartened or grow cold through discouragement or slackening of heart, but that, on the contrary, you will take fresh courage and life, humble yourself and correct your faults by the help of God's grace.

Then calmly and quietly examine how you have conducted yourself towards God, your neighbor, and yourself, up to the present hour.

CHAPTER FOUR

Examination of
The State of Our Soul towards God

———— • ————

HOW does your heart stand with regard to mortal sin? Have you a fixed resolution never to yield to it under any circumstances whatever? Have you persevered in this resolution since your profession until now? In this resolution lies the foundation of the spiritual life.

1. What is the state of your heart with regard to God's commandments? Do you find them easy, light, and pleasant? He who is in good health and has a healthy digestion likes good food and rejects that which is unwholesome.

2. What is the state of your heart with regard to venial sins? You cannot altogether prevent the occasional commission of some such, but are there none to which you are specially inclined or, what is worse, in which you take delight and which you love?

3. What is the state of your heart with regard to spiritual exercises? Do you value and love them? Are you never disgusted with those in which you take least delight?—hearing or reading the Word of God, pondering and meditating thereon, longing after God, Confession, spiritual direction, preparation for Communion and Communion itself, the restraint of your passions—what in all these is repugnant to your heart? And if you discover that you are disinclined to any of them, examine whence such disinclination arises, and what is its cause.

4. What is the state of your heart as regards God Himself? Does it delight in remembering Him? Does it draw thence a soothing pleasure? as David says, "I remember, O Lord, Thy judgments of old: and I was comforted." (*Ps.* 118:52). Do you feel within your heart a readiness to love Him, and a taste to rejoice in that love? Does your heart seek repose in reflecting upon the immensity, the goodness, the sweetness of God? If amidst the occupations or vanities of the world the remembrance of God comes over you, does it find room in your heart? Does it seize upon you? Does your heart turn gladly towards it, and as it were go to meet it? There are some souls that experience this.

5. If a wife sees her husband who has been long absent, returning, and hears his voice, however she may be absorbed in business, or detained by some urgent occupation, her heart must speak and act. She forsakes all other thoughts for that one, her returning husband. So with souls that love God, although they may be engrossed with other things when the remembrance of God comes upon them, they will forget everything else, so glad are they to regain that beloved remembrance. This is an extremely good sign.

6. How is your heart affected towards Jesus Christ, both God and man? Do you delight in being near Him? Bees hover round their honey with delight, but wasps feed upon every kind of corruption. Thus holy souls find their delight in Jesus Christ, and are kindled with an ardent love towards Him; but the wicked seek their joys in vanity.

7. What is the state of your heart with regard to the Blessed Virgin, the Saints, and your Guardian Angel? Do you love them greatly? Have you special confidence in their good will? Do you take delight in their lives, their praises, and in thoughts of them?

8. As regards your tongue, how do you speak of God? Do you delight in praising Him according to your powers, and do you love to sing His praise?

9. As to works, examine whether you have God's external glory at heart, and seek to honor Him by your deeds; for those who love God, also love to adorn His house.

Can you remember any affection which you have forsaken, or anything which you have renounced, for God's sake? For it is a sure sign of love when we renounce anything for the sake of Him we love. What, then, have you abandoned for the love of God?

CHAPTER FIVE

Examination of Your Condition
With Regard to Yourself

———•———

1. How do you love yourself? Is your love a purely worldly one? If so, you will desire always to abide here, and your cares will all be given to your establishment on earth; but if your love for yourself is a heavenly love, you will desire, or at least be ready and glad, to depart hence whensoever it shall please the Lord.

2. Do you keep your self-love in good control? for ill-regulated self-love ruins us. Well-regulated love requires us to love the soul more than the body, to endeavor to acquire virtue more than aught else, and to esteem heavenly honor far above all low, earthly honor. A well-regulated heart oftener asks itself, "What will the angels say if I do or think thus?" than, "What will men say?"

3. What love do you bear your own soul? Are you willing to tend it in its maladies? You owe this care to it, and should leave all else in order to procure it aid when it is harassed by its own passions.

4. For what do you count yourself in the sight of God? Doubtless, nothing. Now, there is no great humility in a fly which holds itself as nothing when compared to a mountain, or a drop of water as compared to the sea, or in a cornflower or a spark which counts itself nought when compared to the sun; but humility lies in not esteeming ourselves

more than others, and not desiring to be so esteemed by others. How are you on this score?

5. In word, do you boast of yourself in one way or another? Do you flatter yourself when speaking of yourself?

6. In your recreations, do you indulge in pleasures which can injure your health? I mean useless, vain pleasures; unprofitable watching, and suchlike?

CHAPTER SIX

Examination of the Soul as Regards Our Neighbor

———————•———————

THE Christian should love husband or wife with a calm, tranquil, firm and constant love, chiefly because God desires and enjoins us to do so. The same reason holds good as to children and other relatives and friends, each one according to his rank. But as a general thing, what is the state of your heart with regard to your neighbor? Do you love him from your heart and for the love of God? In order to prove this, you must call to mind certain disagreeable, troublesome individuals, for with such it is that we practice the love of God towards our neighbor, and still more towards those who do us any injury either in word or deed. Try whether your heart is clear with regard to such, and whether you have to force it to love them.

Are you slow to speak evil of your neighbor, especially of those whom you do not like? Do you never injure him either directly or indirectly? A very little reflection will easily satisfy you on these points.

CHAPTER SEVEN

Examination of the Soul's Affections

———————————•———————————

I HAVE gone into detail on these points. On them depends our knowledge of our spiritual progress, for, as to the examination of sins, that applies rather to the Confessions of those who do not seek to advance. And on each of these heads you must sift yourself gently but carefully, examining how your heart has been with regard to them since your resolution, and what evident failures you have to reproach yourself with.

But you may shorten the examination by inquiring into the passions of the heart; and if you are weary of the above-detailed process, you can examine what you have done, and how you stand, thus:

In your love towards God, your neighbor, and yourself.

In your hatred of your own sin and that of others, for we ought to seek to do away with both the one and the other.

In your desire of worldly goods, pleasures, and honors.

In your fear of the dangers of sin, and of the loss of this world's goods: men fear the one too much, and the other all too little.

In your hope, which has perhaps been centered overmuch on the world and the flesh, and too little on God and the things of eternity.

In sadness, whether it was inordinate.

In joy, whether it was excessive for vain and empty trifles.

Finally, what affections hinder your heart, what passions rule it, and what most distracts it.

Thus, one's condition may be tested by examining the passions one after another; just as one who plays the lute tries the several strings and tunes those that are false, either tightening or loosening them: so when we have tested the love and hatred, the desire, fear, hope, sadness and joy of our soul, if we find these ill-tuned to the song we would raise, which is the glory of God, we can by His grace and the help of our spiritual father tune them afresh.

CHAPTER EIGHT

Affections after the Examination

———— • ————

HAVING deliberately considered each point of this examination and ascertained your own position, you should proceed to the stirring up of such affections as the following: thank God for whatever little improvement you find in your life since your resolutions were made, and acknowledge that it has been wrought in you and for you by His grace alone.

Humble yourself before God, acknowledging that it is your own fault that you have not made greater progress, inasmuch as you have not cooperated faithfully with the inspirations, illuminations, and impulses which He has given you in prayer and by other means.

Promise that you will ever praise Him for His favors towards you and for having led you even so far contrary to your natural inclinations.

Ask forgiveness for the want of faith and loyalty in your return for His goodness, offer your heart to Him, that He alone may be its Lord.

Entreat Him to make you truly faithful. Invoke the Saints, the Blessed Virgin, your good Angel, your patron Saint, St. Joseph and others.

CHAPTER NINE

Reflections Suitable to the
Renewal of Our Good Resolutions

———————●———————

A FTER this examination, and after having taken counsel of some wise guide concerning your faults and their correction, use the following reflections, taking one daily as in meditation, devoting your season of prayer to it, and making use of the same method of preparation, and arousing your affections as with the meditations given before: Above all, place yourself in the presence of God, and entreat His grace to keep you faithful in His holy love and service.

CHAPTER TEN

First Reflection:
The Excellence of the Soul

———————•———————

CONSIDER the nobility and excellence of your soul, which has an understanding capable not only of knowing the things of this visible world, but knows that there are angels and a Paradise; knows that there is an all-mighty, all-good, and ineffable God, knows that there is an eternity, and further knows that which is required to lead a good life here, to be numbered with the angels in Paradise and to rejoice forever in God.

Furthermore, your soul has a noble will which can love God, and cannot hate Him in Himself. Consider how generous your heart is, and that as nothing corrupt can allure bees, which linger only over sweet flowers, so your heart can find no repose save in God alone, and can be subject to no creature. Resolutely call to mind the most attractive and delightful amusements which once filled your heart, and see whether they were not full of disquieting fears, anxious thoughts, and importunate cares, amidst which your poor heart was wretched. Alas! When our heart seeks the things of the flesh, it pursues them eagerly, expecting in them to satisfy its longings; but as soon as it finds them it also finds that it has to begin again, and that nothing can satisfy it. For God has ordained that our heart should no more find a resting-place than did Noah's dove, in order that it may return unto its God, whence it came forth. What natural beauty is there in our heart? Why then do we force it against its will to serve the creature?

O my soul (so should you say), thou art able to know, love and long after God, why wilt thou take pleasure in anything short of Him? Thou canst aim at eternity, why wilt thou trifle away thine energies on time? It was one of the Prodigal Son's sorrows, that whereas he might have lived sumptuously at his father's table, he ate the coarse food of swine. My soul, thou art capable of seeking God; woe be to thee if thou restest in aught less. Raise your soul with this reflection, prove to it that it is immortal and worthy of eternity, and fill it, therefore, with courage.

CHAPTER ELEVEN

Second Reflection:
The Excellence of Virtue

———— • ————

REFLECT that virtue and devotion alone can satisfy your soul in this world; behold how lovely they are; consider the virtues and their opposing vices. How precious is patience compared with revenge, gentleness compared with anger and passion, humility compared with arrogance and ambition, liberality compared with avarice, charity compared with envy, temperance compared with excess! For one admirable property attendant on acts of virtue is, that they leave an exceeding delight and sweetness in the soul after their practice, whereas acts of vice leave her injured and enfeebled. Why, then, do we not seek to acquire such satisfaction?

In vice, he who has made some progress is not satisfied, and he who has made much is dissatisfied; but he who follows after virtue is well pleased from the first, and his contentment constantly increases. O life of devotion! How lovely and pleasant, how soothing and winning thou art! Thou softenest our trials and enhancest our delights! Without thee good is evil, pleasure full of uneasiness, fears, and failures: truly whosoever knoweth thee might say with the woman of Samaria, "Lord, give me this water": an aspiration very frequently on the lips of the holy mother Teresa, and of St. Catherine of Genoa, in their various needs.

CHAPTER TWELVE

Third Reflection:
The Example of the Saints

———————•———————

CONSIDER the example of all the Saints: what have they not done for the love of God, and in order to be His devout servants? Think of those martyrs! How steadfast in their resolutions! What tortures they suffered in order to be faithful! Think, too, of those holy and blessed women, whiter than lilies in their purity, redder than roses in their charity, who when twelve, fifteen, twenty, or twenty-five years old, underwent all manner of martyrdom rather than renounce their resolutions, not only their profession of faith, but also their profession of devotion; some dying rather than sacrifice their virginity, others, rather than abandon their ministries of love, tending the sick, comforting the mourners, and burying the dead. What marvelous constancy was displayed under such circumstances by this tender sex!

Consider all those holy confessors, how utterly they despised the world, how invincible they were in their resolutions. Nothing could induce them to lay them aside; they embraced them without reserve, and maintained them without faltering. Remember what St. Augustine tells us of his mother, Monica, with what firmness she kept to her resolution to serve God, first in her married life, and afterwards in her widowhood. Recall how St. Jerome speaks of his beloved daughter, Paula, and her constancy amidst so many trials and adverse circumstances.

What may not we do with such examples before our eyes? They were what we are, they performed their holy deeds in order to serve the same God, and to attain the same graces. Why, then, may not we do the like, according to our circumstances and vocation, in behalf of our cherished resolution and solemn protestation?

CHAPTER THIRTEEN

Fourth Reflection:
The Love that Jesus Christ Bears Us

———— • ————

REFLECT with what love Jesus Christ our Lord endured so many sufferings on earth, especially in the Garden of Olives and on Mount Calvary. That love embraced you, and through all its pains and travail won for your heart good resolutions and professions from God the Father, and by the same means obtained all that you need in order to maintain, nourish, strengthen, and confirm these resolutions. O resolution! How precious art thou, the offspring of my Saviour's Passion! How should my soul cherish thee, since thou wert so dear to my Lord! O Saviour of my soul! Thou didst die to win for me my good resolutions, grant me Thy grace that I may die sooner than forsake them. Remember the Heart of Jesus beheld your heart and loved it, even whilst He hung upon the Cross; and by that love He obtained for you all good things which you will ever possess; amongst others, your good resolutions. Well may we all say with the Prophet Jeremias, "O Lord, before I had a being Thou knewest me and calledst me by my name." (*Jer.* 1:5). Inasmuch as His Divine Goodness through love and mercy prepared for us all the means of salvation both in general and in particular, and therefore our good resolutions also. Just as a woman prepares for her child making ready the cradle and swaddling clothes, and engaging a nurse even before it is yet in the world, so the grace of Our Lord, preparing for your spiritual birth, seeking to bring you forth into salvation, made ready upon the Cross all that was needful for you, your spiritual cradle, your swaddling clothes, your nurse, and all that was required for your happiness. By these means, these graces and allurements, He leads your soul and would fain draw it unto His own perfection. When He hung upon the Cross He was as a woman in travail.

How deeply should this be graven in our memory. Is it possible that I have been thus loved, thus tenderly loved by my Saviour, even that He should remember me individually, and in all the little events by which He has drawn me to Himself? How, then, ought we not to prize, cherish, and avail ourselves of all such favors? It is a soothing thought that the loving Heart of God remembered you, Philothea, loved you, and prepared a thousand means of forwarding your salvation, as carefully as though He thought of no other soul in the world: just as the sun lights up one part of the earth as brightly as though it shone nowhere else, save there alone. Even so our Blessed Lord thought and cared for all His cherished children, caring for each one of us as though He cared for none beside. "Who loved me, and gave himself for me," says St. Paul, as though he said, "for me alone, as much as if He had done nothing for others." Let this be graven in your soul, in order to cherish and feed your resolution, which is so precious to our Saviour's Heart.

CHAPTER FOURTEEN

Fifth Reflection: God's Eternal Love for Us

— • —

CONSIDER the eternal love which God had borne you; for even before our blessed Lord Jesus Christ became man and suffered on the Cross for you, His Divine Majesty foresaw you in His sovereign goodness and loved you exceedingly. When did He begin to love you? When He began to be God. And when was His beginning? Never, for He has always been, without beginning and without end: wherefore He has always loved you, and from eternity prepared the favors and graces which He has bestowed upon you. And by His prophet He says (and He speaks to you as much as to any), "I have loved thee with an everlasting love; therefore have I drawn thee, taking pity on thee." (*Jer.* 31:3). Amongst other things, then, He thought to lead you to resolve on serving Him.

What mighty resolutions are these, then, on which God thought and meditated, which He foresaw from eternity! How dear and precious should they be to us! What should we not suffer sooner than lose one particle thereof! Rather let the whole world perish, for the whole world is not worth one soul, and that soul is worth nothing without its steadfast resolutions.

CHAPTER FIFTEEN

General Affections Following These Reflections, And Conclusion of the Exercise

———————•———————

O CHERISHED resolutions! You are as the tree of life which God has with His own hand planted in the midst of my heart, and which my Saviour waters with His own blood that it may bring forth fruit. Rather would I die a thousand deaths than suffer any blast of wind to uproot you. No, neither vanity nor pleasure, neither poverty nor wealth shall ever alter my intentions.

O my Lord, Thou has planted this lovely tree, and hast preserved it for my garden from eternity in Thy paternal breast. Alas! How many souls have not been thus richly blest? How then can I humble myself sufficiently before Thy tender pity and compassion?

Good and holy resolutions I will keep you, and you shall keep me: if you live in my soul, my soul will live in you. Live forever then. O good resolutions! Since through God's mercy you are from all eternity, continue and dwell forever in me; let me never forsake you.

After such affections you should specify the means requisite for the maintenance of your good resolutions, and promise to use them faithfully; such as frequent use of prayer, the Sacraments and good works; the amendment of your faults ascertained under the second head; the cutting off of occasions of sin, and the following of those counsels given to you for this end.

After this take as it were new courage and strength with reiterated protestations that you will abide steadfast in your resolutions, and dedicate, consecrate, sacrifice, and immolate your heart, your soul, and will to God, as though you held them in your hand; protesting that you will never take them back, but leave them in His holy hands, ever following His Will everywhere and in all things. Ask God to deign to renew all that is in you, to bless your renewed protestation and confirm it.

In such a frame of mind go and kneel at the feet of your spiritual father, accuse yourself of the chief faults of which you have been guilty since your General Confession, receive absolution as you did then, reiterate your protestation before him, and sign it; and then proceed to unite your heart thus renewed to its Beginnings and its Saviour, in the most holy Sacrament of the Eucharist.

CHAPTER SIXTEEN

The Feelings to Be Retained after This Exercise

———— • ————

THE day after this renewal, and indeed, on many subsequent days, you should frequently repeat those burning words of St. Paul, St. Augustine, and others: I am no more mine own, whether I live or die I am my Saviour's! There is no more any "I" or "mine"— "I" am Christ's—"mine" is to be His. O world, thou art ever thyself, and hitherto I have been myself, but henceforth I will no longer be myself! Truly, we shall no longer be ourselves, because our hearts will be changed, and the world which deceives so many will itself be deceived in us; for as it perceives our change only little by little, it will believe us still to be Esau, whilst we are really Jacob.

These exercises must sink into our hearts, and laying aside our reflections and meditations, we must return to our wonted society and occupations soberly, for fear the wine of our good resolutions be suddenly spilled; because it must saturate and penetrate every corner of our soul, yet without any effort either of body or mind.

CHAPTER SEVENTEEN

Answer to Two Objections Which
May Be Made against This Introduction

———————•———————

THE world will tell you that these rules and exercises are so numerous, that whoever seeks to follow them must give up all other occupation. And, indeed, if we did nothing else, we should do enough, since we should fulfill our duty in this world; but do you not perceive the fallacy? If it were needful to perform all these exercises every day, undoubtedly they would wholly engross us, but they are required only at certain times and places, according to circumstances. What an accumulation of laws is contained in our codes and digests, to which obedience is enjoined? But then they affect only peculiar circumstances, and do not come into use every day. Besides, David, a king, and one cumbered with many weighty cares, practiced many more pious exercises than I have set before you. St. Louis, who was so admirable a monarch both in peace and war, and who governed and administered justice with unsurpassed diligence, heard Mass twice daily, said Vespers and Compline with his Chaplain, devoted a time to meditation, visited the hospitals every Friday, went to Confession and took the discipline, frequently attended sermons, and engaged in spiritual conferences, yet never lost any opportunity of promoting the public welfare, and the court was more brilliant and flourishing than under any of his predecessors. Do you then courageously persevere in the exercises I have set before you, and God will provide you with strength and leisure for your worldly affairs, even if it necessitated His stopping the sun in its course, as in the time of Josue. If God works with us, we are sure to do enough.

It will further be said that I have assumed everyone to possess the gift of mental prayer, which is not common to all, and that therefore this book will not be serviceable to everyone. I have certainly assumed such to be the case, and it is also true that everyone has not the gift of mental prayer, but it is likewise true that almost everyone, even the most unlearned, may obtain it with the help of good guides, if they will labor as much as the acquisition of so excellent a thing deserves. And if there be some who are entirely devoid of this gift (which I imagine to be a very rare occurrence), a wise spiritual guide will easily remedy the deficiency by teaching them to be very diligent in reading or hearing read suitable reflections and meditations.

CHAPTER EIGHTEEN

Three Final and Chief Rules

———————•———————

O N THE first day of every month renew the protestation given in Part I after the meditations, and at all times, protest that you will observe it, saying with David, "Thy justifications I will never forget, for by them Thou hast given me life" (*Ps.* 118:93), and when you feel any slackening in your soul, take up your protestation, and, prostrating yourself in all humility, offer it with your whole heart, and you will find great relief.

Make open profession of your desire to be devout. I do not say *to be devout*, but of *desiring* to be so; and never be ashamed of the ordinary and necessary actions which conduct us towards the love of God. Boldly acknowledge that you try to meditate, that you would rather die than commit mortal sin, that you desire to frequent the Sacraments and to follow the guidance of your director (although for various reasons it may be unadvisable to mention his name). For God, who will have no one be ashamed of Him or of the Cross, is well pleased with this readiness to confess that we desire to serve Him, and have dedicated ourselves to His love with especial affection. Moreover, such an open profession does away with many of the hindrances with which the world would fain molest us, and for the sake of our own reputation we are bound to persevere. The philosophers of old gave out that they were philosophers, in order that they might be left to lead a philosophic life, and we should give out that we aim at leading a devout life, in order that we may be permitted to lead a devout life. And if you are told that it is possible to lead a devout life without following all these rules and exercises, do not deny it, but answer meekly that your great infirmity requires more support and aid than others do.

Finally, Philothea, I beseech you in the name of all that is sacred in Heaven and earth, by the Baptism which you received, by the tender Heart with which Jesus loves you, and by those bowels of compassion which are your hope, abide and persevere in this blessed undertaking of a devout life. Our days glide by; death is at our door. "The trumpet sounds," says St. Gregory Nazianzen; "let everyone make ready, for judgment is at hand." When the mother of St. Symphorian saw him led to his martyrdom, she exclaimed, "My son, my son, remember life eternal! Look up to heaven, and remember Who reigns there! Your approaching end will soon and quickly close your brief career here below." So would I say to you, Philothea: Look up to Heaven, and do not forsake it for earth; look down into Hell, and for the sake of the present moment do not plunge therein. Look to Jesus Christ and do not deny Him for the world; and if the trials of a devout life seem hard to you, say with St. Francis: "How sweet these momentary trials and sorrows, for they lead to Heaven's never-ending joys!"

Glory be to the Father, and to the Son, and to the Holy Ghost, now, henceforth, and forever. Amen.

The End

🛡 SAINT BENEDICT✝PRESS

Saint Benedict Press, founded in 2006, is the parent company for a variety of imprints including TAN Books, Catholic Courses, Benedict Bibles, Benedict Books, and Labora Books. The company's name pays homage to the guiding influence of the Rule of Saint Benedict and the Benedictine monks of Belmont Abbey, North Carolina, just a short distance from the company's headquarters in Charlotte, NC.

Saint Benedict Press is now a multi-media company. Its mission is to publish and distribute products reflective of the Catholic intellectual tradition and to present these products in an attractive and accessible manner.

🛡 TAN·BOOKS

TAN Books was founded in 1967, in response to the rapid decline of faith and morals in society and the Church. Since its founding, TAN Books has been committed to the preservation and promotion of the spiritual, theological and liturgical traditions of the Catholic Church. In 2008, TAN Books was acquired by Saint Benedict Press. Since then, TAN has experienced positive growth and diversification while fulfilling its mission to a new generation of readers.

TAN Books publishes over 500 titles on Thomistic theology, traditional devotions, Church doctrine, history, lives of the saints, educational resources, and booklets.

For a free catalog from Saint Benedict Press
or TAN Books, visit us online at
saintbenedictpress.com • tanbooks.com
or call us toll-free at
(800) 437-5876